This is a ground-breaking volume which is a must-read for anyone interested in furthering their understanding of, and capacity to work with, LGBT older adults living with dementia. It addresses an area that is underrepresented in current research, policy and practice in dementia and does so with a sensitivity to intersectional identity, lived experience, service delivery, and social and political rights. The contributors represent a variety of disciplines and perspectives across geographic regions and bring together a vast array of knowledge from queer studies and social gerontology. Of particular note is the inclusion of the experiences and perspectives of those living with or caring for someone living with dementia. The inclusion of multiple perspectives makes this edited volume unique and highly relevant. The volume pays important attention to tensions and absences within current LGBT research and counters these through the inclusion of bisexual, and trans voices and concerns. This book lays down a strong theoretical foundation for the reader which facilitates common understandings of the concepts, terms and ideas presented in the various chapters. As a social work scholar working with LGBT older adults and their families, I was touched by the diversity and depth of the material presented, the links developed between theory, research, social policy and practice, and the particular sensitivity to complex ideas and realities including advocacy, social action and rights-based considerations, issues which are often absent in work on dementia and dementia care, particularly within health and social care literature. This is a pioneering book that will undoubtedly have an important impact upon the field. It can both foster best practice guidelines for working with LGBT older adults with dementia and those that provide care to them *and* encourage the development of coordinated local and international efforts to advance equity and social inclusion for these previously marginalized communities. This book is a first of its kind – contributing important information to enhance our understanding of the lived experiences of dementia and our capacity to provide dementia care to LGBT people. It is a must-read for anyone engaged in ageing and/or LGBT studies, and for a wide variety of practitioners and policy makers interested in developing more comprehensive programs and practices that pay attention to equity and diversity. As a social worker scholar in the field, I can say without hesitation, that I will recommend *Lesbian, Gay, Bisexual and Trans* Individuals Living with Dementia: Concepts, Practice and Rights* to my students and colleagues in the health and social care field in the coming years. Thank you to the authors for such a well written, comprehensive volume which deepens our understanding of the diversity and complexity of aging in LGBT communities.

Associate Professor Shari Brotman,
School of Social Work, McGill University, Canada

This book will prove to be an invaluable tool to service providers, advocates, caregivers and researchers alike. Westwood and Price curated an exceptional group of experts to understand, humanize and ultimately effect change in the lives of LGBT people living with dementia.

Hilary Meyer, *Director, Social Enterprise & National Projects,*
SAGE (Services & Advocacy for GLBT Elders)

Lesbian, Gay, Bisexual and Trans* Individuals Living with Dementia

This groundbreaking collection is the first to focus specifically on LGBT* people and dementia. It brings together original chapters from leading academics, practitioners and LGBT* individuals affected by dementia. Multi-disciplinary and international in scope, it includes authors from the UK, USA, Canada and Australia and from a range of fields, including sociology, social work, psychology, health care and socio-legal studies.

Taking an intersectional approach – i.e. considering the plurality of experiences and the multiple, interacting relational positions of everyday life – *Lesbian, Gay, Bisexual and Trans* Individuals Living with Dementia* addresses topics relating to concepts, practice and rights. Part I addresses theoretical and conceptual questions; Part II discusses practical concerns in the delivery of health and social care provision to LGBT* people living with dementia; and Part III explores socio-legal issues relating to LGBT* people living with dementia.

This collection will appeal to policy makers, commissioners, practitioners, academics and students across a range of disciplines. With an ageing and increasingly diverse population, and growing numbers of people affected by dementia, this book will become essential reading for anyone interested in understanding the needs of, and providing appropriate services to, LGBT* people affected by dementia.

Sue Westwood is a socio-legal and gerontology scholar. She is a researcher at the University of Oxford, Honorary Research Fellow at the Centre for Research on Ageing and Gender, University of Surrey and teaches Law at Coventry University. Sue previously managed a dementia adviser service for a UK charity.

Elizabeth Price is Senior Lecturer in Social Work at the University of Hull, UK. She is a registered social worker and her research interests currently include the lived experience of chronic illness, sexualities and dementia, and the use of music as a therapeutic intervention.

Routledge Advances in Sociology

Lesbian, Gay, Bisexual and Trans* Individuals Living with Dementia

Concepts, practice and rights

**Edited by
Sue Westwood and
Elizabeth Price**

LONDON AND NEW YORK

First published 2016
by Routledge
2 Park Square, Milton Park, Abingdon, Oxon OX14 4RN

and by Routledge
711 Third Avenue, New York, NY 10017

First issued in paperback 2018

Routledge is an imprint of the Taylor & Francis Group, an informa business

British Library Cataloguing-in-Publication Data
A catalogue record for this book is available from the British Library

Library of Congress Cataloging-in-Publication Data
Names: Westwood, Sue, editor.
Title: Lesbian, gay, bisexual and trans individuals living with dementia / [edited by] Sue Westwood, Elizabeth Price.
Description: New York : Routledge, 2016. | Series: Routledge advances in sociology
Identifiers: LCCN 2015046998| ISBN 9781138840690 (hardback) | ISBN 9781315732718 (e-book)
Subjects: LCSH: Dementia–Patients–Sexual behavior. | Older sexual minorities. | Sexual minorities.
Classification: LCC RC521 .L47 2016 | DDC 616.8/3008664–dc23
LC record available at http://lccn.loc.gov/2015046998

ISBN 13: 978-1-138-34334-4 (pbk)
ISBN 13: 978-1-138-84069-0 (hbk)

Typeset in Times New Roman
by Wearset Ltd, Boldon, Tyne and Wear

Sue dedicates this book to her father,
Basil Alexander Westwood (1920–2007).
Basil lived well with, and eventually died from, dementia.
Being his 'carer' eventually led me, via a rather circuitous
route, to this book.

Contents

Contributors

Catherine Barrett is the Chief Investigator and Coordinator of the Sexual Health and Ageing Programme at the Australian Research Centre in Sex, Health and Society at La Trobe University. She has over 30 years' experience in gerontology and, for the past 20 years, has been working to promote recognition of the sexual rights of older people, including the rights of older LGBTI people. In 2009, Catherine established Val's Café, a national programme to promote the health and wellbeing of older LGBTI Australians.

Jenny-Anne Bishop is a 69-year-old married trans* woman, living with her partner Elen in North Wales. She has been out as a trans* person for over 44 years and transitioned completely eight years ago. Jenny-Anne is an active campaigner for the Trans and LGBT communities. This includes being a lay pastoral leader and board member of the Metropolitan Church, a member of both the Westminster Parliamentary Forum on Gender Identity and the Welsh Government Strategic Equality Plan Board, and trustee for several LGBT organisations. She helps manage Unique, the largest transgender social and mutual support group in Wales, and coordinates TransForum Manchester. Jenny-Anne is a Trustee and member of Sparkle Manchester's organising team and is also on several equality steering groups and stakeholder steering groups for Gender Dysphoria Care. She regularly delivers trans awareness and equality training (so far to around 90 organisations), provides support for parents and children of trans* people, is researching the care of older trans people, was a stakeholder member of the Rainbow Lives project (Merseyside) and, with her partner Elen, runs a community house for trans people. She has appeared many times on various radio stations, many national and regional television programmes and in over 50 magazine and newspaper articles. Jenny-Anne was recently awarded an OBE for Services to the Trans Community (2015) and the Homo Heroes Volunteer of the Year trophy for 2014.

Pauline Crameri is a Research and Community Liaison Officer in the Sexual Health and Ageing programme at the Australian Centre in Sex, Health and Society, La Trobe University and the coordinator of Val's Café, a national programme to promote the health and wellbeing of older LGBTI Australians.

Pauline has over 15 years' experience in the aged and disability sector in local government and has practical experience in LGBTI service development including leading a service to achieve a Rainbow Tick.

Mark Hughes is Associate Professor in Social Work in the School of Arts and Social Sciences, Southern Cross University, Australia. Mark's research interests are the organisational dimensions of social work practice, social work with older people, and LGBT ageing. Mark is the co-author of six books as well as a range of journal publications. He is also editor of the journal *Australian Social Work*.

Wendy Hulko is an Associate Professor in the School of Social Work and Human Service at Thompson Rivers University in Kamloops, BC, Canada and is affiliated with the Institute for Intersectionality Research and Policy at Simon Fraser University and the Centre for Research on Personhood in Dementia at the University of British Columbia. She holds a BA (Hon) in Sociology and Spanish (Trent University), a Masters in Social Work (University of Toronto), and a PhD in Sociology and Social Policy (University of Stirling) and has worked in the field of aging since 1993 – as a nursing assistant, hospital social worker, government policy advisor, researcher, and educator. Wendy teaches Bachelor of Social Work courses on sexual orientation and gender expression, theory and ideology, research, and ageing, an MEd course on diversity and equity, and runs an interdisciplinary field school in Cuba. She is an active researcher in the area of ageing and dementia, working in collaboration with equity-seeking groups (e.g. First Nation Elders, LGBT youth, older women), and has published in a wide variety of journals and edited books.

Chryssy Hunter is a trans* researcher and activist, in the final stages of writing her PhD thesis investigating the relationships between trans* and non-normative sexgender identities and expressions, and their representation, repression and significance in discourses of contemporary culture and law. She was one of the organisers of the Radical Transfeminisms stream at the 2015 London Conference of Critical Theory. She is also active in organising for the Transgender and Gender Nonconforming Swimming Group (TAGS) and the Bent Bars Project, a pen pal organisation for LGBTQ prisoners. She lives in London.

Andrew King is a Senior Lecturer in Sociology at the University of Surrey, UK. He has been undertaking sexualities research for over ten years and researching LGBT ageing for over seven. His LGBT ageing research has been funded by the Economic and Social Research Council (ESRC) and has addressed the relationship between older LGBT people and service providers. He has published widely on LGBT ageing, in a range of edited collections and articles in *Sociology, Ageing and Society, International Social Work* and *Social Policy and Society*. He identifies as a gay man whose late father had dementia.

Nancy J. Knauer is the I. Herman Stern Professor of Law and Director of Law & Public Policy Programmes at Beasley School of Law, Temple University, Philadelphia. She is an internationally recognised scholar writing in the areas of identity, sexuality, and gender. Professor Knauer was selected as one of 26 law professors from across the nation to be featured in the book *What the Best Law Teachers Do*, published by Harvard University Press in 2013. Professor Knauer received a Dukeminier Award and the Stu Walter Prize from the Williams Institute at UCLA Law School for her article 'LGBT Elder Law: Toward Equity in Aging', 32 *Harvard Journal of Law & Gender 1* (2009). Her book, *Gay and Lesbian Elders: History, Law, and Identity Politics in the U.S.* (Ashgate Publishing, Ltd. 2010) focuses on the unique challenges facing gay and lesbian elders. Professor Knauer is the co-founder of the *Aging, Law & Society Collaborative Research Network* of the Law & Society Association.

Sally Knocker is Head of Tailored Training and a consultant trainer at Dementia Care Matters with 25 years' experience working in the dementia care field and 15 years as a specialist trainer. She is the author of Age UK's publication *The Whole of Me* and Joseph Rowntree Foundation's *Perspectives on Ageing: Lesbians, Gay Men and Bisexuals* and was also one of the independent evaluators of the *Opening Doors London* project. She offers training to managers and care staff on a range of dementia care issues including exploring sexuality and intimacy needs, and has delivered awareness training for both staff and older people themselves on thinking about the needs of people living with dementia who are also lesbian, gay, bisexual or transgender. The focus of *Dementia Care Matters* on 'feelings matter most' fits well with her own philosophy that, as cognition deteriorates, our emotional needs for safety and for our core identity to be valued are integral to genuinely 'person-centred' care.

Sally Lambourne is a Senior Project Manager with Alzheimer's Australia NSW. Her career has spanned a wide range of sectors, including aged care, women's health, youth health, LGBT health, evaluation and organisational development. Sally holds a Master of Policy from the University of NSW where she was the winner of the prize in Policy Studies. Sally is passionate about fairness and equity and committed to inclusive health and social services.

J. R. Latham is completing his PhD at the Australian Research Centre in Sex, Health and Society, La Trobe University and is project coordinator for Val's Café Intersex and Trans Ageing research. He has published essays in the journals *Sexualities*, *Feminist Theory* and *Studies in Gender and Sexuality*.

Tracey Maegusuku-Hewett is Senior Lecturer in Social Work at Swansea University, Wales. Tracey has worked within nursing, residential, community, voluntary and statutory sector roles with children and adults in her capacity as a support worker, a nurse with people with learning disabilities and, latterly, as a qualified social worker. Her research interests include LGBT people's wellbeing, equality and social work practice, and evidence enriched practice.

Roger Newman is a married, retired teacher from Margate, Kent. Resulting from the experience of caring for his first partner, David, he was active in co-founding an LGBT carers' group within the Alzheimer's Society. He has been a trustee of OPAAL, the Older People's Advocacy Alliance, a member of Age UK national committees for engagement and policy, a member of the ITV Meridian diversity group, and a member of the dementia management group of the Royal Surgical Aid Society. He was a co-founder, and was recently chair, of the trustees of the East Kent Independent Dementia Support organisation. In 2007, he was awarded the MBE for services to charity. He is a keen blogger and is a co-author of chapters in *Telling Tales about Dementia* (ed. L. Whitman, 2009) and *Lesbian, Gay, Bisexual and Transgender Ageing – Biographical Approaches for Inclusive Care and Support* (ed. R. Ward *et al.*, 2012) both published by Jessica Kingsley Publishers.

Elizabeth Price is Senior Lecturer in Social Work at the University of Hull. As a registered social worker, she specialised in work with people living with dementia and she has a particular interest in the ways in which the condition is experienced by, and impacts upon, LGBT* people. Her research interests also focus upon the experience of chronic illness and the use of music as a healing intervention.

Michele Raithby is Senior Lecturer in Social Work at Swansea University, Wales. Following working in a variety of educational, research and residential care settings, Michele qualified in social work at the University of Oxford. Her qualified practice experience included generic neighbourhood-based social work, specialist mental health social work and inspection. Her research interests include provision of domiciliary care services with older people, implementation of evidence-based practice, and social work with LGBT adults.

Richard Ward is a Senior Lecturer in Dementia Studies at the University of Stirling, where he currently teaches on the Masters in Dementia Studies. He is a qualified social worker with a particular interest in social care practice. His research focuses upon the everyday experience of living with dementia using participatory approaches. He is currently leading a five-year study, funded jointly by the ESRC and NIHR exploring the experience of neighbourhood for people living with dementia and their carers. He is also piloting a novel approach to investigating household disbandment for people making the transition to long-stay care and extra-care housing using visual and object-elicitation methods. Richard is the co-founder of an international online hub for sharing evidence and good practice regarding dementia, place and space: http://memoryfriendly.org.uk/.

Sue Westwood is a socio-legal and gerontology scholar with a particular interest in ageing and equality. With a PhD in Law, Sue is a researcher at the University of Oxford, Honorary Research Fellow at the Centre for Research on Ageing and Gender, University of Surrey and teaches Law at Coventry

University Law School. She is also a contract-based researcher, most recently with the University of Leeds and the Faculty of Health Sciences, University of Surrey. Sue was previously a manager of dementia adviser and befriending services for a UK charity and has conducted research on dementia provision for a local authority and on dementia advocacy for a UK dementia advocacy organisation. Her monograph *Ageing, Gender and Sexuality: Equality in Later Life* is also published by Routledge.

Carolyn Whyte is a researcher and the former coordinator of Val's Café, a national programme to promote the health and wellbeing of older LGBTI Australians. Carolyn has been involved in Australian research exploring the experiences and needs of older LGBTI people including experiences of discrimination, mental wellbeing, dementia and carers.

Paul Willis is Senior Lecturer in Social Work at Swansea University, Wales. Prior to working in academia, Paul qualified in social work at the University of Tasmania, Australia, and his practice experience included supporting LGBTQ young people in counselling and community development roles in rural Tasmania. His research interests include sexuality and care in adult relationships, sexuality and ageing, and the social identities and wellbeing of LGBTQ youth.

Tarynn M. Witten, PhD, LCSW, FGSA, is a Fellow of the Gerontological Society of America and holder of the Inaugural Nathan W. and Margaret Shock New Investigator Research Award from the Gerontological Society of America. She is currently an Associate Professor of Biological Complexity, Emergency Medicine, and an Adjunct Associate Professor, Social Work and Women's & Gender Studies, at Virginia Commonwealth University. Tarynn has also served on the National Gay and Lesbian Task Force on Aging and serves as a member of the Virginia Commission on Aging. She is the founder and director of the Transgender Longitudinal Aging Research Study. She has published over 40 research papers, books and book chapters related to gender-identity issues in older people. Her newest co-edited book is *Gay, Lesbian, Bisexual & Transgender Aging: Challenges in Research, Practice and Policy*.

Foreword

There has never been more hope for realising people's full potential to live well with dementia. In the UK the launch of the *Living Well with Dementia: A National Dementia Strategy* in 2009 was followed by the *Prime Minister's Challenge on Dementia* in 2012 and most recently by the *Prime Minister's Challenge on Dementia 2020*, published in 2015 (London: Stationary Office). The latter's vision is:

> to create a society by 2020 where every person with dementia, and their carers and families, from all backgrounds, walks of life, and in all parts of the country – people of different ages, gender, sexual orientation, ability or ethnicity for example, receive high quality, compassionate care from diagnosis through to end of life.
>
> (p. 6)

Yet whilst there is lots of attention paid to supporting this diverse group of people to live well with dementia, there is limited attention – in research, policy or practice – paid to the perspective and experience of lesbian, gay, bisexual and trans* individuals. This neglect is all the more striking because within the field of dementia policy and practice there is a commitment to addressing the diversity of experience of living with dementia. This edited collection is a landmark in redressing this neglect.

This timely edited collection includes contributions from a range of disciplinary perspectives including social work, law, education, disability studies, gerontology, gender studies, and perhaps not surprisingly, dementia studies. Many of the contributors bring additional perspectives from working across fields, for example gender and ageing studies. The breadth of disciplinary perspectives is further enriched by the breadth of countries represented including Australia, Canada, the UK and the US.

This edited collection has several highlights for me. First, I am struck by the complexity of language and terminology in this field. The editors in their introduction are refreshingly frank about the tensions among their own contributors about the language to be used. The collection is explicit about the concern with the marginalisation of bisexuality and trans* issues in the LGBT* discourse.

Second, we know that the experience of living with dementia is affected by societal and community understanding and attitudes. This edited collection directly confronts the compound effect of the stigma and discrimination associated with being old, lesbian, gay, bisexual and/or trans* and living with dementia. Third, the collection pays attention both to people living with dementia who are lesbian, gay, bisexual and/or trans* and also family carers who are lesbian, gay, bisexual and/or trans*. Fourth, the book addresses the tension between being visible and being hidden; reminding us that many old people living with dementia today will have felt the need to hide their sexual identity and/or gender identity in the past in order to avoid stigma, discrimination and prejudice. Fifth, the book challenges us to question not only our assumptions of heterosexuality, but also ways in which we privilege and prioritise heterosexuality. This collection not only points out the error in such assumptions but spells out the unnecessary hurt and suffering caused by these assumptions. Truly taking the person's perspective means being open to a diverse range of sexualities, sexual identities and gender identities. It is important that we see and engage with the *whole* person. While many of us recognise that this requires a concern with knowing the person's biography (life experience to date), personality, preferences and aspirations, we may be guilty of assuming heterosexuality and/or gender congruence.

For these reasons this edited collection is a milestone in our field. Focussing on concepts, care, services and rights it is a timely and compelling resource addressing the paucity of research and scholarship in this area and inequalities in service provision.

Murna Downs
Professor in Dementia Studies
School of Dementia Studies
University of Bradford

Acknowledgements

Many thanks to Emily Briggs for commissioning this book and to Anne Halliday for another superb piece of copyediting. The idea for this edited collection originated from a 2013 seminar on lesbian, gay, bisexual and trans* (LGBT*) people and dementia, which was held in London by The Dementia Engagement & Empowerment Network (DEEP). It was chaired by Sue, and Liz was one of the keynote speakers. Our thanks go to DEEP and, in particular, Nada Savitch for creating such a brilliant forum, and for inspiring us to take things further.

We want to acknowledge the invaluable help we received from Jenny-Anne Bishop and Chryssy Hunter, who provided editorial input on the trans* aspects of the book as a whole, as well as contributing to their own chapter. We would like to thank all of the contributors, of course. Our thanks, in particular, go to Richard Ward, for telling us we could do this, and for his wise counsel and support at various stages of the book's development.

1 Introduction

Sue Westwood and Elizabeth Price

Why a book about lesbian, gay, bisexual and trans* people and dementia? What makes their experiences of dementia different from those of anyone else? With an ageing population, dementia, which is age related (Knapp *et al.*, 2007), is on the increase and is a growing social concern. An estimated 44.35 million people worldwide were living with dementia in 2013 and this is predicted to rise to 75.62 million by 2030 and 135.46 million by 2050 (Alzheimer's Disease International, 2013). Women are disproportionately affected by dementia (Alzheimer's Disease International, 2015), primarily because of ageing demographics: women tend to live longer than men, (Bamford, 2011). Individuals aged over 80 living with dementia are twice as likely to be women as men, and individuals reaching 100 who are living with dementia are four times as likely to be women as men (World Health Organization (WHO), 2007).

An estimated 7.5 to 10 per cent of the population identify as lesbian, gay and bisexual (LGB), the exact figures not being known, partly because sexuality/sexual identity is not routinely surveyed (Aspinall, 2009) and partly because they comprise, to a certain degree, a hidden population (Meyer and Wilson, 2009). Given that 'dementia does not discriminate' (Newman and Price, 2012: 183), a significant proportion of people with dementia, and the families, friends and carers of people with dementia, will be lesbian, gay and bisexual. Moreover, given that more women than men are affected by dementia, lesbians and bisexual women will be disproportionately affected compared with gay and bisexual men (Westwood, 2015). An increasing number of people openly identify as trans*, although, again, the exact figures are not yet known and estimates are even more imprecise (Bailey, 2012). Trans* people are at least as likely as cisgender people to develop dementia, and may even, because of psychosocial stressors, be at increased risk of doing so (Witten, 2014).

While LGBT* people living with dementia will share many of the experiences and concerns of non-LGBT* people living with dementia, theirs will also be informed by gender, sexuality/sexual identity and gender identity, and the social marginalisation associated with each of these intersecting social positions. Their experiences and concerns will also be informed by the readiness, or not, of services for people with dementia and those who care for them, to recognise, understand and be equipped to meet the needs of LGBT* people (Ward *et al.*, 2005; Cook-Daniels, 2006; Price, 2008, 2010, 2012; Witten, 2008).

This edited collection brings together original authorship from academics, practitioners and LGBT* individuals affected by dementia. Taking an intersectional approach (Taylor *et al.*, 2011) – that is considering the plurality of experiences and the multiple, interacting relational positions of everyday life – it addresses topics relating to concepts, practice and rights. Multidisciplinary and international in scope, it includes authors from the UK, USA, Canada and Australia, from a range of disciplinary backgrounds (including sociology, social work, psychology, health care and socio-legal studies). By bringing together this wide-ranging authorship, the collection will appeal to policy makers, commissioners, practitioners, academics and students across a range of disciplines.

In this introductory chapter, we shall first consider the marginalisation of LGBT* people living with dementia in dementia studies. We will then introduce and outline each of the parts and chapters in this edited collection. Lastly, we will reflect on links and interconnections between chapters, identifying conceptual, policy, practice, rights and research implications.

Terms and abbreviations

We need to briefly address the issue of language. Many authors writing in this field seek to avoid using fixed identity categories if possible. Despite modern day binary constructions of hetero- homo- and bi-sexualities, sexuality is far more complex, fluid and socially, historically and contextually contingent (Weeks, 2010). Since Kinsey's early work (Kinsey *et al.*, 1948, 1953), there has been a growing recognition of the overlap between the 'hetero' and the 'homo' and of sexual fluidity in individual lives (Sedgwick, 1990), particularly the lives of women (Kitzinger, 1987; Diamond, 2008). Sexuality itself is a contested term (Weeks, 2007), in relation to whether it describes a behaviour, an orientation (innate or acquired), a strategic identity (Bernstein, 2009), an actual identity (Calzo *et al.*, 2011), with/out a politicised component (Adam, 1995; Power, 1995), a broader ethos (Blasius, 1994), or possible combinations of all. In more recent years, those individuals who identify as intersex or asexual (Pinto, 2014) have also further complicated and contested simplistic notions of sexuality, including in relation to dementia (Alzheimer's Australia, 2014).

Those members of the trans* community who do not ascribe to binary notions of gender, but engage far more with gender fluid notions, and hence sexuality fluid notions too (given that 'same' and 'opposite' sex are predicated on either/or notions of gender) have demonstrated how gender too is not a fixed category. They have extended the logic of Judith Butler's (1999) arguments about gender performance as a normative social construction to demonstrate, through lived experience, the diversity, complexity, fluidity and creativities of gender (Williams, 2014). Some authors have resisted sexuality categories by mobilising the term queer (e.g. Warner, 2000) However, queer is not a unilaterally popular term and, indeed, many non-heterosexual individuals, especially older individuals (Fox, 2007) and/or feminists are uneasy with its use (Fineman *et al.*, 2009). We have chosen to avoid using the term queer in the chapters in this book. This has not necessarily sat comfortably with some of the authors contributing to chapters, and we appreciate their forbearance in this editorial decision.

Reflecting this diversity of discourse, there is an ever-expanding range of terms and abbreviations in use to describe non-heterosexual and/or non-gender-normative individuals, including LGBT (lesbian, gay, bisexual and trans); LGBTI (lesbian, gay, bisexual, trans and intersex); GLBT (gay, lesbian, bisexual and trans); GLBTI (gay, lesbian, bisexual, trans and intersex); LGBTQ (lesbian, gay, bisexual, trans and queer); LGBTQI (lesbian, gay, bisexual, trans, queer and intersex); LGBTTQ (lesbian, gay, bisexual, transsexual, transgender and queer); and LGBTQQIA (lesbian, gay, bisexual, transgender, queer, questioning, intersex, asexual). Almost all these terms and abbreviations were present in the first drafts of chapters submitted by the authors. Some authors suggested that we might keep them all in order to emphasise the diversity and non-homogeneity of this 'population'. However, we had in mind those readers who are new to this topic, who might be confused, and even put off, by this plethora of different terms, and decided that one term/abbreviation should be used consistently across the book. The issue then, of course, became which one to use.

In terms of sexuality only, we have employed LGB (lesbian, gay and bisexual) for convenience, rather than as an indication that we ascribe to notions of fixed sexual identity categories for all, although they may apply to some individuals. We have avoided using 'queer' because it is a contested term (as above). Trans* (T*) is an umbrella term which is increasingly deployed to cover the gender identity spectrum: including (but not limited to) transgender, transsexual, transvestite, genderqueer, genderfluid, non-binary, genderless, agender, non-gendered, third gender, two-spirit and bigender (Tompkins, 2014; Stonewall, 2015). We decided to use the term trans* in order to be as inclusive as possible. So, we have concluded that LGBT* would be our abbreviation of choice. The exception to this (there are always exceptions!) is Chapter 7, where Catherine Barrett and colleagues have used the term lesbian, gay and trans* (LGT*) to formally acknowledge that they have not included bisexual-identifying people in their study.

Ways of using this book

This book can be read in a variety of ways. For those who have an overarching interest in the subject, it can, of course, be read from beginning to end. For those with a more pragmatic focus on understanding and meeting the needs of LGBT* people affected by dementia in care contexts, Part II, 'Practice' might be approached as a standalone section if preferred. For those who have particular interests in certain topics, each chapter can be read in isolation, as well as an inter-connected part of the whole collection.

LGBT* people and dementia in context

Silences and similarities

Whilst there has been a growth in literature on LGBT* ageing (Cronin and King, 2010; Stein *et al.*, 2010; Ward *et al.*, 2012; Witten and Eyler, 2012; Finkenauer *et al.*, 2012; Sears, 2013; Kimmel, 2014; de Vries and Croghan, 2014) and on LGBT* mental health in later life (Fredriksen-Goldsen *et al.*, 2013, 2014), very little of it has, so far, addressed issues of dementia (McGovern, 2014). Similarly, while there is an emergent awareness of the significance of diversity in the experience of living with dementia (Innes *et al.*, 2009), very little attention has been paid to diversity relating to sexuality/sexual identity (Price, 2008; Ward *et al.*, 2012), gender (Westwood *et al.*, 2015) and/or gender identity (Witten, 2014). Indeed, there appears to be a silence on these issues among the extensive body of health and social care literature on ageing and dementia (Concannon, 2009; Eliason *et al.*, 2010; Ward *et al.*, 2011; McGovern, 2014). Most notable of all has been an absence of the voices of LGBT* people living with dementia themselves (Peel and McDaid, 2015).

Existing literature on LGBT* people living with dementia

The very limited research so far on LGBT* dementia has come from a small number of authors. McGovern, writing in 2014, identified 16 academic articles about LGBT* dementia, although while articles may use the LGBT* abbreviation, their content often only addresses lesbian and gay concerns. This reflects the wider marginalisation of bisexuality and trans issues in LGB/LGBT* discourse particularly in relation to health and social care provision (Jones, 2010; Ward *et al.*, 2012; Witten, 2014; Westwood *et al.*, 2015). The bulk of the literature in this area has been produced by two separate researchers. Richard Ward (2000) first highlighted over 15 years ago how the 'gay community' is fearful about dementia-related care needs and having to try to conceal their sexualities in care spaces to avoid prejudice and discrimination. Ward has gone on to identify with colleagues (Ward *et al.*, 2005) the assumptions of heterosexuality among care home staff and how this, together with the surveillance of sexuality, particularly men's sexuality, serves to exclude the experiences of gay men with dementia in particular.

Elizabeth Price's work has highlighted the invisibility of gay men and lesbians in dementia nursing (Price, 2005); how dementia can compound the stigma and social marginalisation experienced by older gay men and lesbians (Price, 2008); and how disclosure of sexuality can be a 'critical issue' (Price, 2010: 160) for carers of a lesbian or gay person with dementia, informing how they perceive health and social care provision in the light of how such disclosures are dealt with. More recently, Price (2012) has described research findings which suggest that lesbian and gay people who care, or have cared for, a person with dementia, are very fearful of dementia care spaces. They anticipate that these spaces will privilege and prioritise heterosexuality, resulting in a split between those who want mainstream provision to become more attuned to lesbian and gay identities, and those who see specialist provision as a solution. Price has also written with Roger Newman about the development and demise of the UK Alzheimer's Society's LGBT* network (Newman and Price, 2012).

Current theoretical models of dementia

In terms of mainstream dementia theorising, the four main models of dementia – biomedical, gerontological, psychosocial and disability – each frame dementia, and the person living with dementia, in ways which are LGBT* exclusionary. The biomedical model (Gubrium, 1986), with its emphasis on bodies, pathologies, symptoms and symptom management, has been widely critiqued for failing to take into account the person in the body (Lyman, 1989), and how individual experiences of living with dementia are shaped by socio-cultural contexts (Downs, 2000). Such socio-cultural contexts include issues of gender, sexuality and gender identity. Moreover the biomedical model of dementia constructs bodies with dementia as deviating from 'normal' bodies. Such constructions of the 'normal' body are highly contingent on socio-cultural norms, inclusions and exclusions and can be quite arbitrary at times (Burns and Iliffe, 2009). They are, in particular, embedded in values which assume heteronormativity, gender conformity and bodies which have temporal consistency (McRuer, 2006). This is especially excluding with regard to the bodies of trans* people (Wahlert and Fiester, 2014) including those with dementia: their gender may not conform with the sex assigned at birth; they may not have genital congruence with their gender identity; and, in advanced dementia, may experience shifting conceptions of a gendered, sexual, self (Marshall *et al.*, 2015).

The gerontological model of dementia (O'Reilly *et al.*, 2011), which is based on the notion that dementia is a natural part of the ageing process, is also problematic for LGBT* people. Mainstream gerontological discourse is based on a heteronormative (Cronin, 2006) and heterosexist (Clarke *et al.*, 2010) 'rhetorical silencing' (Brown, 2009: 65) of ageing LGB sexualities, while older trans people are 'both underserved and understudied' in mainstream gerontology (Persson, 2009: 633). Similarly, the field of disability, while showing an increased interest in dementia and intellectual disability (Janicki and Dalton, 2014) has been repeatedly critiqued for failing to take into account the needs of LGBT* people with an intellectual disability (Noonan and Gomez, 2011). Indeed 'queer' critiques of disability more generally have interrogated notions of normal within disability discourse, including from the perspectives of gender and sexuality (Clare, 2001; McRuer, 2006), as well as in terms of trans* issues:

> Transgender studies, much like disability studies, works with the lived bodily experiences of people who fit outside of hegemonic gender norms and the ways in which people negotiate corporeal experiences that run up against societal barriers that only privilege certain bodies.
>
> (Mog and Lock Swarr, 2008: Para 4)

The psychosocial model of dementia (Kitwood, 1990, 1993, 1997), by contrast, holds greater potential for understanding sexuality, gender and gender identity diversity in the context of dementia. 'Central to this is the concept of personhood in which subjectivity and intersubjectivity are fully recognised ... the key psychological task in dementia care is that of keeping the sufferer's personhood in being' (Kitwood and Bredin, 1992: 269). This model has generated wide-ranging philosophical debates about what constitutes personhood, particularly in the context of dementia, especially advanced dementia (Hughes *et al.*, 2006). Central to this is whether there is a core stable self, a central personhood, which may or may not endure at the point of profound cognitive decline (Cowdell, 2006). Those who argue that it does, also assert that this personhood should be at the core of dementia care:

> Whilst mood and behaviour may be profoundly affected, personhood is not; the individual remains the same equally valuable person throughout the course of the illness. Interventions to support the person with dementia should honour their personhood and right to be treated as a unique individual.
>
> (Kinnaird, 2012: 9)

However, personhood is itself a problematic concept, not least for the notions of a fixed and stable self which endures across time. Queer theorists (Butler, 1993, 1999, 2004) have critiqued such notions, arguing that identity is fluid, unstable, contingent and discursively and performatively reproduced in variable ways according to time, space and context (see Chapter 4). They emphasise, '[t]he importance of physical embodiment of intersecting identities and ... how the narratives of lived experiences integrate the socially constructed, embodied and self-constructed aspects of identity' (Nagoshi and Brzuzy, 2010: 437). Emerging from such critiques, intersectionality theorists have advocated instead an understanding of the person affected by dementia in the context of intersecting identities and social locations (see Hulko, 2004, 2009; and Chapter 3). The growing appreciation of dementia as a contextually contingent, embodied experience and of the disciplining of the body in dementia care (Twigg, 1999, 2000) 'collectively destabilizes dementia as a taken-for-granted category and has generated critical texts on the interrelationship between the body and social and political processes in the production and expression of dementia' (Kontos and Martin, 2013: 288).

Each of the main theoretical models of dementia, then, not only fail to take LGBT* people with dementia into account, but are also structured in such a way as to make them unthinkable. The purpose of this book is to make them thinkable and to consider the conceptual, practice and rights implications of taking LGBT* people living with dementia into account.

Chapter outlines

This book is divided into three sections. Part I, 'Concepts', comprises four chapters addressing theoretical and/or conceptual issues. In Chapter 2, 'Gender, sexuality, gender identity and dementia: (in)equality issues', Sue Westwood takes a socio-legal approach to the marginalisation of LGBT individuals living with dementia. Drawing upon the work of Nancy Fraser (1997), Westwood argues that LGBT* individuals affected by dementia have unequal access to resources, recognition and representation, compared with non-LGBT* individuals affected by dementia. She considers the legal and ethical implications of these inequalities.

In Chapter 3, 'LGBT* individuals and dementia: an intersectional approach', Wendy Hulko explains and considers intersectionality, which offers a framework to understand how multiple social positions can work with and through one another to produce complex in/equalities. Hulko uses the narratives of an older trans* bisexual woman to explore how she might be affected were she to have dementia. By doing so, Hulko is able to explore how intersectionality can offer an important framework for understanding the diversity of experiences of dementia and services for people with dementia, their families, friends and carers. She highlights how the social locations of gender, sexuality and gender identity might intersect to produce uneven outcomes for LGBT* people living with dementia.

In Chapter 4, 'Queer(y)ing dementia – bringing queer theory and studies of dementia into dialogue', Andrew King offers an analysis of the conceptual construction of gender, sexuality/sexual identity and gender identity and of people with dementia, from the perspective of queer theory and queer studies. He critically interrogates the categories which are deployed in such conceptualisations, arguing for the need for a deconstruction of such categories in order to resist the norms and normativities which underpin them, and which in turn produce sites of both inclusion and exclusion in LGBT* and dementia discourse.

In Chapter 5, 'Reconceptualising dementia: towards a politics of senility', Richard Ward and Elizabeth Price bring together key concepts from dementia studies and LGBT* studies to open up a more radical critique of dementia discourse. In particular they interrogate notions of personhood and citizenship as sites of normative social inclusions and exclusions which serve to marginalise LGBT* people living with dementia. Drawing upon disability, feminist and queer theories, they argue for a reconceptualising of dementia which offers greater opportunities to create connections between individuals both 'with' and 'without' dementia, and, crucially, those who occupy the spaces in between.

Part II, 'Practice', comprises six chapters addressing practice issues in relation to the delivery of health and social care provision to LGBT* people living with dementia. In Chapter 6, 'Providing responsive services to LGBT* individuals with dementia', Mark Hughes explores how mainstream health and social services providers could and should respond to the diverse needs of LGBT* people with dementia. He highlights the importance of appreciating the complexity of gender, sexuality and gender expression. Hughes also considers the challenges of negotiating privacy in health and social care contexts and the need to address the impact of discrimination on service use. The chapter explores ways to promote the rights of LGBT* people receiving services and opportunities to facilitate organisational change in order to improve service delivery.

In Chapter 7, 'Person-centred care and cultural safety: the perspectives of lesbian, gay and trans (LGT) people and their partners on living with dementia', Catherine Barrett and colleagues report on their research with lesbian, gay and trans* (LGT*) people affected by dementia. Their analysis of this rich data demonstrates the challenges faced by LGT* people living with dementia, including the challenges of managing the disclosure of sexuality/sexual identity and/or gender identity and of encountering services which are under-prepared to meet the needs of LGBT* people living with dementia. Barrett and colleagues highlight the importance of health and social care organisations providing dementia services which recognise and are responsive to the needs, wishes, and concerns of LGBT* people.

Chapters 8 and 9 address issues relating to trans* people with dementia. In Chapter 8, 'Trans* people anticipating dementia care: findings from the Transgender MetLife Survey', Tarynn Witten describes the findings from a recent USA survey which explored trans* people's fears and concerns about dementia care provision. In Chapter 9, 'The complexity of trans*/gender identities: implications for dementia care', Chryssy Hunter, Jenny-Anne Bishop and Sue Westwood explore the implications of dementia for trans* identities and trans* dementia care.

Many LGBT* people care for and support both LGBT* and non-LGBT* people who are living with dementia. In Chapter 10, 'Looking back whilst moving forward: LGBT* carers' perspectives', Elizabeth Price considers the very limited accounts of the experience of lesbian and gay carers of people with dementia and the silences about bisexual and trans* carers of people with dementia. Price reflects on her own pioneering research on lesbian and gay carers of people with dementia, spanning 15 years, which was prompted by a (surprised) colleague questioning why caring for someone with dementia is any different for a LGBT* person than a non-LGBT* person. Price's work has demonstrated very clearly that the differences relate to: a lack of recognition and support for LGBT* carers; a lack of appreciation among health and social care providers of the histories, lived experiences, identities and cultures of LGBT* people; the need to deal with prejudice and discrimination at times of extreme stress; and the loss of privacy for (LGBT*) people with dementia and their LGBT* carers, whose identities are still often stigmatised and marginalised in society at large.

One of the main strategies among LGBT* activists to address shortcomings in health and social care provision for LGBT* people, including those with dementia, relate to staff training and education, often in the form of one-off training events. This approach is considered in Chapter 11, 'One-day training courses on LGBT* awareness – are they the answer?' in which Sue Westwood and Sally Knocker consider its advantages (increase awareness; promote sensitisation to relevant issues; encourage reflective practice; open up a dialogue, and offer a language and framework for, discussing older LGBT* issues and care practices; increase knowledge of local and national agencies with expertise in older LGBT* issues) and disadvantages (does not tackle systemic and/or organisational issues; does not overcome entrenched negative attitudes towards LGBT* people; tends to mobilise a collective narrative, for strategic convenience, which promotes – positive – stereotyping and obscures diversity among and between LGBT* people). Westwood and Knocker argue for the need for more comprehensive, organisation-focused interventions which promote lasting organisational change and afford greater opportunity to represent the wide range of lives, and interests (sometimes competing) which fall under the LGBT* umbrella.

Part III, 'Rights', is made up of four chapters addressing socio-legal issues relating to LGBT* people living with dementia. In Chapter 12, 'LGBT* individuals living with dementia: rights and capacity issues in the United States', Nancy Knauer considers how the unique challenges facing LGBT* individuals living with dementia have been largely overlooked by USA national policy initiatives and the LGBT* rights movement. Knauer explores the rights issues affecting LGBT* people with dementia in the USA, and gives a number of examples of cases where those rights have recently been violated. Knauer proposes a range of socio-legal reforms to address these inequalities. She emphasises the importance of using legal mechanisms for advance planning in order to ensure that the rights, wishes and needs of LGBT* individuals living with dementia are recognised and respected even if they should lose capacity.

The experience of living with and supporting someone living with dementia is always a deeply personal one. In Chapter 13, 'The needs and rights of LGBT* carers of individuals with dementia: a personal journey', Roger Newman reflects on his experiences as a gay man caring for a partner with dementia in the 1990s and the insights gleaned from those experiences. He charts his journey from becoming first 'a carer' and then an activist on behalf of LGBT* people living with dementia, their carers, and wider LGBT* care and ageing issues. Roger reflects on his experiences, the lessons he has learned, and concludes with a wish list for addressing the rights and needs of LGBT* people living with dementia, and LGBT* carers, in the future.

In Chapter 14, 'Navigating stormy waters: consent, sexuality and dementia in care environments in Wales', Paul Willis, Michele Raithby and Tracey Maegusuku-Hewett report on their recent research with residential care staff in Wales working with older people, many of whom have dementia. They consider how the staff understand and manage issues of sexual consent and capacity and the implications for their provision of care to older lesbian, gay or bisexual (LGB) adults. Their findings highlight how, in facilitating relationships between residents with declining mental capacity, and in managing issues of capacity to consent and of risk, the staff mobilise narratives which do not take into account the possibility that some of their residents will be lesbian, gay or bisexual. Willis and his colleagues conclude with recommendations for developing 'LGB affirmative' approaches to negotiating care, consent and dementia.

LGBT* rights and dementia rights often overlap. In Chapter 15, 'To equality – and beyond? Queer reflections on an emerging rights-based approach to dementia in Scotland', Richard Ward explores an emerging rights-based agenda for dementia in Scotland and the tensions and limitations associated with this rights-based approach. Drawing upon queer theory, Ward considers: the import-ance of spaces of advantage and disadvantage among collective groups of people; the risk that focussing on a single identity category (in this case 'demen-tia') can obscure inequalities among and between people within that category (in this case people living with dementia); and thus the need to move away from identity categories in order to conceptualise the lives and experiences of people affected by dementia more broadly (which would include LGBT* people living with dementia). Ward advocates a more radical agenda for dementia policy, practice and activism in order to reduce normative marginalisation and increase inclusivity for all people affected by dementia.

Interconnections

The chapters are linked in several ways. First, they highlight the importance of multiple social locations, and their intersections, for experiences of dementia, and of dementia services. In the context of this book the social locations which are of particular relevance are gender, sexuality, gender identity, and the over-arching framework of age and ageing. Second, they emphasise the significance of recognition for people with dementia (whose voices are often not heard) and for LGBT* people, who are affected by multiple and interacting sites of non-recognition (i.e. not being conceptualised in theory or practice) or mis-recognition (Lovell, 2007) (i.e. being mis-understood as heterosexual and/or cisgender). These two sites overlap for LGBT* people with dementia who are multiply marginalised as a result. Recognition is also extremely important in terms of actual and/or anticipated stigma, that is, being recognised in ways which involve prejudice and discrimination, which are, again, issues for people living with dementia and for LGBT* people separately and are then compounded for LGBT* people living with dementia.

   The third linked theme relates to notions of belonging and social inclusion. Per-sonhood and citizenship are key concepts in attempts to create greater social inclu-sion for people with dementia, and also afford greater rights to them. Similarly identity rights-based claims have advanced the legal recognition (and regulation, Harding, 2011) of LGBT* individuals and same-sex couples. However, critics of these concepts have highlighted how they are not only inclusionary but also exclu-sionary processes: whenever a boundary of socio-legal inclusion is drawn, it deter-mines not only who lies within it, but also who lies without it too (Smart, 1989). The chapters variously question and challenge the use of categories, and the norms and normativities which underpin them, emphasising in particular those individuals whose lives and experiences may be excluded by them.

   All of the chapters, implicitly or explicitly, address issues of equality and inequality, for people with dementia, for LGBT* people, and for LGBT* people with dementia. The privileging of heterosexuality and cisgender identities in dementia theory, practice and rights discourse has produced profound sites of inequality for LGBT* people with dementia. As a consequence, their (varied) experiences are not recognised or understood, their particular and specific needs not addressed, and their rights undermined. This has produced profound social injustices which must be addressed, by creating theories which are LGBT* inclusive, services which understand and serve well the needs of LGBT* people affected by dementia, and rights discourse which encompass intersectionality, and, in particular, gender, sexuality and gender identity in relation to dementia. Until this is achieved, a significant sub-section of people affected by dementia will have the distress associated with dementia compounded by marginalisation, social exclusion and the anxiety, fear and pain which accompany them.

Future implications

The first and most obvious implication from the chapters is the need for more research on the experiences of LGBT* people living with dementia (Kimmel, 2014), both collectively, and separately. There is in particular a need to better understand bisexuality and dementia. Wendy Hulko's case study involves a bisexual woman, but her chapter is the only one in this collection to foreground issues of bisexuality. Catherine Barrett and colleagues deliberately drop the 'B' from the LGBT* abbreviation in their 'LGT*' chapter in recognition that their sample did not include people who identified as bisexual. But other chapters often refer to LGBT* without addressing bisexuality beyond the abbreviation, reflecting Rebecca Jones' (2010) observation that the 'B' in LGBT* rarely gets addressed beyond the title. There is an urgent need for bisexuality-specific dementia research but also dementia research which includes participants across the sexuality/sexual identity spectrum, including bisexual people.

Another critical silence to be addressed is in relation to LGBT* people from Black, Asian and minority ethnic (BAME) communities living with dementia. There is a growing appreciation of: the significance of dementia for people from BAME communities (Moriarty *et al.*, 2011); the need for dementia services in particular to understand how 'race', culture and religion mediate the experiences of living with dementia (Regan *et al.*, 2013); and the need for providers to develop 'cultural competence'. There is a nascent appreciation of the significance of dementia in the lives of LGBT* people. However, BAME dementia authorship does not address LGBT* issues, reflecting the wider silences and absences about LGBT* people living with dementia. Similarly, while there is a small amount of literature on BAME/LGBT* ageing and mental health coming from the USA (SAGE, 2013), non-USA authorship on LGBT* issues associated with dementia has not addressed issues affecting LGBT* people from BAME communities (Westwood *et al.*, 2015). This reflects a wider silencing of the voices of LGBT* people from BAME communities in mainstream gerontological discourse (Van Sluytman and Torres, 2014). This silence needs to be addressed, and indeed critical race theory (Delgado and Stefancic, 2012) has much to offer in terms of understanding not only the silence about LGBT* people from BAME communities who are living with dementia but also the wider silences and absences in dementia discourse about all LGBT* people living with dementia.

In terms of future recommendations, the respective Parts of this collection reflect the key areas which need to be addressed: dementia theory needs to take gender, sexuality/sexual identity and trans identities into account; dementia research must routinely and proactively include both LGBT* and non-LGBT* people in samples, and analyses should always consider the dimensions of gender, sexuality/sexual identity and trans identities; dementia practice must become far more equipped to recognise and respond appropriately to the needs of LGBT* people living with dementia; the violation of the rights of LGBT* people living with dementia in health and social care spaces require much closer attention. Impartial advocacy for LGBT* individuals living with dementia who have not nominated someone to represent them is an essential means of ensuring their best interests are represented on an ongoing basis.

The need for effective advocacy is not, of course, unique to LGBT* people with dementia, but to all people living with dementia who lack capacity and have no one to speak up for them. However, as Ward and colleagues have pointed out, policy and services for LGBT* individuals have the potential to serve as a 'litmus test' (Ward *et al.*, 2011: 26) for how well social care providers respond to equality and diversity issues and the needs of all marginalised people. In this way, addressing the inequalities which affect LGBT* people living with dementia will benefit other marginalised people living with dementia as well.

References

Adam, B. (1995) *The Rise of a Gay and Lesbian Movement.* New York: Twayne.

Alzheimer's Australia (2014) *Dementia, Transgender and Intersex People: Do Service Providers Really Know What Their Needs Are?* Melbourne: Alzheimer's Australia.

Alzheimer's Disease International (2013) *The Global Impact of Dementia 2013–2050.* London: Alzheimer's Disease International.

Alzheimer's Disease International (2015) *Women and Dementia: A Global Research Review.* London: Alzheimer's Disease International.

Aspinall, P. J. (2009) *Estimating the Size and Composition of the Lesbian, Gay, and Bisexual Population in Britain.* London: Equality and Human Rights Commission.

Bailey, L. (2012) Trans Ageing. In R. Ward, I. Rivers and M. Sutherland (eds) *Lesbian, Gay, Bisexual and Transgender Ageing: Biographical Approaches for Inclusive Care and Support*, pp. 51–66. London and Philadelphia: Jessica Kingsley Publishers.

Bamford, S. (2011) *Women and Dementia – Not Forgotten.* London: The International Longevity Centre – UK.

Bernstein, M. (2009) The Strategic Uses of Identity by the Lesbian and Gay Movement. In J. Goodwin and J. M. Jasper (eds) *The Social Movements Reader: Cases and Concepts, 2nd edition*, pp. 264–278. Chichester: John Wiley & Sons.

Blasius, M. (1994) *Gay and Lesbian Politics: Sexuality and the Emergence of a New Ethic.* Philadelphia: Temple University Press.

Brown, M. (2009) LGBT aging and rhetorical silence. *Sexuality Research & Social Policy*, **6**(4): 65–78.

Burns, A. and Iliffe, S. (2009) Alzheimer's disease: clinical review. *British Medical Journal*, **338**: b 158.

Butler, J. (1993) *Bodies that Matter: On the Discursive Limits of Sex.* New York: Routledge.

Butler, J. (1999) *Gender Trouble*. London: Routledge.

Butler, J. (2004) *Undoing Gender*. London: Routledge.

Calzo, J. P., Antonucci, T. C., Mays, V. M. and Cochran, S. D. (2011) Retrospective recall of sexual orientation identity development among gay, lesbian, and bisexual adults. *Developmental Psychology*, **47**(6): 1658–1673.

Clare, E. (2001) Stolen bodies, reclaimed bodies: Disability and queerness. *Public Culture*, **13**(3): 359–365.

Clarke, V., Ellis, S. J., Peel, E. and Riggs, D. W. (2010) *Lesbian, Gay, Bisexual, Trans and Queer Psychology*. Cambridge: Cambridge University Press.

Concannon, L. (2009) Developing inclusive health and social care policies for older LGB citizens. *British Journal of Social Work*, **39**: 403–417.

Cook-Daniels, L. (2006) Trans Ageing. In D. Kimmel, T. Rose and S. David (eds) *Lesbian, Gay, Bisexual and Transgender Ageing*, pp. 20–35. New York: Columbia University Press.

Cowdell, F. (2006) Preserving personhood in dementia research: A literature review. *International Journal of Older People Nursing*, **1**: 85–94.

Cronin, A. (2006) Sexuality in Gerontology: A Heteronormative Presence, a Queer Absence. In S. O. Daatland and S. Biggs (eds) *Ageing and Diversity: Multiple Pathways and Cultural Migrations*, pp. 107–122. Bristol: Policy Press.

Cronin, A. and King, A. (2010) Power, inequality and identification: Exploring diversity and intersectionality amongst older LGB adults. *Sociology*, **44**: 876–892.

De Vries, B. and Croghan, C. F. (2014) LGBT aging: The contributions of community-based research. *Journal of Homosexuality*, **61**(1): 1–20.

Delgado, R. and Stefancic, J. (2012) *Critical Race Theory: An Introduction.* 2nd edition. New York: New York University Press.

Diamond, L. M. (2008) *Sexual Fluidity: Understanding Women's Love and Desire*. Cambridge, MA: Harvard University Press.

Downs, M. (2000) Dementia in a socio-cultural context: An idea whose time has come. *Ageing and Society*, **20**: 369–375.

Eliason, M. J., Dibble, S. and DeJoseph, J. (2010) Nursing's silence on lesbian, gay, bisexual, and transgender issues: The need for emancipatory efforts. *Advances in Nursing Science*, **33**(3): 206–218.

Fineman, M., Jackson, J. and Romero, A. (eds) (2009) *Feminist and Queer Legal Theory: Intimate Encounters, Uncomfortable Conversations*. Aldershot: Ashgate.

Finkenauer, S., Sherratt, J., Marlow, J. and Brodey, A. E. (2012) When injustice gets old: A systematic review of trans ageing. *Journal of Gay and Lesbian Social Services*, **24**: 311–330.

Fox, R. C. (2007) Gay grows up: An interpretive study on aging metaphors and queer identity. *Journal of Homosexuality*, **52**(3–4): 33–61.

Fraser, N. (1997) *Justice Interruptus.* New York: Routledge.

Fredriksen-Goldsen, K. I., Cook-Daniels, L., Kim, H.-J., Erosheva, E. A., Emlet, C. A., Hoy-Ellis, C. P., Goldsen, J. and Muraco, A. (2014) Physical and mental health of transgender older adults: An at-risk and underserved population. *The Gerontologist*, **54**(3): 488–500.

Fredriksen-Goldsen, K. I., Kim, H.-J., Barkan, S. E., Muraco, A. and Hoy-Ellis, C. P. (2013) Health disparities among lesbian, gay, and bisexual older adults: Results from a population-based study. *American Journal of Public Health*, **103**(10): 1802–1809.

Gubrium, J. F. (1986) *Old Timers and Alzheimer's: The Descriptive Organization of Senility.* Greenwich, CT: JAI Press.

Harding, R. (2011) *Regulating Sexuality: Legal Consciousness in Lesbian and Gay Lives.* Abingdon: Routledge.

Hughes, J., Louw, S. and Sabat, S. (eds) (2006) *Dementia: Mind, Meaning and the Person.* Oxford: Oxford University Press.

Hulko W. (2004) Social Science Perspectives on Dementia Research: Intersectionality. In A. Innes, C. Archibald and C. Murphy (eds) *Dementia and Social Inclusion: Marginalised Groups and Marginalised Areas of Dementia Research, Care and Practice,* pp. 237–254. London: Jessica Kingsley Publishers.

Hulko, W. (2009) From 'not a big deal' to 'hellish': Experiences of older people with dementia. *Journal of Aging Studies,* **23**(3): 131–144.

Innes, I., Archibald, C. and Murphy, C. (eds) (2009) *Dementia and Social Inclusion.* London: Jessica Kingsley Publishers.

Janicki, M. P. and Dalton, A. J. (2014) *Dementia and Aging Adults with Intellectual Disabilities: A Handbook.* Abingdon: Routledge.

Jones, R. (2010) Troubles with Bisexuality in Health and Social Care. In R. L. Jones and R. Ward (eds) *LGBT Issues: Looking Beyond Categories,* pp. 42–55. Edinburgh: Dunedin Academic Press.

Kimmel, D. (2014) Lesbian, gay, bisexual, and transgender aging concerns. *Clinical Gerontologist,* **37**(1): 49–63.

Kinnaird, L. (2012) *Delivering Integrated Dementia Care: The 8 Pillars Model of Community Support.* Edinburgh: Alzheimer Scotland.

Kinsey, A. C., Pomeroy, W. B. and Martin, C. E. (1948) *Sexual Behavior in the Human Male.* Philadelphia: W.B. Saunders; Bloomington, IN: Indiana U. Press.

Kinsey, A. C., Pomeroy, W. B., Martin, C. E. and Gebhard, P. H. (1953) *Sexual Behavior in the Human Female.* Philadelphia: W.B. Saunders; Bloomington, IN: Indiana U. Press.

Kitwood, T. (1990) The dialectics of dementia: With particular reference to Alzheimer's disease. *Ageing and Society,* **10**: 177–196.

Kitwood, T. (1993) Towards a theory of dementia care: The interpersonal process. *Ageing and Society,* **13**: 51–67.

Kitwood, T. (1997) *Dementia Reconsidered: The Person Comes First.* Buckingham, UK: Open University Press.

Kitwood, T. and Bredin, K. (1992) Towards a theory of dementia care: Personhood and well-being. *Ageing and Society,* **12**: 269–287.

Kitzinger, C. (1987) *The Social Construction of Lesbianism.* London: Sage.

Knapp, M., Prince, M., Albanese, E., Banerjee, S., Dhanasiri, S., Fernandez, J.-L., Ferri, C., McCrone, P., Snell, T. and Stewart, R. (2007) *Dementia UK: A Report to the Alzheimer's Society on the Prevalence and Economic Cost of Dementia in the UK.* London: Alzheimer's Society.

Kontos, P. and Martin. W. (2013) Embodiment and dementia: Exploring critical narratives of selfhood, surveillance, and dementia care. *Dementia,* **12**(3): 288–302.

Lovell, T. (ed.) (2007) *(Mis)recognition, Social Inequality and Social Justice: Nancy Fraser and Pierre Bourdieu.* London: Routledge.

Lyman, K. A. (1989) Bringing the social back in: A critique of the bio-medicalisation of dementia. *The Gerontologist,* **29**: 597–604.

Marshall, J., Cooper, M. and Rudnick, A. (2015) Gender dysphoria and dementia: A case report. *Journal of Gay & Lesbian Mental Health,* **19**(1): 112–117.

McGovern, J. (2014) The forgotten: Dementia and the aging LGBT community. *Journal of Gerontological Social Work,* **57**(8): 845–857.

McRuer, R. (2006) *Crip Theory: Cultural Signs of Queerness and Disability.* New York: NYU press, 2006. Kindle Edition.

Meyer, I. H. and Wilson, P. A. (2009) Sampling lesbian, gay, and bisexual populations. *Journal of Counseling Psychology*, **56**(1): 23–31.

Mog, A. and Lock Swarr, A. (2008) Threads of commonality in transgender and disability studies. *Disability Studies Quarterly*, **28**(4). Downloaded 19 July 2015 from: www.dsq-sds.org/article/view/152/152.

Moriarty, J., Sharif, N. and Robinson, J. (2011) *Black and Minority Ethnic People with Dementia and their Access to Support and Services*. SCIE Research Briefing 35. London: SCIE.

Nagoshi, J. L. and Brzuzy, S. (2010) Transgender theory: Embodying research and practice. *Affilia*, **25**(4): 431–443.

Newman, R. and Price, E. (2012) Meeting the Needs of LGBT People Affected by Dementia. In R. Ward, I. Rivers and M. Sutherland (eds) *Lesbian, Gay, Bisexual and Transgender Ageing: Biographical Approaches for Inclusive Care and Support*, pp. 183–195. London: Jessica Kingsley Publishers.

Noonan, A. and Gomez, M. T. (2011) Who's missing? Awareness of lesbian, gay, bisexual and transgender people with intellectual disability. *Sexuality and Disability*, **29**(2): 175–180.

O'Reilly, O., Lavin, D. and Coughlan, B. J. (2011) Ageing and Dementia. In P. Ryan and B. J. Coughlan (eds) *Ageing and Older Adult Mental Health: Issues and Implications for Practice*, pp. 89–108. Abingdon: Routledge.

Peel, E. and McDaid, S. (2015) *'Over the Rainbow': Lesbian, Gay, Bisexual, Trans People and Dementia Project. Summary Report*. Worcester: Institute for Health and Society, University of Worcester, UK.

Persson, D. (2009) Unique challenges of transgender aging: Implications from the literature. *Journal of Gerontological Social Work*, **52**(6): 633–646.

Pinto, S. A. (2014) ASEXually: On being an ally to the asexual community. *Journal of LGBT Issues in Counseling*, **8**(4), 331–343.

Power, L. (1995) *No Bath but Plenty of Bubbles: An Oral History of the Gay Liberation Front 1970–73*. London: Cassell.

Price, E. (2005) All but invisible: Older gay men and lesbians. *Nursing Older People*, **17**(4): 16–18.

Price, E. (2008) Pride or prejudice? Gay men, lesbians and dementia. *British Journal of Social Work*, **38**: 1337–1352.

Price, E. (2010) Coming out to care: Gay and lesbian carers' experiences of dementia services. *Health and Social Care in the Community*, **18**(2): 160–168.

Price, E. (2012) Gay and lesbian carers: In the shadow of dementia. *Ageing and Society*, **32**(10): 526–532.

Regan, J. L., Bhattacharyya, S., Kevern, P. and Rana, T. (2013) A systematic review of religion and dementia care pathways in black and minority ethnic populations. *Mental Health, Religion & Culture*, **16**(1): 1–15.

SAGE (Services and Advocacy for GLBT Elders) (2013) *Health Equity and LGBT Elders of Color: Recommendations for Policy and Practice*. New York: SAGE.

Sears, James T. (ed.) (2013) *Growing Older: Perspectives on LGBT Aging*. London: Routledge.

Sedgwick, E. (1990) *Epistemology of the Closet*. Berkeley, CA: California University Press.

Smart, C. (1989) *Feminism and the Power of Law*. London: Routledge.

Stein, G., Beckerman, N. and Sherman, P. (2010) Lesbian and gay elders in long-term care: Identifying the unique psychosocial perspectives and challenges. *Journal of Gerontological Social Work*, **53**(5): 421–435.

Stonewall (2015) *Transgender*. Available from: www.stonewall.org.uk/sites/default/files/ transgender_booklet_2004.pdf [downloaded 13 October 2015].

Taylor, Y., Hines, S. and Casey, M. (eds) (2011) *Theorizing Intersectionality and Sexuality*. Basingstoke: Palgrave Macmillian.

Tompkins, A. (2014) Asterisk. *TSQ: Transgender Studies Quarterly*, 1(1-2): 26–27.

Twigg, J. (1999) The spatial ordering of care: Public and private in bathing support at home. *Sociology of Health & Illness*, 21(4): 381–400.

Twigg, J. (2000) Carework as a form of bodywork. *Ageing and Society*, 20: 389–411.

Van Sluytman, L. G. and Torres, D. (2014) Hidden or uninvited? A content analysis of elder LGBT of color literature in gerontology. *Journal of Gerontological Social Work*, 57(2–4): 130–160.

Wahlert, L. and Fiester, A. (2014) Repaving the road of good intentions: LGBT health care and the queer bioethical lens. *Hastings Center Report*, 44(s4): S56–65.

Ward, R. (2000) Waiting to be heard: Dementia and the gay community. *Journal of Dementia Care*, 8(3): 24–25.

Ward, R., Pugh, S. and Price, E. (2011) *Don't Look Back? Improving Health and Social Care Service Delivery for Older LGB Users*. London: Equality and Human Rights Commission.

Ward, R., Rivers, I. and Sutherland, M. (eds) (2012) *Lesbian, Gay, Bisexual and Transgender Ageing: Biographical Approaches for Inclusive Care and Support*. London: Jessica Kingsley Publishers.

Ward, R., Vass, A. A., Aggarwal, N., Garfield, C. and Cybyk, B. (2005) A kiss is still a kiss? – The construction of sexuality in dementia care. *Dementia*, 4(1): 49–72.

Warner, M. (2000) *The Trouble with Normal: Sex, Politics, and the Ethics of Queer Life*. New York: Harvard University Press.

Weeks, J. (2007) *The World We Have Won: The Remaking of Erotic and Intimate Life*. London: Routledge.

Weeks, J. (2010) *Sexuality*. 3rd edition. London: Routledge.

Westwood, S. (2015) Dementia, women and sexuality: How the intersection of ageing, gender and sexuality magnify dementia concerns among lesbian and bisexual women. *Dementia*, DOI: 1471301214564446.

Westwood, S., King, A., Almack, K. and Suen, Y.-T. (2015) Good Practice in Health and Social Care Provision for Older LGBT People. In J. Fish and K. Karban (eds) *Social Work and Lesbian, Gay, Bisexual and Trans Health Inequalities: International Perspectives*, pp. 145–159. Bristol: Policy Press.

Williams, C. (2014) Judith Butler on trans issues. *TransAdvocate*, 1 May 2014. Available from: www.transadvocate.com/gender-performance-the-transadvocate-interviews-judith-butler_n_13652.htm#sthash.CqUOVktP.dpuf [accessed 3 January 2015].

Witten, T. M. (2008) Transgender Bodies, Identities, and Healthcare: Effects of Perceived and Actual Violence and Abuse. In J. J. Kronenfeld (ed.) *Research in the Sociology of Healthcare: Inequalities and Disparities in Health Care and Health – Concerns of Patients*. v. 25, pp. 225–249. Oxford, England: Elsevier JAI.

Witten, T. M. (2014) End of life, chronic illness, and trans-identities. *Journal of Social Work in End-of-Life & Palliative Care*, 10(1): 34–58.

Witten, T. M. and Eyler, A. (eds) (2012) *Gay, Lesbian, Bisexual and Transgender Aging: Challenges in Research, Practice and Policy*. Baltimore: Johns Hopkins University Press.

World Health Organization (WHO) (2007) *Women, Ageing and Health: A Framework for Action*. Geneva: World Health Organisation.

Part I

Concepts

Introduction to Part I

Sue Westwood and Elizabeth Price

This section encompasses a range of theoretical approaches to LGBT* people living with dementia. In Chapter 2, Sue Westwood take a socio-legal approach to the marginalisation of LGBT* individuals living with dementia, considering the implications of their unequal access to resources, recognition and representation, compared with non-LGBT* individuals. In Chapter 3, Wendy Hulko explains and explores intersectionality, using an example of a trans* bisexual woman (with hypothetical dementia) as a lens through which to explore how multiple social locations might inform the experience of dementia and services for people with dementia, their families, friends, carers and supporters. In Chapter 4, Andrew King offers an analysis of the conceptual construction of gender, sexuality/sexual identity and gender identity and of people with dementia, from the perspective of queer theory and queer studies. He critically interrogates the categories which are deployed in such conceptualisations, arguing for the need for their deconstruction. In Chapter 5, Richard Ward and Elizabeth Price offer a wider radical critique of dementia discourse. They interrogate notions of personhood and citizenship as sites of normative social inclusions and exclusions which serve, in particular, to marginalise LGBT* people living with dementia.

All four chapters seek to understand and explain how the experiences, needs and concerns of LGBT* people affected by dementia have been so far neglected, both in LGBT* studies and in dementia studies. In particular, each chapter offers insights on the various silences and absences regarding dementia in LGBT* discourse and, conversely, regarding LGBT* issues in dementia discourse. They approach these issues through a wide theoretical lens, including crip (disability) theory, feminist theories, models of intersectionality, queer studies/theories, and socio-legal analyses of the legal (dementia) subject in formal law (statute and social policy) and disciplinary law (the social reproduction of norms and normativities which informally, and yet powerfully, regulate individuals and groups). The chapters also serve to highlight the similarities and dissimilarities of LGBT* individuals' experiences of living with dementia and how these are also informed by multiple other social locations, including age, gender, 'race', ethnicity, class, culture, religion and non-dementia-related disabilities.

The chapters offer a broad theoretical foundation from which to approach the subsequent sections on practice and rights issues. They offer intellectual spaces through and against which the notion of LGBT* people living with dementia moves from being unthinkable to 'thinkable'. In that 'thinkability', issues concerning LGBT* people living with dementia can shift from being silenced to being heard, from being invisible to being visible, from an absence to a critical presence. That increased hearing, visibility and presence thus creates a space where it becomes possible to begin to address the experiences, needs, wishes and rights of LGBT* people living with dementia.

2 Gender, sexuality, gender identity and dementia

(In)equality issues

Sue Westwood

Introduction

This chapter explores the equality implications of the absences and silences about LGBT* people affected by dementia, in dementia theory, practice and rights discourse. It does so by first mapping those absences and silences. It then goes on to consider what they mean for equality of recognition, resources and representation, drawing upon the work of the socio-legal theorist Nancy Fraser (1997). The argument being put forward is that LGBT* people affected by dementia are systemically disadvantaged in comparison with non-LGBT* people who are affected by dementia. This disadvantage is produced by multiple intersecting factors. First, people with dementia are often conceptualised, implicitly or explicitly, as heterosexual, cisgender and sex/gender binary (McGovern, 2014). Second, there is a lack of research about LGBT* people with dementia (Kimmel, 2014) which means this heterosexual bias remains unchallenged by evidence. Third, services for people living with dementia generally do not recognise or meet the needs of LGBT* people (Price, 2008; Witten, 2014). Fourth, dementia rights discourse does not take LGBT* people with dementia into account and there is a lack of impartial advocacy services for LGBT* people with dementia (Knauer, 2009, 2010). These, I would suggest, work together to create a web of inequalities for LGBT* people affected by dementia.

Conceptualisations of equality fall under three main categories: equality of 'how', equality of 'what' and equality 'for whom' (Fredman and Spencer, 2003). Equality of 'how' involves (Baker *et al.*, 2009): consistency, (everyone being treated the same); opportunity (everyone having the same chances in life); and results (everyone having the same outcomes). A sameness approach can be problematic because it does not take individual variations into account. Equality of opportunity can be over-simplistic, because it does not take into consideration structural disadvantages which may impinge upon being able to access opportunities. Equality of outcome, which emphasises equalising the end result, can be controversial in that it may require positive discrimination. A further problem with equality of outcome is when the outcome itself is poor.

Numerous lists and categories have been proposed to define the 'what' of equality (Baker *et al.*, 2009). Nancy Fraser (Fraser, 1996, 1997, 2000) has offered a tripartite model of equality involving: resources (economic); recognition (social status, cultural visibility and cultural worth); and representation (social and political participation and access to justice). Fraser refers to the inter-related nature of these concepts. She controversially asserted, in 1996, that lesbian, gay and bisexual equality was a problem of recognition, not redistribution (Fraser, 1996: 13–14). This, not surprisingly, aroused considerable debate. Judith Butler, in her paper 'Merely Cultural', for example, emphasised the inter-relatedness of 'the reproduction of goods as well as the social reproduction of persons' (Butler, 1997: 40). Fraser eventually acknowledged, in a footnote in a paper in 2007, 'even sexuality, which looks at first sight like the paradigm of pure recognition, has an undeniable economic dimension' (Fraser, 2007: 27, footnote 3), indicating that she had somewhat shifted her position. Despite her uneasy relationship with sexuality, Fraser's central framework is extremely helpful in structuring an analysis of equality and I will use this here. However, Fraser's notion of resources is expanded here to include not only economic resources but also the affective resources of 'love, care and solidarity' (Lynch, 2010: 3) and safe environments and housing (Barnes, 2012).

In terms of 'equality for whom', in order to discuss the rights and needs of particular individuals and/or social groups, it is necessary to mobilise identity categories to be able to explore particular elements of inequality. However, the use of fixed identity categories is problematic, as they can suggest a homogen-eity which does not exist and can mask fluidities, specificities and contingencies of experiences. Queer theorists, in particular, have challenged the use of identity categories (Cronin et al., 2011). However, I share Yuval-Davis's view (Yuval-Davis, 2006) that some degree of categorisation is necessary in order to locate and distinguish between processes of inequality. Such an analysis must take into account intersectionality: 'Intersectional approaches look at forms of inequality which are routed through one another, and which cannot be untangled to reveal a single cause' (Grabham et al., 2009: 1).

For a more detailed analysis of intersectionality, see Chapter 3 by Wendy Hulko in this volume. Intersectionality involves both temporal and spatial dimensions. Temporality engages with 'the interplay of the social context and historical times as well as the nature and consequences of linked and interde-pendent lives' (Fredriksen-Goldsen and Muraco, 2010: 402). In terms of spatial-ity, Gill Valentine has observed, 'the ability to enact some identities or realities rather than others is highly contingent on the power-laden spaces in and through which our experiences are lived' (Valentine, 2007: 19). In her case study with a deaf lesbian, Valentine demonstrated how that woman felt marginalised by dis-ablism when among hearing lesbians and gay men, and by heteronormativity and homophobia when among heterosexual deaf people (Valentine, 2007). Valentine observed, '[w]hen individual identities are "done" differently in particular tem-poral moments they rub up against, and so expose, these dominant spatial order-ings that define who is in place/out of place, who belongs and who does not' (p. 19). Despite the significance of temporality and spatiality for equality, inequalities associated with care spaces for older people and/or people with dementia (Kontos and Martin, 2013) have so far been under-interrogated from these perspectives (Milligan and Wiles, 2010).

As I shall argue in this chapter, all three types of equality are engaged in relation to LGBT* people affected by dementia. Resources are relevant, in terms of LGBT* individuals' uneven access to appropriate dementia care and support (Price, 2008, 2010, 2012; Newman and Price, 2012; Withall, 2014; Westwood, 2015a, 2015b). Recognition is of significance in terms of the lack of recognition of LGBT* issues in dementia discourse (McGovern, 2014). Representation is also relevant, in terms of the injustices experienced by many LGBT* people affected by dementia and a lack of advocacy or support in relation to those injustices (Knauer, 2009, 2010; Witten, 2014; Marshall *et al.*, 2015). Each will now be examined more closely.

Absences and silences

In this section, I shall consider the absences and silences regarding, in turn, gender, sexuality, gender identity and dementia. The distinction between the three is, in many ways, an arbitrary one, with gender and sexuality being closely interconnected, with gender and gender identity often being read as synonymous, and with trans* people being affected by issues of sexuality as well as gender identity. I have broken them down, however, to try and disentangle some of the intersections which can be obscured in generic LGBT* discourse. In particular, I am keen to highlight the perspectives of cisgender lesbians who are disproportionately affected by dementia (Westwood, 2015a) and whose gendered concerns about dementia are often lost both in narratives about women and dementia and about LGBT* people and dementia.

Gender

There is a growing awareness that dementia is a gendered concern, and that dementia, particularly dementia among the oldest old, is a women's issue (Alzheimer's Disease International, 2015). Twice as many women as men are affected by dementia and individuals reaching the age of 100 who are living with dementia are four times as likely to be women as men (WHO, 2007). What is less well recognised is that this issue affects lesbians and bisexual women as much as, if not more than, heterosexual-identifying women (Westwood, 2015a). What is also less well recognised is that, while all men living with dementia are in a minority, gay and bisexual men are, in effect, a minority within a minority (Westwood, 2015b). What this gender dimension means for trans* women and men is not at all clear as yet (Witten, 2014) as is explored further in the section on gender identity.

Lesbian and bisexual women with dementia may not only be proportionately represented among women with dementia (an estimated 7.5 to 10 per cent of the population) (Aspinall, 2009), they may be at increased risk of dementia and thus disproportionately represented in two key ways. First, in terms of risks, smoking, alcohol use and depression have been linked to dementia. While the evidence on smoking and alcohol is mixed (Rusanen *et al.*, 2011; Panza *et al.*, 2012), the link between depression and dementia would appear to be stronger (Kessing, 2012). Lesbian and bisexual women smoke more, use alcohol more, and have increased rates of depression, compared with heterosexual-identifying women (Guasp, 2011). This would suggest that they may also be at a concomitant increased risk of dementia compared with heterosexual-identifying women.

Older women (who are most likely to have dementia) who are never-married, single and have no children are more likely to spend the final years of their life in residential and/or nursing home provision (Glaser *et al.*, 2009). Older lesbians and bisexual women are more likely than older heterosexual-identifying women to be never-married, single and not have children (50 per cent of lesbian and bisexual women have children compared with 90 per cent of older heterosexual women) (Guasp, 2011). This suggests that not only are older lesbian and bisexual women more likely to be living in residential care than older gay and bisexual men, they are also more likely to do so than heterosexual women. This, in turn, means that they are more likely than gay and bisexual men and heterosexual women to be exposed to the deficiencies of care provision for older people/people with dementia and to care provision which is 'heteronormative at best and homophobic at worst' (Westwood, 2015a: 1).

Despite the significance of dementia and dementia care provision for lesbians and bisexual women, their voices are under-represented in dementia research, policy and practice (Price, 2008). Women affected by dementia are generally discursively produced as heterosexual women in a wide range of dementia literature. To give an example,

> Gender differences in spousal care are highly prevalent for patients with dementia, more so than with other illnesses. Husbands with AD [Alzheimer's Disease] and related dementias (ADRD) receive an average of 31% more hours of spousal care than ADRD wives do from their husbands. Wives also continue to provide care longer and at greater levels of disability than husbands and with less help from adult children. Adult children, usually daughters, intervene more to help husbands caring for ADRD wives, particularly as needs increase and the disease progresses...
>
> (Carter *et al.*, 2012: 4–5)

In this extract, gender is discursively produced as a binary ('men' and 'women' tacitly assumed to be cisgender) and relationships between men and women to be heterosexual (husbands and wives). This completely excludes the possibility of even thinking about the gendering of dementia as experienced by lesbian, gay and bisexual women and men, and by same-sex couples. The abstract is representative of much of the literature on gender and dementia; lesbians and bisexual women are either not referred to at all or only as remarkable 'others' (Price, 2008), a notable exception to this being the recent report produced by Alzheimer's Disease International (2015) which includes references to lesbian and bisexual women throughout the report. However, even in that report, the 'women' affected by dementia are by default heterosexual (i.e. heterosexuality is assumed, not made explicit) and only lesbian and bisexual women located (by special mention) in terms of their sexuality/sexual identities. In this way, lesbian and bisexual women are marginalised. The taken-for-grantedness and normativity of hetero-sexuality (Wilkinson and Kitzinger, 1993), and its implications for heterosexual women with dementia, remains un-interrogated.

Moreover, even when LGBT* issues are raised in relation to dementia (e.g. McGovern, 2014), the gendering of those issues tends to get lost amidst con-cerns relating to sexuality and gender identity, reflecting a wider marginalisation of lesbian (Traies, 2012) and bisexual (Jones, 2010) narratives in LGBT* dis-course. The marginalisation of gender issues echoes longstanding feminist cri-tiques of the lesbian and gay, and more recently LGBT*, political movements, for failing to recognise and/or prioritise gender inequalities experienced by les-bians and bisexual women including in relation to gay and bisexual men (Adam, 1995). The voices, and concerns, of lesbians and bisexual women with dementia are thus obscured *both* in discourse about women and dementia *and* in discourse about LGBT* people and dementia.

Sexuality

Lesbians and gay and bisexual (LGB) women and men affected by dementia are significantly under-represented in the literature (McGovern, 2014; Westwood, 2015a) in several ways. First, there continues to be a 'queer absence' (Cronin, 2006: 107) produced by a 'rhetorical silencing' (Brown, 2009: 65) of LGB sexualities (this includes both trans* and cisgender LGB-identifying people) in mainstream ageing discourse. This silencing means that older people are discursively produced, explicitly or implicitly, as heterosexual. This is in stark contrast with a burgeoning body of literature about ageing in LGB scholarship, which has, in particular, high-lighted a range of concerns about the unmet health and social care needs of older LGB people (Brotman *et al.*, 2003, 2007; Harrison, 2006; Hughes, 2007, 2009; Fredriksen-Goldsen and Muraco, 2010; Stein *et al.*, 2010; Ward *et al.*, 2011, 2012; Fredriksen-Goldsen *et al.*, 2013; Gendron *et al.*, 2013). Second, within that body of literature about LGB ageing, dementia has, surprisingly, remained on the margins. This is perhaps, in part, because much of the research with older LGB people has focussed so far on the 'younger old' rather than the 'oldest old' (Kimmel, 2014), but may also involve a reluctance to engage with the very diffi-cult issues dementia raises. This includes the implications of memory loss for (sexual) identity as well as stigma and marginalisation associated with both dementia and LGB sexualities (Price, 2008). Third, sexuality in older age, and the expression of any sexuality/sexual identity by older people, especially older people with dementia, has been, until quite recently, and in some ways still remains, a taboo subject (Bauer *et al.*, 2014). The expression of sexuality in res-idential care spaces for people with dementia has posed a range of significant challenges for care staff, particularly in relation to issues of consent (Bauer *et al.*, 2013) and is often simply constructed as a problem which needs to be managed (Ward *et al.*, 2005; Mahieu *et al.*, 2014).

The majority of previous academic work on LGB people and dementia has been conducted by Richard Ward and Elizabeth Price. Ward (2000) first raised the issue of lesbian and gay concerns about dementia and dementia care spaces and subsequently, with colleagues, explored the responses of residential care staff to the expression of sexuality in dementia care spaces (Ward *et al.*, 2005). Price has written about the lack of visibility of gay men and lesbians in dementia care (Price, 2005); the intersection of stigma and social marginalisation associated with both dementia and lesbian and gay identities (Price, 2008); issues of disclosure of sexuality (Price, 2010) and of support (Newman and Price, 2012) for lesbian and gay carers of people with dementia (Price, 2010); and the fears those carers have for their own possible dementia care futures (Price, 2012). More recently, Nancy Knauer has written about the socio-legal implications for LGBT* people in the USA (Knauer, 2009, 2010) and I have focussed on how dementia disproportionately affects lesbians and bisexual women (Westwood, 2015a) and, with colleagues, on good practice guidelines for older LGBT* people, including those with dementia (Westwood *et al.*, 2015).

Despite this growing body of work, it is not yet reflected in more mainstream academic literature addressing theory, practice or rights issues and dementia. What has emerged instead is an increasing amount of grey (i.e. non-academic) literature which has primarily focussed on highlighting gaps in knowledge and/ or practice issues in relation to the provision of care to LGB and/or LGBT* people with dementia (Birch, 2009; Alzheimer's Association, 2012; Alzheimer's Society, 2013; Peel and McDaid, 2015; National LGB&T Partnership, 2014). However, this also does not appear to have been translated so far into the mainstream literature on dementia. Innes *et al.*, (2004) have suggested that 'within the study of dementia there is a tendency to relegate certain issues, which are often difficult and challenging, to the margins of academic and professional discourses' (Innes *et al.*, 2004: 11). As standpoint theorists have also demonstrated (Hill Collins, 2000), the dominant majority can also construct knowledge networks which render minority narratives not only to the margins, but off the entire map. Either way, LGBT* women and men remain positioned profoundly at the margins and/or off the dementia map.

Gender identity

There has been a resounding silence about trans* issues and dementia in the literature (McGovern, 2014; Withall, 2014), apart from the grey literature referred to in the previous section and one recent academic exception: Tarynn Witten has reported from the Transgender MetLife Survey (TMLS) that trans* people are concerned about 'discrimination by caregivers, fears of cruelty and abuse, fears of being homeless and of dementia, and fears of not being allowed to live their final years as their true selves' (Witten, 2014: 17–18). (See also Witten Chapter 8 in this volume). The exclusion of trans* people's issues and concerns from dementia discourse and of dementia from trans* discourse not only creates impoverished theory but also privileges the lives and experiences of cisgender people with dementia (see Hunter, Bishop and Westwood, this volume, Chapter 9) and those of trans* people not affected by dementia. This, in turn, leaves care providers under-informed and ill-equipped to meet the needs of trans* people with dementia.

A recent paper by Marshall *et al.* (2015) highlights some of the challenges which can be faced by a trans* person with dementia, and by care teams attempting to provide them with appropriate care and support, when they lack the necessary 'cultural competence' (Gendron *et al.*, 2013) to do so. The paper describes Jamie, a 94-year-old trans woman in Canada, who had been living openly as a woman since the age of 80, although Jamie had been wearing women's clothing for much longer, and had said when transitioning that 'she had felt this inclination her entire life' (p. 115). After transitioning, Jamie had written a leaflet about trans* issues and circulated it to all their neighbours (Jamie's wife was supportive), among whom Jamie was apparently accepted. Jamie had also been 'a prominent figure in her local transgender society' (p. 115).

Jamie was diagnosed with dementia and admitted to a residential care facility for older people after Jamie's wife died. Jamie had been taking oestrogen and steroids, but this was discontinued upon her admission for unknown reasons. Upon admission, Jamie was referred to a psychiatrist because of apparent gender confusion: 'She was confused as to whether she was male or female, asking, "What am I?" She frequently looked down at her breasts and asked, "Where did these come from?" ' (p. 113). Jamie sometimes expressed a wish to live as a man and sometimes as a woman. Jamie would ask to wear men's clothing, but would then point to items of women's clothing in the wardrobe. The staff did not know how to respond: 'What pronoun should they use? Should her clothing and haircut be feminine or masculine?' (p. 113). The other residents 'found Jamie's gender ambiguity difficult to accept, and as a result she became socially isolated' (p. 114). Jamie's daughter, who visited (removing 'some of the more effeminate clothing' from Jamie's closet, p. 113) did not accept Jamie's (now apparently ambivalent) gender identity as a woman: 'She [his daughter] stated, "He's putting aside the facade that he had been maintaining.... He never really was a transsexual, because he never had the surgery and physically he is male"' (p. 114).

The psychiatric assessment concluded that Jamie's history was 'consistent with a diagnosis of Gender Dysphoria–Posttransition according to the DSM-5' (American Psychiatric Association, 2013: 116). The assessment also concluded that Jamie exhibited 'considerable gender identity ambivalence'. In terms of how the staff should respond to this ambivalence, the most obvious solution, that they should respond to Jamie's presentation at any given moment in time, and not try to get Jamie to conform to 'either/or' binary notions of gender, does not appear to have been considered. Instead, the possibility of a 'gender neutral' approach had been suggested, whereby 'staff would avoid the use of pronouns and dress Jamie in a gender neutral manner' (p. 116). However, because it was thought that Jamie's co-residents would find this difficult, resulting in further ostracism, it was decided that a (gender) 'choice had to be made' on Jamie's behalf. Jamie died before such a choice was made.

Marshall *et al.*'s (2015) paper eloquently demonstrates so many of the unaddressed issues which concern trans* people in relation to dementia. First, Jamie is pathologised by care providers, her experiences being labelled and categorised as a psychiatric disorder. Second, Jamie loses Jamie's own (gendered) voice and history through memory impairment. Third, Jamie is taken off medications which support her chosen gender identity. Fourth, Jamie has an unsupportive family member who denies her gender identity and who wields power over Jamie's life. Fifth, the care staff are intent on shoehorning Jamie into an 'either/ or' gender binary and this is informed by collusion with the other residents' transphobia (rather than it being challenged). Jamie's history is unacknowledged, Jamie's needs not understood, and there is also no independent advocate to speak on Jamie's behalf. Jamie ended up dying in a residential care facility, rejected by fellow residents, with staff not knowing how to respond, a daughter openly opposed to Jamie's gender identity, and without legal representation. Jamie died confused, frightened, and alone. And much of that has to be attributed to the silences and absences in dementia discourse about LGBT* people – particularly trans* people in this case.

Equality implications

Having outlined the absences and silences relating to LGBT* people affected by dementia, I shall now consider their equality implications. I shall do so using Fraser's framework of resources, recognition and representation. The conceptual absences and silences about LGBT* people in dementia theory is a profound inequality of recognition. Not being seen, not being heard, and not being thought about is a fundamental intellectual exclusion. Dorothy Smith (1990) and related standpoint theorists (e.g. Harding, 2004) have emphasised the power of hegemonic ideological structures to allow knowledge which protects and supports the dominant discourse while excluding knowledge which threatens to undermine the dominant 'paradigmatic thought of a more powerful insider community' (Hill Collins, 2000: 76). In dementia discourse, the dominant insider community is heterosexual and cisgender, the dominant norms heteronormative and cisnormative, and all are constructed on 'either/or' binary notions of gender, sexuality and gender identity. The knowledge which is thereby excluded is that of LGBT* people affected by dementia.

In her classic essay, 'Compulsory Heterosexuality', Adrienne Rich (1980) powerfully demonstrated how 'the lie' (p. 657) of compulsory heterosexuality – the unquestioning assumption that all women are, and should be, heterosexual and the privileging of heterosexual women – pervades every layer of society, including scholarly analysis. This 'lie' can also be extended to cisgenderism and binarism, i.e. the privileging of cisgender and/or gender binary individuals and the unquestioning assumption that all people are, and should be, cisgender and/or gender binary. The 'lie' can be so all-pervasive that it evades recognition itself. This chapter, and this book, is an attempt to reveal the lie, make it recognised and recognisable, and move it into conceptual spaces where it can be critically interrogated. Doing so necessitates critically interrogating the powerful overarching backcloth of heterosexuality and cisgender norms and normativities which shape understandings of non-LGBT* people with dementia as well as LGBT* people with dementia.

The unthinkability of LGBT* people with dementia has had profound implications for dementia services. The lack of appropriate health and social care provision for older LGBT* people, including those with dementia, is clearly a site of affective and spatial inequalities. A 'sameness' approach to care for people with dementia – a 'one size fits all' model (Eaglesham, 2010) – clearly does not work when diversity, including gender, sexuality and gender identity diversity, is taken into account. Similarly, an 'equality of opportunity' approach to dementia care provision also does not work: having equal access to provision which is equipped to understand heterosexual and cisgender people's needs, but not the needs of LGBT* people, is no equality at all. What is needed is 'equality of outcome', so that LGBT* people have dementia care that is equally as good as that of non-LGBT* people, which inevitably involves recognising their differences as well as their shared concerns. Moreover, when dementia care provision is deficient, it does not mean LGBT* people should receive equally poor services, but that services for all should be improved.

Recognition is central to improving health and social care provision for LGBT* people with dementia. Poor recognition involves being unseen, unheard, disrespected, misunderstood and one's needs not identified. Good recognition involves being seen, heard, respected, and having needs identified. Without recognition, the issue of resources becomes redundant: we cannot interrogate how needs are or are not being met before those needs have been identified. Dementia, as it progresses, often deprives an individual of the ability to assert their own needs and rights. People with dementia are often reliant upon their informal social support networks to advocate on their behalf. For LGBT* people, those networks may involve strong friendship as well as biological family connections (Roseneil and Budgeon, 2004). If those friendships are not equally recognised alongside biological family members, this can deprive people with dementia of a vital source of community support (Westwood, 2015b), which is another affective inequality (Lynch, 2010).

Often, however, those individuals with the least amount of community support are those who live in residential care spaces. In those spaces, at a time when they most need someone to speak on their behalf, there is no one, which is a crucial inequality of representation. The lack of appropriate formal advocacy and support for all people with dementia, is particularly problematic for LGBT* people with dementia. They may need formal advocacy more than non-LGBT* people, both because they are more likely to lack informal advocacy, and because, as minority groups, they are more likely to need their rights to be asserted within care environments dominated by a heterosexual and cisgender majority.

Conclusion

The absences and silences relating to LGBT* people affected by dementia have produced, and are producing, significant inequalities for LGBT* people, conceptually, in terms of practices, and in terms of rights. This edited collection is intended to render LGBT* people affected by dementia visible, heard, thinkable, and to move them, and the issues affecting them, into conceptual, practice and rights-based spaces in dementia discourse. However, throwing light on these issues is not enough. As the standpoint theorists have shown us, dominant majority narratives are very difficult to shake. It will be important to insert LGBT* issues into every dementia conversation, at every level of theory, practice and rights discourse. We need to make LGBT* issues an 'ordinary' everyday occurrence in dementia discourse. Sandra Fredman (2014) has recently argued that there are four main elements in achieving substantive equality: to redress disadvantage; to address stigma, stereotyping, prejudice and violence; to embrace difference and achieve structural change; and to enhance voice and participation. And to achieve that for LGBT* people affected by dementia, we still have a very long way to go.

Acknowledgements

Many thanks to: Ruth Fletcher and Rosie Harding, my PhD supervisors, for developing my critical thinking skills; to Chryssy Hunter and Jenny-Anne Bishop for their very thoughtful and thought-provoking insights about trans* issues; and to Chryssy Hunter for her feedback on this chapter.

References

Adam, B. (1995) *The Rise of a Gay and Lesbian Movement*. New York: Twayne.

Alzheimer's Association (2012) *LGBT Caregiver Concerns*. Washington, DC: Alzheimer's Association.

Alzheimer's Disease International (2015) *Women and Dementia: A Global Research Review*. London: Alzheimer's Disease International.

Alzheimer's Society (2013) *Supporting Lesbian, Gay and Bisexual People with Dementia*. Alzheimer's Society Factsheet 480. London: Alzheimer's Society.

American Psychiatric Association (2013) *Diagnostic and Statistical Manual of Mental Disorders (DSM-5®)*. American Psychiatric Pub.

Aspinall, P. J. (2009) *Estimating the Size and Composition of the Lesbian, Gay, and Bisexual Population in Britain*. London: Equality and Human Rights Commission.

Baker, J., Lynch, K. and Cantillon, S. (2009) *Equality: From Theory to Action*. 2nd edn. Basingstoke: Palgrave Macmillan.

Barnes, M. (2012) *Care in Everyday Life: An Ethic of Care in Practice*. Bristol: Policy Press.

Bauer, M., Fetherstonhaugh, D., Tarzia, L., Nay, R., Wellman, D. and Beattie, E. (2013) ' "I always look under the bed for a man". Needs and barriers to the expression of sexuality in residential aged care: the views of residents with and without dementia'. *Psychology & Sexuality*, **4**(3) 296–309.

Bauer, M., Nay, R., Tarzia, L. and Fetherstonhaugh, D. (2014) ' "We need to know what's going on": views of family members toward the sexual expression of people with dementia in residential aged care'. *Dementia*, **13**(5) 571–585.

Birch, H. (2009) *It's Not Just About Sex! Dementia, Lesbians and Gay Men*. Adelaide, Australia: 2009 Alzheimer's Australia Conference.

Brotman, S., Ryan, B., Collins, S., Chamberland, L., Cormier, R., Julien, D. and Richard, B. (2007) 'Coming out to care: Caregivers of gay and lesbian seniors in Canada'. *The Gerontologist*, **47**(4) 490–503.

Brotman, S., Ryan, B. and Cormier, R. (2003) 'The health and social services needs of gay and lesbian elders and their families in Canada'. *The Gerontologist*, **43** 192–202.

Brown, M. (2009) 'LGBT aging and rhetorical silence'. *Sexuality Research & Social Policy*, **6**(4) 65–78.

Butler, J. (1997) 'Merely cultural'. *Social Text*, **52**(53) 265–77.

Carter, C. L., Resnick, E. M., Mallampalli, M. and Kalbarczyk, A. (2012) 'Sex and gender differences in Alzheimer's disease: Recommendations for future research'. *Journal of Women's Health*, **21**(10) 1018–1023.

Cronin, A. (2006) 'Sexuality in Gerontology: A Heteronormative Presence, a Queer Absence'. In S. O. Daatland and S. Biggs (eds). *Ageing and Diversity: Multiple Pathways & Cultural Migrations*. Bristol: Policy Press, pp. 107–122.

Cronin, A., Ward, R., Pugh, S., King, A. and Price, E. (2011) 'Categories and their consequences: Understanding and supporting the caring relationships of older lesbian, gay and bisexual people'. *International Social Work*, **54**(3) 421–435.

Eaglesham, P. (2010) 'The Policy Maze and LGBT Issues: Does One Size Fit All?'. In R. Jones and R. Ward (eds). *LGBT Issues: Looking Beyond Categories*. Edinburgh: Dunedin, pp. 1–15.

Fraser, N. (1996) 'Social Justice in the Age Of Identity Politics: Redistribution, Recognition And Participation'. *The Tanner Lectures on Human Values*. New York: Stanford University.

Fraser, N. (1997) *Justice Interruptus*. New York: Routledge.

Fraser, N. (2000) 'Rethinking recognition'. *New Left Review*, **3** 107–120.

Fraser, N. (2007) 'Feminist politics in The Age of Recognition: A two-dimension approach to gender justice'. *Studies In Social Justice*, **1**(1) 23–35.

Fredman, S. (2014) 'Substantive Equality Revisited'. *Oxford Legal Studies Research Paper No. 70/2014*. [Online] available at: http://dx.doi.org/10.2139/ssrn.2510287 [accessed 12 August 2015].

Fredman, S. and Spencer, S. (eds) (2003) *Age as an Equality Issue*. Portland: Hart.

Fredriksen-Goldsen, K. I. and Muraco, A. (2010) 'Aging and sexual orientation: A 25-year review of the literature'. *Research on Aging*, **32**(3) 372–413.

Fredriksen-Goldsen, K. I., Emlet, C. A., Kim, H.-J., Muraco, A., Erosheva, E. A., Goldsen, J. and Hoy-Ellis, C. P. (2013) 'The physical and mental health of lesbian, gay male, and bisexual (LGB) older adults: The role of key health indicators and risk and protective factors'. *The Gerontologist*, **53**(4) 664–675.

Gendron, T., Maddux, S., Krinsky, L., White, J., Lockeman, K., Metcalfe, Y. and Aggarwal, S. (2013) 'Cultural competence training for healthcare professionals working with LGBT older adults'. *Educational Gerontology*, **39**(6) 454–463.

Glaser, K., Price, D., Willis, R., Stuchbury, R. and Nicholls, M. (2009) *Life Course Influences on Health and Well-being in Later Life: A Review*. Manchester: Equality and Human Rights Commission with Age Concern and Help the Aged.

Grabham, E., Herman, D., Cooper, D. and Krishnadas, J. (2009) 'Introduction'. In E. Grabham, D. Cooper, J. Krishnadas and D. Herman (eds). *Intersectionality and Beyond: Law, Power and the Politics of Location.* Abingdon: Routledge-Cavendish, pp. 1–17.

Guasp, A. (2011) *Lesbian, Gay and Bisexual People in Later Life.* London: Stonewall.

Harding, S. (ed.) (2004) *The Feminist Standpoint Theory Reader: Intellectual and Political Controversies.* New York: Routledge.

Harrison, J. (2006) 'Coming out ready or not! Gay, lesbian, bisexual, transgender and intersex ageing and aged care in Australia: Reflections, contemporary developments and the road ahead'. *Gay & Lesbian Issues and Psychology Review*, 2(2) 44–53.

Hill Collins, P. (2000) *Black Feminist Thought: Knowledge, Consciousness and the Politics of Empowerment.* 2nd edn. London: Routledge.

Hughes, M. (2007) 'Older lesbians and gays accessing health and aged-care services'. *Australian Social Work*, 60(2) 197–209.

Hughes, M. (2009) 'Lesbian and gay people's concerns about ageing and accessing services'. *Australian Social Work*, 62(2) 186–201.

Innes, A., Archibald, C. and Murphy, C. (2004) 'Introduction'. In A. Innes, C. Archibald and C. Murphy (eds). *Dementia and Social Inclusion: Marginalised Groups and Marginalised Areas of Dementia Research, Care and Practice.* London: Jessica Kingsley Publishers, pp. 1–17.

Jones, R. (2010) 'Troubles with Bisexuality in Health and Social Care'. In R. Jones and R. Ward (eds). *LGBT Issues: Looking Beyond Categories.* Edinburgh: Dunedin, pp. 42–55.

Kessing, L. V. (2012) 'Depression and the risk for dementia'. *Current Opinion in Psychiatry*, 25(6) 457–461.

Kimmel, D. (2014) 'Lesbian, gay, bisexual, and transgender aging concerns'. *Clinical Gerontologist* 37(1) 49–63.

Knauer, N. (2009) 'LGBT elder law: Toward equity in aging'. *Harvard Journal of Law and Gender*, 32 301–358.

Knauer, N. (2010) 'Gay and lesbian elders: Estate planning and end-of-life decision making'. *Florida Coastal Law Review*, 12 163–215.

Kontos, P. and Martin, W. (2013) 'Embodiment and dementia: Exploring critical narratives of selfhood, surveillance, and dementia care'. *Dementia*, 12(3) 288–302.

Lynch, K. (2010) 'Affective inequalities: challenging (re)distributive, recognition and representational models of social justice'. Paper presented at *RCO2 Economy and Society Session 1 New Approaches to Understanding Inequalities and their Significance ISA XVII World Congress of Sociology*, Gothenburg, Sweden 11–17 July 2010. [Online] available at: http://researchrepository.ucd.ie/handle/10197/2479 [accessed 11 June 2013].

Mahieu, L., Anckaert, L. and Gastmans, C. (2014) 'Intimacy and sexuality in institutionalized dementia care: Clinical-ethical considerations'. *Health Care Analysis*, 1–20.

Marshall, J., Cooper, M. and Rudnick, A. (2015) 'Gender dysphoria and dementia: A case report'. *Journal of Gay & Lesbian Mental Health*, 19(1) 112–117.

McGovern, J. (2014) 'The forgotten: Dementia and the aging LGBT community'. *Journal of Gerontological Social Work*, 57(8) 845–857.

Milligan, C. and Wiles, J. (2010) 'Landscapes of care'. *Progress in Human Geography*, 34(6) 736–754.

National LGB&T Partnership (2014) *The Dementia Challenge for LGBT Communities.* Manchester: National LGB&T Partnership.

Newman, R. and Price, E. (2012) 'Meeting the Needs of LGBT People Affected by Dementia'. In R. Ward, I. Rivers and M. Sutherland (eds). *Lesbian, Gay, Bisexual and Transgender Ageing: Biographical Approaches for Inclusive Care and Support.* London: Jessica Kingsley Publishers, pp. 183–195.

Panza, F., Frisardi, V., Seripa, D., Logroscino, G., Santamato, A., Imbimbo, B. P. and Solfrizzi, V. (2012) 'Alcohol consumption in mild cognitive impairment and dementia: Harmful or neuroprotective?'. *International Journal of Geriatric Psychiatry*, **27**(12) 1218–1238.

Peel, E. and McDaid, S. (2015) *'Over the Rainbow': Lesbian, Gay, Bisexual, Trans People and Dementia Project. Summary Report.* Worcester: Institute for Health and Society, University of Worcester, UK.

Price, E. (2005) 'All but invisible: Older gay men and lesbians'. *Nursing Older People*, **17**(4) 16–18.

Price, E. (2008) 'Pride or prejudice? Gay men, lesbians and dementia'. *British Journal of Social Work*, **38** 1337–1352.

Price, E. (2010) 'Coming out to care: Gay and lesbian carers' experiences of dementia services'. *Health and Social Care in the Community*, **18**(2) 160–168.

Price, E. (2012) 'Gay and lesbian carers: In the shadow of dementia'. *Ageing and Society*, **32**(10) 526–532.

Rich, A. (1980) 'Compulsory heterosexuality and lesbian existence'. *Signs*, 631–660.

Roseneil, S. and Budgeon, S. (2004) 'Cultures of intimacy and care beyond "The Family": Personal life and social change in the early 21st century'. *Current Sociology*, **52**(2) 135–159.

Rusanen, M., Kivipelto, M., Quesenberry, C. P. Jr, Zhou, J. and Whitmer, R. A. (2011) 'Heavy smoking in midlife and long-term risk of Alzheimer disease and vascular dementia'. *Archives of Internal Medicine* **171**(4) 333–339.

Smith, D. (1990) *The Conceptual Practices of Power: A Feminist Sociology of Knowledge.* Boston: Northeastern University Press.

Stein, G. L., Beckerman, N. L. and Sherman, P. A. (2010) 'Lesbian and gay elders and long-term care: Identifying the unique psychosocial perspectives and challenges'. *Journal of Gerontological Social Work*, **53**(5) 421–435.

Traies, J. (2012) 'Women Like That: Older Lesbians in the UK'. In R. Ward, I. Rivers and M. Sutherland (eds). *Lesbian, Gay, Bisexual and Transgender Ageing: Biographical Approaches for Inclusive Care and Support.* London and Philadelphia: Jessica Kingsley Publishers, pp. 76–82.

Valentine, G. (2007) 'Theorizing and researching intersectionality: A challenge for feminist geography'. *The Professional Geographer*, **59**(1) 10–21.

Ward, R. (2000) 'Waiting to be heard: Dementia and the gay community'. *Journal of Dementia Care*, **8**(3) 24–25.

Ward, R., Pugh, S. and Price, E. (2011) *Don't Look Back? Improving Health and Social Care Service Delivery for Older LGB Users.* London: Equality and Human Rights Commission.

Ward, R., Rivers, I. and Sutherland, M. (eds) (2012) *Lesbian, Gay, Bisexual and Transgender Ageing: Biographical Approaches for Inclusive Care and Support.* London: Jessica Kingsley Publishers.

Ward, R., Vass, A. A., Aggarwal, N., Garfield, C. and Cybyk, B. (2005) 'A kiss is still a kiss? – The construction of sexuality in dementia care'. *Dementia*, **4**(1): 49–72.

Westwood, S. (2015a) 'Dementia, women and sexuality: How the intersection of ageing, gender and sexuality magnify dementia concerns among lesbian and bisexual women'. *Dementia*, DOI: 1471301214564446.

Westwood, S. (2015b) '"We see it as being heterosexualised, being put into a care home": Gender, sexuality and housing/care preferences among older LGB individuals in the UK'. *Health and Social Care in the Community*, DOI: 10.1111/hsc.12265.

Westwood, S., King, A., Almack, K. and Suen, Y.-T. (2015) 'Good Practice in Health and Social Care Provision for Older LGBT People'. In J. Fish and K. Karban (eds). *Social Work and Lesbian, Gay, Bisexual and Trans Health Inequalities: International Perspectives*. Bristol: Policy Press, pp. 145–159.

Wilkinson, S. and Kitzinger, C. (eds) (1993) *Heterosexuality: A Feminism & Psychology Reader*. London: Sage.

Withall, L. (2014) *Dementia, Transgender And Intersex People: Do Service Providers Really Know What Their Needs Are?* Melbourne: Alzheimer's Australia.

Witten, T. M. (2014) 'End of life, chronic illness, and trans-identities'. *Journal of Social Work in End-of-Life & Palliative Care*, **10**(1) 34–58.

World Health Organization (WHO) (2007) *Women, Ageing and Health: A Framework for Action*. Geneva: World Health Organization.

Yuval-Davis, N. (2006) 'Intersectionality and feminist politics'. *European Journal of Women's Studies*, **13**(3) 193–209.

3   LGBT* individuals and dementia

An intersectional approach

Wendy Hulko

Introduction

Intersectionality, as a way of framing the lives and experiences of those impacted by more than one domain of oppression, was taken up by both gerontologists and queer studies scholars long ago and, since then, has been applied to dementia studies both in Canada (see Hulko, 2002, 2009a, 2011; O'Connor *et al.*, 2010) and the UK (Price, 2008, 2010; Westwood, 2014), often with an additional focus on privilege. Intersectionality posits that social-identity categories like sexual orientation, gender expression, race, ethnicity, age, and social class cannot be pulled apart in order to locate the source of discrimination – as racism versus sexism for example – to which a minoritised individual may be subject. As Warner and Shields (2013) argue in their review of identity research regarding the intersections of sexuality, gender and race, 'intersectionality is the embodiment in theory of the real-world fact that systems of inequality, from the experiential to the structural, are interdependent' (p. 804). This theory also posits that belonging to more than one equity-seeking group (e.g. Indigenous woman) is qualitatively different than belonging to only one such group (e.g. Indigenous man) and therefore any outcomes – in the form of violence, poor health status and/or poverty – can/should not be added together.

This theoretical framework has much to offer research and practice with older lesbian, gay, bisexual, transgender (LGBT*) individuals living with dementia. This is primarily as it accounts for the complexity of people's lives and directs attention towards people with dementia who may be invisible, like older lesbian and bisexual women and trans* people (see Rich, 1980; Witten, 2003) or 'too visible' in the case of racialized LGBT* folk, particularly men. Older LGBT* people are more likely to experience dementia due to a higher prevalence of smoking, depression and obesity (Fredricksen-Goldsen *et al.*, 2013; Mulé *et al.*, 2009) which have been linked to Alzheimer's disease (Norton *et al.*, 2014). In addition, there are unique ethical, legal and medical concerns facing this population. Further, if we contest the biomedicalization of dementia (Binney and Swan, 1991), then we will shift our focus beyond the medical realm to the social aspects of the lives of older LGBT* adults, including living conditions, financial resources, and social connectedness. As this is a nascent field, research to date has not addressed these topics.

In this chapter, I provide an overview of the history of intersectionality theorizing and its contemporary articulation, including models, and discuss its relevance to the lives and experiences of older adults with dementia. This discussion is brought alive through the use of a case study of an older Métis[1] woman who identifies as both bisexual and trans* and is awaiting gender affirmation[2] surgery. Through socially locating Joan and imagining her as a person with dementia, intersectionality becomes more understandable and potential issues are raised in the discussion section. The chapter concludes with implications for research and practice with older LGBT* individuals living with dementia, including a recommendation to view liminality and border crossing as strengths.

Intersectionality – historical and contemporary theorizing

In spite of the fact that sexual orientation was foregrounded in early intersectionality scholarship (Combahee River Collective, 1977; Lorde, 2007, [1984]), it (was) largely disappeared from subsequent writing on intersectionality by feminist and critical race theorists of the 1990s and early 2000s, who focused mainly on the trilogy of race, class, and gender (see Brotman and Kraniou, 1999 for a notable exception; see Hulko, 2009b for an analysis of the categories addressed in intersectional scholarship). Since its re-entry, there has been a great deal of intersectionality research on women and LGBT* people – as diverse, overlapping, or monolithic groups (see Bowleg, 2008; Diamond and Butterworth, 2008; Mehrotra, 2010). However, age and the ways in which it structures experiences of being a woman, a man, or a transgender person, is still addressed infrequently, as is geographic context (Hulko, in press) and the presumed or actual subject in much of the – albeit limited – literature on LGBT* persons with dementia is white, majority ethnic and middle class, as will be shown in the literature review that follows.

McCall's (2005) framing of intersectional scholarship as 'intra-categorical', 'inter-categorical', or 'anti-categorical' has been widely adopted as a way of distinguishing between different forms of intersectional analysis, though it may be more difficult to apply than the theory to which it refers. For example, anti-categorical intersectionality research in which social group membership categories (e.g. LGBT* people, older adults) are not used at all is uncommon or not recognized as such. Most intersectionality research is of the intra-categorical type, with the focus being one particular social group marked by differences or intersections (e.g. older LGBT* people with or without dementia; see Cronin and King, 2010; Westwood, 2014). An inter-categorical approach, that is research that looks at the relations within and across multiple social groups (e.g. sub-groups of older people with dementia based on factors like gender, race, ethnicity, and social class; see Hulko, 2011), is less common. What tends to happen with the intra-categorical approach is that particular intersections get missed and, in the case of LGBT* persons with dementia, the (invisible or unmarked) white Anglo-European or Anglo-Canadian subject becomes reified. This is particularly ironic given that intersectional scholarship arose from Black lesbian women calling for attention to all of these aspects of their beings, not only, or primarily, one.

Intersectionality is used as a framework, theory, and/or approach to social activism in psychological research, with the first being the most popular and the last being the most uncommon (Warner and Shields, 2013). In sociological research, intersectionality is seen to be more closely bound to both feminist theory and social justice activities (see Hill Collins, 2012). Several models have been developed or proposed as a means of depicting intersectionality (see Dhamoon, 2011, for a review) and distinguishing this form of theorizing social life from a cumulative or additive approach. This includes Enid Lee's (1985) flower of power (as cited in Bishop, 2001), Patricia Hill Collins' (2000) matrix of domination, Adams, Bell, and Griffin's (2007) identity wheel and Sisneros and colleagues' web of oppression (as cited in Mullaly, 2010). Most of these models take a binary approach, with one being either the oppressor (advantaged) or the oppressed (disadvantaged). The flower of power, in its adapted and less dichotomous form, has been made into an online interactive version for a cultural safety training module for nursing,[3] for example.

Figure 3.1 is an updated version of the social location diagram that I developed during my doctoral research on dementia and intersectionality (Hulko, 2002, 2009a, 2011) to enable me to compose a sample more accurately reflective of the theoretical framework that I was using. It was informed by the first of the above-mentioned models as well as anti-oppression workshops and dialogues in which I had been participating since entering the field of social work in 1996. While I devised a model of my own for research purposes, and continue to use it to compose samples, I have been using this model more in teaching as a way for Bachelor of Social Work and Master of Education students to determine their own social location and that of the people with whom they work, and recently updated it for re-publication (Hulko, 2015a).

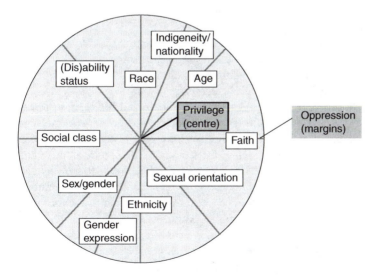

Figure 3.1 Social location diagram (source: Hulko, 2015a).

This model treats privilege and oppression as relative, rather than assigning either/or positions, and as multidimensional, with the labelling of each individual axis of privilege and oppression grounded in theories of, and research into, the social world and how it operates, rather than subjective feelings (see Hulko, 2015a for further explanation). It allows us to capture the complexity and relativity of intersectionality and determine the extent to which a person may be multiply privileged and/or multiply disadvantaged. Later in this chapter, the model is used to socially locate Joan based on the case study description and an awareness of which groups hold more or less power in relation to the varied axes. With this theoretical background in mind, the relevant – and limited – literature related to LGBT* persons with dementia is now briefly reviewed.

Literature review

There are two main strands of extant literature related to LGBT* persons living with dementia: (1) sexuality and dementia; and (2) LGBT* ageing. Very few articles bring these two topics together as this chapter attempts to do, with the exceptions being those noted in the Introduction and discussed in this section. As sub-themes of these topics, the literature also addresses attitudes and fears about ageing and dementia as well as risk factors for dementia in relation to LGBT* communities.

The challenge in identifying and accessing LGBT* older adults is an overriding theme in the literature with authors noting that this is likely to change with future cohorts of older adults who are accustomed to having attained and guarded legal rights and social recognition, particularly those who came of age during or after the 1969 Stonewall rebellion in New York City. The latter event is acknowledged as having birthed a twentieth century social movement for queer rights (distinct from the homophile and daughters of Bilitis movements in the US, for example) and launching annual Pride celebrations. However, not many realize that it was mostly Black and Puerto Rican transwomen and gay men who fought back against police harassment on that hot June night, putting their lives on the line to advance all of our interests.

In discussing the invisibility of older LGBT* people and the relationship to social work practice, Stern (2015) notes the need for workers to acknowledge the existence of, and reason for, an 'invisibility cloak', the history of oppression which older LGBT* people have endured, the worker's own self-awareness, and the diversity within the older LGBT* community with bisexual, transgender, racialized and lower income older adults being relatively absent in the literature. McGovern (2014) echoes these recommendations in her review of the literature on LGBT* older adults with dementia and recommends social workers adopt an intersectional lens. However, two-spirit older people are not discussed in the literature with the little attention paid to Indigenous people who are sexual and/ or gender minorities being focused mainly on youth.

Two-spirit people

Two-spirit people are researching and writing about their historical/traditional and contemporary roles in their First Nation or Native American communities and thereby advancing our knowledge of an identity concept created by Indigenous people in 1992 (see Thomas and Jacobs, 1999). Two-spirit people embody feminine and masculine spirits and as such are gender-transgressive; they may or may not experience same-sex attractions and/or engage in same-sex intimacy (see Adams and Phillips, 2009: 960). Indigenous scholars have noted that two-spirit is an inherently intersectional term or identity (McNeil-Seymour, 2015) and caution against using it in a simplistic/descriptive fashion (i.e. to name/label LGBT* Indigenous people) as it references not only culture, sexuality, gender, and spirituality, but also community and relationship to the land. For example, McNeil-Seymour discovered through interviewing 15 LGTB/Two-Spirit Secwepemc individuals that their role and responsibility is *yucamin'min*, meaning 'to protect the earth and protect the people' (p. 92). This word, and the role it describes, is specific to this Nation, however.

One participant in Adams and Phillips' (2009) study of two-spirit Native Americans was in her sixties, yet she is not quoted in their article nor do the authors mention this participant other than to identify her age and note that she recently discovered she was Native American. The latter is a common phenomenon with the growing acceptance of, and reduced hostility towards, Indigenous peoples making it safer to identify now. It was far riskier to acknowledge one's ancestry (and easier to pass for white if one could) when children could be taken away to residential schools for much of the twentieth century and/or apprehended by child welfare authorities during the sixties scoop in Canada, for example.

Sexuality and dementia

The literature on sexuality and dementia focuses on sexual expression in care home settings and related legal issues, with the person with dementia usually cast as either the initiator/craver (of physical affection and/or sexual intimacy) or the recipient/potential victim of another resident's sexual expressiveness (see Bauer *et al.*, 2014; Benbow and Beeston, 2012; Breland, 2013; Di Napoli *et al.*, 2013; Heath, 2012). Rarely is the person with dementia positioned as an agentic being involved in a consensual and mutually satisfying relationship. For example, Heath (2012) briefly touches on LGB issues, yet only in the context of sexual expression and the need for care staff to be non-judgemental.

The participants in the empirical studies and subjects in the theoretical or practice-focused articles related to this topic are most often white, heterosexual, cisgender, opposite-sex partnered, and belong to the dominant ethnic group in their country of residence. Thus, while they may be older and disabled due to their dementia diagnosis, their gender (as man or woman) is usually the only factor by which this group is diversified. Exceptions include Benbow and

Beeston (2012) who note the invisibility and unique concerns of lesbian, gay, bisexual and transgender individuals, Bauer and colleagues' (2014) study on family members' views of sexual expression by persons with dementia in residential care which included a same-sex partner, and Breland (2013), a review of legal issues in the US in which the author notes the existence of private care homes for members of the LGBT* community. While family members in Bauer *et al.*'s (2014) study differentiated between degrees of intimacy, being okay with kissing, touching, and hugging, but not sex, residential care staff in Di Napoli *et al.*'s (2014) research distinguished between sex and gay sex and felt the latter should be discouraged.

LGBT ageing*

While the issues addressed in the literature on LGBT* ageing or older adults are more expansive and include caregiver support, residential care or institutionalization, health care needs and access, and pensions and other benefits (Stern, 2015; see also Brotman *et al.*, 2003; Fredriksen-Goldsen *et al.*, 2013; Fredriksen-Goldsen and Muraco, 2010; Westwood, 2014; Witten, 2015a), the limitations with respect to the person with dementia are similar. However, this time, the white majority ethnic person happens to be lesbian or gay and either involved in a long-term same-sex relationship or single at this stage of their life (see Hutchins, 2014; Rawlings, 2012). For example, Hutchins (2014) offers useful tips for residential care nurses in the UK and includes a case study of a same-sex couple, one of whom has dementia (Mr. Smith) and the other who is possibly Indian (Mr. Chowdry), yet neither the latter's ethnicity nor the former's dementia are discussed. As noted previously, there is much less research on bisexual and transgender older adults (Fredriksen-Goldsen *et al.*, 2015; Persson, 2009; Witten, 2015a), whether they have dementia or not.

Attitudes and fears about ageing and dementia

The MetLife survey (MetLife Mature Market Institute, 2010) of Americans in the age group 45–64 years old, on their attitudes towards ageing and retirement, discovered that 29 per cent of the LGBT* respondents feared becoming confused or getting dementia compared to 37 per cent of the general population. At the same time, a higher proportion of the LGBT* participants had made plans for the loss of their decision-making capacity by preparing a living will (38 per cent versus 28 per cent) or appointing a substitute decision-maker (34 per cent versus 19 per cent), for example. Anxiety about being diagnosed with dementia was also a shared concern for the 21 gay and lesbian carers in Price's (2012) narrative research in which participants also expressed a need for specialist service provision. This is undoubtedly a reflection of the hetero/cis-normativity and/or homo/bi/transphobia that characterizes most interactions between LGBT* folk and health care providers (see Brotman *et al.*, 2003; Cronin and King, 2010; Witten, 2015b). That is, a same-sex partner is less likely to be recognized by a health care provider without a document appointing them to act on their partner's behalf and/or outlining their partner's wishes for care should they lose their capacity to make decisions.

Risk factors for dementia

LGBT* populations have higher rates of depression than do heterosexuals and lesbians in particular have higher rates of smoking and obesity (Mulé *et al.*, 2009), as do transgender older adults (Fredriksen-Goldsen *et al.*, 2013). These are three of the seven (ranked four through six) main risk factors for Alzheimer's disease (Norton *et al.*, 2014), the others being (1) lack of exercise, (2) diabetes, (3) high blood pressure in middle age, and (7) low education. This finding has led Norton and colleagues to argue that one-third of all cases of Alzheimer's disease are preventable. I would further argue that dementia is of particular concern for older LGBT* persons, not only based on these risk factors, but also due to the unique ethical, medical and legal concerns facing older sexual and/or minorities which have been touched upon with respect to care settings and/or interactions with health care providers. There are other areas that require attention as well, including living conditions, financial resources, and social connectedness, as noted in the introduction.

Social connectedness can slow the onset of dementia and social isolation is connected to cognitive decline. This is of particular concern for older LGBT* folk who live on their own and do not have a support network whether composed of their families of choice or their families of origin or some combination of the two. For this subset of the LGBT* community in particular, programmes like Generations – a peer-led group for older adults run by Qmunity, British Columbia's queer resource centre based in Vancouver[4] are critically important. Support groups like those offered through the Transgender Health Programme or Qmunity's Generations, along with the latter's social events and friendly visiting, create opportunities for social connectedness, and reduce the social isolation of older LGBT* persons. The latter can have tragic consequences, particularly for those living in care homes, as a 2010 report by the LGBT Movement Advancement Project (MAP) and Services and Advocacy for Gay, Lesbian, Bisexual and Transgender Elders (SAGE) (LGBT* MAP and SAGE, 2010) illustrates:

> an openly gay man in a nursing home was regularly the target of protests from other patients (and their family members) on his floor. The facility moved him to a floor for patients with severe disabilities and/or dementia. Without any family or friends to advocate for him, he eventually hanged himself.
>
> (p. 36)

As has been shown, the literature on the topic of LGBT* persons with dementia is sparse (and growing), yet there are insights to be drawn from research on sexuality and dementia and LGBT* ageing, including awareness of the increased risk for dementia to which LGBT* people may be subject and their fears about and plans for the future should they develop dementia. The subjects contained within this literature need to be made more complex, however, which is what intersectionality theorizing prompts us to do. It calls us to 'ask the other question'. This is what I have done in relation to Joan, the subject of the case study that follows a brief note on methodology.

A note on data sources

While this chapter is largely theoretical, I include empirical data in order to ground the theoretical discussion, and demonstrate the applicability of this theory to practice, as I have done previously (Hulko, 2009b). As such, a note on methodology is warranted. The case study that follows was drawn from feminist research based on an intersectionality and interlocking oppressions paradigm (see Hulko, in press; Hulko, 2015b; Hulko and Hovanes, 2013). The purpose of this pilot study was to explore the experiences of younger and older women on identifying as a sexual and/or gender minority in a small city or rural area. Data were gathered through interviews and focus groups and were analysed through an intersectional lens. The sample was comprised of 14 lesbian or bisexual women and 7 transgender persons ($n=21$), including 6 older lesbians and 1 older transgender and bisexual woman (Joan), who is the subject of this case study. The older participants ranged in age from 52 to 61 years with an average of 56 years[5] and all were white and either Anglo-Canadian or Northern European, except for Joan. None of the participants had a diagnosis of dementia nor reported having memory problems.

Case study – 'I walk with one foot as female, one foot as male, so I have both wisdoms'

Joan is a 53-year-old trans and bisexual woman living in a small city in Western Canada who is awaiting approval for gender affirmation (sexual reassignment) surgery. She knew from a young age that she was 'a female trapped inside a man's body', yet Joan did not start transitioning until the age of 45, at which point she began identifying as a straight female. She has been married to a woman for the past 14 years and her partner fully supports her transition and the bisexual identification that Joan adopted a year ago. At this time Joan also began working in the sex trade, serving both male and female clients, to supplement the disability pension she receives through income assistance. In addition, Joan volunteers with two local social service agencies that support people who are living and/or working on the street and mentors a transgender youth. Having been raised as Pentecostal and left the church when she was young, Joan joined the United Church three years ago and attends services every Sunday. She believes that it is having *courage* (Joan's emphasis) and the strength to endure disrespect and judgement for being different that has made a difference to her life as a transwoman living in a small city.

Joan is Métis, as was her mother, and refers to herself as more in touch with her Aboriginal roots than her white ones; she intends to apply for her Métis status as she thinks this will open up doors for her. In addition, she feels an affinity with Indigenous views on sexuality and gender expression, having learned about two-spirit people from Aboriginal Elders.

> And they said 'you would be classified as a two-spirited person, with wisdom that was the wisdom of a woman and the strength of a man' and I'm going 'you know what, you're right'! Because … the Aboriginal people back in the old days they had their own culture, their own way of life, and in the modern day Aboriginal people they have one foot in the white man's way, and one foot in the Aboriginal, in their roots and I'm the same way. I've got one foot, I walk with one foot that [i]s female, one foot as a male, so I have both wisdoms and I have them, and when they say to me that two-spirit people – it doesn't matter what native culture it is – two-spirited people are regarded as … as medicine men, as Shamans because they possess the knowledge of both ways, of both male and female, but they pick up and they draw in negativity, and, and, positive, positive vibes and they pull in, and they're very strong when they pull them in, and that's exactly the way it was with me.
>
> (Interview, July 2008)

Since starting the process of transitioning eight years ago, Joan has spent one year taking hormones and four years of 'real life experience' (RLE). After she completed her initial two years of RLE, she underwent a psychiatric evaluation and was told that she needed a few more years of experience to become comfortable with herself and to start to look and dress more her age. In addition, although the surgery is covered by the provincial medical services plan, including travel to the closest surgeon who could be in another province, there are likely to be additional costs for which Joan needs time to save money. As she awaits surgery, she has benefited from the support offered by the Transgender Health Programme (http://transhealth.vch.ca), including attending their weekly support group when she is in Vancouver and connecting with both her peers and the support worker by phone and the Internet.

Discussion

In the discussion that follows, I will first socially locate Joan using the model depicted in Figure 3.1, and then reimagine Joan as a person living with dementia. Through doing the latter, I aim to bring to light issues that may be faced by older sexual and/or gender minorities experiencing cognitive impairment in later life, particularly those who inhabit liminal space and/or do not live at either end of gender expression and sexual orientation continua.

Locating Joan

This rich case study indicates several intersections that Joan needs to navigate in her daily life, in addition to sexual orientation, gender expression and age. These include social class, Indigeneity, ethnicity, faith, and dis(ability). The social location diagram, Figure 3.2, indicates where Joan lies on the various axes of privilege and oppression (see Hulko, 2015a) in terms of how much privilege and oppression we can expect she might face due to her membership in particular social groups, all of which are marginalized to a certain extent.

The axes upon which Joan may fall between the centre (privilege) and the margins (oppression) rather than all the way at the margins are those for sexual orientation, age, race, and Indigeneity as she is bisexual, middle-aged, mixed race and Métis; Joan appears white though she has Indigenous ancestry. Faith and disability status are other axes upon which Joan may experience a degree of marginalization as she was raised Pentecostal and practises First Nations spirituality, and has an invisible disability. Joan's ethnicity (as Métis), social class, and gender expression place her more firmly on the margins. Transitioning from being a cisgender man to living and being recognized as a transgender woman entailed a loss of the only truly privileged position Joan had held in her life. The clustering of the explosive dots in the diagram depicts visually Joan's relationship to privilege and oppression – farther from the former and closer to the latter.

Reimagining Joan as a person with dementia

In the following section, Joan is reimagined as a person living with dementia and her possible concerns regarding ageing and dementia, as well as the challenges and strengths dementia may pose to her life as an older bisexual transwoman are

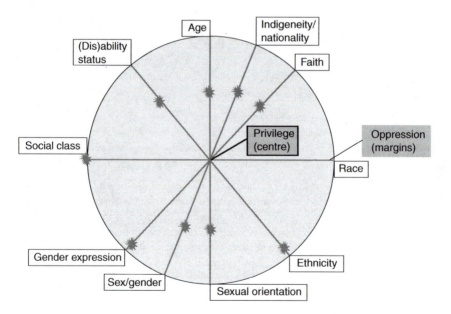

Figure 3.2 Joan's social location.

addressed. The three themes identified in Westwood's (2014) synthesis of the literature and her own empirical research on lesbian and bisexual women with dementia partially structure this analysis: early diagnosis and treatment, community support, and residential care provision.

Given the negative experiences in accessing health care that transgender persons routinely face and the surveillance or gender policing that Joan herself has endured, she may be reluctant to seek the assistance of a health care provider in addressing any memory problems or other symptoms of dementia that she is experiencing. If her partner is also a member of the LGBT* community (e.g. transgender, bisexual, intersex and/or lesbian), then Joan may not have a support person to attend medical appointments with her or to take advantage of caregiver support programmes, for similar reasons. Joan's financial situation certainly would impact on her ability to obtain assistance with her activities of daily living on top of being afraid of disclosure and what that may entail. As Warner and Shields (2013) note, 'particular intersectional locations affect how others' respond to the transperson's gender presence in social interactions' (p. 809) and thus the degree of gender affirmation needed will vary.

Dementia may complicate Joan's desires with respect to 'living her truth', or it could make it clearer or easier as she has felt like a man trapped inside a woman's body 'since a young age'. This would depend on the degree of acceptance of herself that Joan felt at that time and the extent to which her social environment constrained or enabled her to express her gender as woman rather than man. Given the reminiscence bump – memories of one's late teens and early twenties being retained longer – Joan may experience comfort or discomfort. We know that she was involved with the Pentecostal church when she was young and could have traumatic memories associated with that time – that may resurface with dementia – if her gender identity was questioned by the Church or she was pressured to take part in conversion therapy, for example. It is notable that her returning to a religious affiliation involved joining the United Church which is known across Canada for being accepting and inclusive of LGBT* persons. The local church has even hosted workshops aimed at increasing awareness of sexual orientation and gender expression and sensitivity towards LGBT* members of the congregation.

There could be pressure on Joan's already precarious financial resources and living conditions with having a dementia diagnosis in addition to the costs of her transition, particularly the gender affirmation surgery. Moreover, dementia could negatively affect her sources of support given her geographic location. Accessing virtual support and travelling to Vancouver would be difficult without the assistance of a trusted confidant who could accompany her on her travels through both the virtual and the real world (see Purves *et al.*, 2014 for insights on the former).

Clothing and beauty in the lives of people with dementia is a relatively new area of research (Twigg and Buse, 2013) and is highly relevant to gender nonconformative older adults, whether they be transgender, lesbian, or two-spirit for example. Westwood (2014) provides an example of a lesbian woman who had always worn trousers being made to wear a dress in a care home setting, probably as it was easier for the staff, both in terms of their gendered expectations of womanhood and ease of removal. Joan already confronted sexist and ageist assumptions about dress and comportment after completing two years of RLE when the doctor determined that she was not dressing in an age-appropriate fashion. I wonder if these expectations were classed as well. Perhaps there are other middle-aged women working the sex trade and frequenting street outreach agencies in the small city where Joan lives who dress as she does.

Residential care is not required at this point in either Joan's real or her imagined life, yet she and her partner are likely to have started contemplating future care and housing arrangements and the implications Joan's transgender and bisexual identity and their partnership status will have on their wishes and options. Affirmation of gender identity, support of intimacy desires/needs, and inclusion of partner/chosen family in decision-making are likely to be significant issues in a residential care environment.

Person-centred care may be the best way forward, as advocated by Benbow and Beeston (2012) who assert that, when dealing with sexual behaviours, 'the best strategy to adopt is one of openness, thoughtfulness, inclusion, and discussion' (p. 1031). At the same time, we need to adopt an intersectional approach to avoid falling into the trap of assuming that persons with dementia and/or older LGBT* adults are homogeneous. Intersectionality can help 'illustrate the complex interrelationship between biographical diversity and social context that the identification "older LGB adult" can obscure' (Cronin and King, 2010: 880).

This brief glimpse into a possible future with dementia for a transgender and bisexual older adult indicates the importance of focusing on sub-populations within LGBT* communities and teasing out the particular strengths and concerns they may have. As McGovern (2014) notes, 'the onset of the disease often heightens and multiplies challenges for both LGBT* carers and persons with dementia in specific ways' (p. 847).

Conclusion and implications

This chapter provided an overview of intersectionality theorizing and demonstrated its application to the lives of older LGBT* people. It provided the reader with a tool to identify an individual's social location and a concrete example of its application to an older bisexual and transgender woman named Joan. Socially locating Joan and analysing the ways in which dementia might impact her, not only as a sexual and gender minority, but also as someone marginalized on the basis of her social class (low income), race (mixed), ethnicity (Métis) and Indigeneity, highlights the importance of attending to all aspects of an individual's identity and the ways in which they may interact. While the literature has mainly focused on legal and ethical issues related to residential care and interactions with health and social service providers, there are as many areas to be addressed as lives to be lived.

Our task as researchers and practitioners is to peel back the 'cloak of invisibility' so that we can work in collaboration with older LGBT* persons to ensure their later years are marked by dignity, love, and respect. Celebration rather than tolerance should be social and health care professionals' overriding goal of practice with LGBT* persons with dementia. A starting point would be seeing the value in having 'both wisdoms', which Joan and other two-spirit people achieve by being able to 'walk with one foot as female [and] one foot as male'. Having border crossed or negotiated liminal space in such a way should lend itself nicely to living well with dementia.

Acknowledgements

The research from which the Joan case study was drawn was funded through several small grants awarded to the author by the Social Sciences and Humanities Research Council (Aid to Small Universities) and the Michael Smith Foundation for Health Research (Women's Health Research Network; Rural and Remote Health Research Network). I would like to thank everyone who was part of the research, particularly the research participants and co-investigator Natalie Clark, as well as students who worked with this case in my Bachelor of Social Work (BSW) sexual orientation and gender expression course at Thompson Rivers University (TRU). Thank you to former BSW student and research assistant Anna Parkscott for assistance with the literature review for this chapter.

Notes

1 The Métis are one of three Canadian Indigenous peoples, the others being First Nations and Inuit. To be a member of the Métis Nation, one must self-identify as Métis, have an ancestral connection to the historic Métis community and be accepted by the Métis Nation (Métis National Council, 2015). There are 35 chartered Métis communities in British Columbia (Métis Nation BC, 2015).
2 I prefer to use this language as gender affirmation surgery reinforces that a transgender person's gender identity does not change, rather it is affirmed through body modification surgery to ensure congruence between their gender identity and expression.
3 http://web2.uvcs.uvic.ca/courses/csafety/mod2/media/flower.html.
4 http://qmunity.ca/get-support/olderadults/.
5 Through snowball and convenience sampling we aimed to recruit women under the age of 25 and over the age of 60. When we had difficulty locating women over the age of 60 and after several women in their fifties asked to participate, we dropped the age to 50 for the older group. All but the transgender participant were known to the author through the local queer community.

References

Adams, H. L. and Phillips, L. (2009). Ethnic related variations from the Cass model of homosexual identity formation: The experiences of two-spirit, lesbian and gay Native Americans. *Journal of Homosexuality*. **56**(7): 959–976.
Adams, M., Bell, L.-A., and Griffin, P. (2007) *Teaching for diversity and social justice* (2nd edn). New York: Routledge.
Bauer, M., Nay, R., Tarzia, L., Fetherstonhaugh, D., Wellman, D., and Beattie, E. (2014) 'We need to know what's going on': Views of family members toward the sexual expression of people with dementia in residential aged care. *Dementia*. **13**(5): 571–585.

Benbow, S. M. and Beeston, D. (2012) Sexuality, ageing, and dementia. *International Psychogeriatrics.* **24**(7): 1026–1033.

Binney, E. and Swan, J. (1991) The political economy of mental health care for the elderly. In M. Minkler and C. Estes (eds). *Critical perspectives on ageing: The political and moral economy of growing old*, pp. 165–188. Amityville, NY: Baywood.

Bishop, A. (2001) *Becoming an ally: Ending the cycle of oppression* in people (2nd edn). Halifax, NS: Fernwood Publishing.

Bowleg, L. (2008) When Black + lesbian + women = Black lesbian woman: The methodological challenges of qualitative and quantitative intersectionality research. *Sex Roles.* **59**: 312–225.

Breland, L. (2013) Lost libido, or just forgotten? The legal and social influences on sexual activity in long-term care. *Law & Psychology Review.* **38**: 177–211.

Brotman, S. and Kraniou, S. (1999) Ethnic and lesbian: Understanding identity through the life-history approach. *Affilia: Journal of Women & Social Work.* **14**(4): 417–438.

Brotman, S., Ryan, B., and Cormier, R. (2003) The health and social services needs of gay and lesbian elders and their families in Canada. *The Gerontologist.* **43**: 192–202.

Combahee River Collective. (1977) *The Combahee River Collective Statement.* Available at http://historyisaweapon.com/defcon1/combrivercoll.html.

Cronin, A. and King, A. (2010) Power, inequality and identification: Exploring diversity and intersectionality amongst older LGB adults. *Sociology.* **44**(5): 876–892.

Di Napoli, E. A., Breland, G. L., and Allen, R. S. (2013) Staff knowledge and perceptions of sexuality and dementia of older adults in nursing homes. *Journal of Ageing and Health.* **25**(7): 1087–1105.

Diamond, L. M. and Butterworth, M. (2008) Questioning gender and sexual identity: Dynamic links over time. *Sex Roles.* **59**: 365–376. DOI 10.1007/s11199-0089425-30.

Dhamoon, R. K. (2011) Considerations on mainstreaming intersectionality. *Political Research Quarterly.* **64**(1): 230–243.

Fredriksen-Goldsen, K. I. and Muraco, A. (2010) Ageing and sexual orientation: A 25-year review. *Research on Ageing.* **32**(3): 372–413.

Fredriksen-Goldsen, K. I., Cook-Daniels, L., Kim, H.-J, Erosheva, E. A., Emlet, C. A., Hoy-Ellis, C. P., Goldsen, J., and Muraco, A. (2013) Physical and mental health of transgender older adults: An at-risk and underserved population. *The Gerontologist.* **54**(3): 488–500.

Heath, H. (2012) Intimate relationships for people with dementia. *Nursing & Residential Care.* **14**(11): 593–596.

Hill Collins, P. (2000) *Black feminist thought: Knowledge, consciousness, and the politics of empowerment* (2nd edn). New York: Routledge.

Hill Collins, P. (2012) Looking back, moving ahead: Scholarship in service to social justice. *Gender & Society.* **26**(1): 14–22.

Hulko, W. (2002) Making the links: Social theories, experiences of people with dementia, and intersectionality. In A. Leibing and L. Scheinkman (eds). *The diversity of Alzheimer's disease: Different approaches and contexts*, pp. 231–264. Rio de Janeiro, Brazil: CUCA-IPUB.

Hulko, W. (2009a) From 'not a big deal' to 'hellish': Experiences of older people with dementia. *Journal of Ageing Studies.* **23**(3): 131–144. DOI:10.1016/j.jageing.2007.11.002.

Hulko, W. (2009b) The time and context contingent nature of intersectionality and interlocking oppressions. *Affilia: Journal of Women and Social Work.* **24**(1): 44–55. DOI: 10.1177/0886109908326814.

Hulko, W. (2011) Intersectionality in the context of later life experiences of dementia. In O. Hankivsky (ed.). *Health inequities in Canada: Intersectional frameworks and Practices*, pp. 198–220. Vancouver, BC: UBC Press.

Hulko, W. (2015a) Operationalizing intersectionality in feminist social work research: Reflections and techniques from research with equity-seeking groups. In S. Wahab, B. Anderson-Nathe and C. Gringeri (eds). *Feminisms in social work research: Promise and possibilities for justice-based knowledge*, pp. 69–89. London: Routledge Press.

Hulko, W. (2015b) Supporting younger lesbian and bisexual women and transgender youth in small cities and rural communities: Collaboration and affirmation. In B. O'Neill, T. Swan, and N. Mulé (eds). *LGBTQ people and social work: Intersectional perspectives*, pp. 193–212. Toronto: Canadian Scholars' Press.

Hulko, W. (in press) Being queer in the small city. In C. Walmsley and T. Kading (eds). *Power and possibility in the small city*. Calgary, AB: Athabaska University Press.

Hulko, W. and Hovanes, J. (2013) Intersectionality in the lives of LGBTQ youth: Identifying and finding community in small cities and rural communities. Manuscript under review for *Journal of Homosexuality*.

Hutchins, T. (2014) Hidden in the home: Supporting same-sex partnerships. *British Journal of Healthcare Assistants*. **8**(1): 34–37.

LGBT Movement Advancement Project (MAP) and Services and Advocacy for Gay, Lesbian, Bisexual and Transgender Elders (SAGE) (2010, March) *Improving the lives of LGBT older adults*. Denver, CO: MAP.

Lorde, A. (2007) Age, race, class and sex: Women redefining difference. In A. Lorde, *Sister outsider: Essays and speeches by Audre Lorde*, pp. 114–123. Berkeley, CA: Crossing Press. (Original work published 1984).

McCall, L. (2005) The complexity of intersectionality. *Signs*. **30**(3): 1771–1800.

McGovern, J. (2014) The forgotten: Dementia and the ageing LGBT community. *Journal of Gerontological Social Work*. **57**(8): 845–857. DOI: 10.1080/01634372.2014.900161.

McNeil-Seymour, J. (2015) Cross-dancing as culturally restorative practice. In B. O'Neill, T. Swan, and N. Mulé, (eds). *LGBTQ people and social work: Intersectional perspectives*, pp. 87–105. Toronto: Canadian Scholars' Press.

Mehrotra, G. (2010) Toward a continuum of intersectionality theorizing for feminist social work scholarship. *Affilia: Journal of Women and Social Work*. **25**(4): 417–430.

Métis National Council (2015) *The Métis nation: Citizenship*. Retrieved 26 August 2015 from www.metisnation.ca/index.php/who-are-the-metis/citizenship.

Métis Nation BC (2015) *Chartered communities*. Retrieved 26 August 2015 from www.mnbc.ca/chartered-communities.

MetLife Mature Market Institute (MMI) (2010, March) *Still out, still ageing. The MetLife Study of Lesbian, Gay, Bisexual, and Transgender Baby Boomers*. Westport, CT: MetLife MMI.

Mulé, N. J., Ross, L. E., Deeprose, B., Jackson, B. E., Daley, A., Travers, A., and Moore, D. (2009) Promoting LGBT health and wellbeing through inclusive policy development. *International Journal for Equity in Health*. **8**(18): 1–11.

Mullaly, B. (2010) *Challenging oppression and confronting privilege* (2nd edn). Don Mills, ON: Oxford University Press.

Norton, S., Mathews, F. E., Barnes, D. E., Yaffe, K., and Brayne, C. (2014) Potential for primary prevention of Alzheimer's disease: An analysis of population-based data. *The Lancet*. **13**(8): 788–794. DOI: http://dx.doi.org/10.1016/S1474 4422(14)70136-X.

O'Connor, D., Phinney, A., and Hulko, W. (2010) Dementia at the intersections: A unique case study exploring social location. *Journal of Ageing Studies*. **24**(1): 30–39.

Persson, D. I. (2009) Unique challenges of transgender ageing: Implications from the literature. *Journal of Gerontological Social Work.* **52**(6): 633–646.

Price, E. (2008) Pride or prejudice? Gay men, lesbians and dementia. *British Journal of Social Work.* **38**(7): 1337–1352.

Price, E. (2010) Coming out to care: Gay and lesbian carers' experiences of dementia services. *Health and Social Care in the Community.* **18**(2): 160–168.

Price, E. (2012) Gay and lesbian carers: Ageing in the shadow of dementia. *Ageing & Society.* **32**: 516–532. DOI: 10.1017/S0144686X11000560.

Purves, B., Phinney, A., Hulko, W., Puurveen, G., and Astell, A. (2014, June 13) Developing CIRCA-BC and exploring the role of the computer as a third participant in conversation. *American Journal of Alzheimer Disease & Other Dementias. On-line first.* 1–7. DOI: 10.1177/1533317514539031.

Rawlings, D. (2012) End-of-life care considerations for gay, lesbian, bisexual, and transgender individuals. *International Journal of Palliative Nursing.* **18**(1): 29–34.

Rich, A. (1980) Compulsory heterosexuality and lesbian existence. *Signs.* **5**(4): 631–660.

Stern, L. (2015) The invisibility paradox: Oppression and resilience in the context of LGBT ageing. In B. O'Neill, T. Swan, and N. Mulé (eds). *LGBTQ people and social work: Intersectional perspectives,* pp. 67–86. Toronto: Canadian Scholars' Press.

Thomas, W. and Jacobs, S. E. (1999) '...And we are still here': From *Berdache* to Two Spirit people. *American Indian Culture and Research Journal.* **23**(2): 91–107. DOI: http://dx.doi.org/10.17953/aicr.23.2.k5255571240t5650.

Twigg, J. and Buse, C. (2013). Dress, dementia and the embodiment of identity. *Dementia* **12**(3): 326–336.

Warner, L. R. and Shields, S. A. (2013) The intersections of sexuality, gender and race: Identity research at the crossroads. *Sex Roles.* **68**: 803–810.

Westwood, S. (2014) Dementia, women and sexuality: How the intersection of ageing, gender and sexuality magnify dementia concerns among lesbian and bisexual women. *Dementia.* 0 (0):1–21. DOI: 10.1177/1471301214564446.

Witten, T. M. (2003) Transgender ageing: An emerging population and an emerging need. *Review Sexologies.* **XII**(4): 15–20.

Witten, T. M. (2015a) Elder transgender lesbians: Exploring the intersection of age, lesbian sexual identity, and transgender identity. *Journal of Lesbian Studies.* **19**(1): 73–89. DOI: 10.1080/10894160.2015.959876.

Witten, T. M. (2015b) End of life, chronic illness and trans identities. *Journal of Social Work in End-of-Life and Palliative Care.* DOI: 10.1080/15524256.2013.877864.

4 Queer(y)ing dementia – bringing queer theory and studies of dementia into dialogue

Andrew King

Introduction

In this chapter I will explore the possibilities and limits of bringing insights and observations from Queer Theory into dialogue with studies and understandings of dementia amongst lesbian, gay and/or bisexual (LGB) people. I consider what it means to queer(y) dementia and what dementia amongst LGB people means for Queer Theory. In order to achieve these aims, the chapter is divided into four, interconnected, sections.

In the first section, I examine Queer Theory, what it is and how it developed. I explain that Queer Theory has its roots in the activism associated with the AIDS pandemic of the late 1980s, the identity politics of the 1990s and academic concerns to challenge understandings of sexuality in the social sciences and humanities. The second section then considers dementia as an object of study, an experiential entity and how it has been conceptualised. This is followed, in the third section, by an overview of a number of themes emanating from studies about dementia and LGB people. The fourth section then moves back to consider Queer Theory and dementia at a more conceptual level, as well as its implications for policy and practice. I conclude that queer(y)ing dementia means a critical reappraisal of Queer Theory and a further re-conceptualisation of dementia.

Queer Theory

Queer Theory is a diffuse and often contradictory body of work that emerged in the late 1980s and 1990s in response to a number of factors, both within and outside of the academic world (Green, 2007). Indeed, Queer Theory blurs the distinctions between the 'academic' and 'real' world, provoking questions about where knowledge is constructed, by whom and in whose name. In part, Queer Theory was evoked by the AIDS-activism of the mid to late 1980s and the new queer activism of the early 1990s – where groups such as Act-Up and Queer Nation, in the US and OutRage, in the UK, sought to challenge heteronormativity, the assumption that heterosexuality is the norm and other sexualities are therefore deviations. It also sought to address the prejudice and complacency of politicians, but also mainstream Lesbian and Gay organisations and what were perceived to be their assimilationist and homonormative tendencies, that is that they accepted a heteronormative, rights-based view of sexuality and were consequently 'fitting in' with mainstream society (Gamson and Moon, 2004).

Queer Theory owes much to the pioneering work of Michel Foucault and his ideas about the history and social construction of sexuality (Foucault, 1978); that is, that sexuality is a modern invention that emerged in the late nineteenth century through a range of techniques designed to control and discipline the body and mind, emanating principally from biomedical and psychoanalytic science. This stance has influenced a generation of queer writers, including Diana Fuss (1991), Eve Kosofsky Sedgwick (1993) and, particularly, Judith Butler (1993, 1999). Giffney (2009) argues, however, that Queer Theory has never been a united theoretical entity. It represents both a perspective towards knowledge, a theory about gender and sexuality, as well as a perspective on the nature of being; a theory produced by, for and about those deemed other because of their gender identity or sexuality. Yet, despite this diversity in outlook, Queer Theorists adopt an approach towards identity, to argue against unitary and hierarchical categories, attending to the inclusions, exclusions and forms of normative and symbolic erasure that such 'fictions' maintain. As Fuss (1991: 2) suggests:

> [t]he language and law that regulates the establishment of heterosexuality as both an identity and an institution, both a practice and a system, is the language and law of defence and protection: heterosexuality secures its self-identity and shores up its ontological boundaries by protecting itself from what it sees as the continual predatory encroachments of its contaminated other, homosexuality.

In other words, the privileging of heterosexuality and the power of such heteronormativity comes from the ability to define and protect heterosexuality by a range of exclusions and elisions associated with its 'other(s)'.

Following its post-structural leanings, language is very important to Queer Theory more generally. The ability to self-define is an important practice. Hence, the use of the term 'queer' is political: to take a term that was formerly used to refer to something as strange, which then became an insult and was then re-appropriated as a form of empowerment, as opposed to abuse (Giffney, 2009).

For Butler, these linguistic manifestations illustrate the performativity of identity; that is, identities are constituted through linguistic and behavioural practices that constitute what they name (Butler, 1999). Butler's famous example is how biomedical (and heteronormative) conceptions of gender produce a subject position from which a sense of self is constituted. As Butler (1993: 232) suggests:

> [gender] is thus not the product of choice, but the forcible citation of a norm, one whose complex historicity is indissociable from relations of discipline,

regulation, punishment. Indeed, there is no 'one' who takes on a gender norm. On the contrary, this citation of the gender norm is necessary in order to qualify as a 'one', to become viable as a 'one', where subject-formation is dependent on the prior operation of legitimating gender norms.

What Butler is suggesting here, is that it is the act of 'citing' a gender identity, drawing upon an existing body of knowledge, or discourse, which brings that identity into being. It does not, for her, exist outside of discourse: there is no doer behind the deed, the deed is the totality. Furthermore, one cannot be a person outside of this discourse; it is regulatory in that it constructs the limits and conditions of (gendered) existence. Similarly, heteronormativity sets the conditions of existence for gendered sexualities, creating hierarchies in the process. To be a 'lesbian' is not to be a 'heterosexual' woman and, arguably, within a heteronormative society is to be a lesser being, since the heterosexual remains the norm from which others are judged as different. However, Butler is adamant that such performativity is not entirely deterministic, as it contains the seeds of identity transgression and social change. Since all identities rely on per-formativity, they are in effect copies of copies, there are not identity beginnings (foundations) or completions – reiteration opens possibilities for doing identity differently. Yet this identity work is also embedded in heteronormative and gender-normative notions of time and the life course, which a queer approach seeks to understand, challenge and disrupt (Binnie and Klesse, 2013; Halberstam, 2005).

It is, therefore, the task of Queer Theory to deconstruct identities, to show how they are unstable, fluidic fictions that are the effects of regimes of power/ knowledge, which regulate bodies and desires (Seidman, 1995). Additionally, those regimes can at the same time be transgressed and transformed. Sullivan (2003: vi) argues that *to queer* is 'to make strange, to frustrate, to counteract, to delegitimise, to camp up – (heteronormative) knowledge and institutions', whilst Edelman (2004: 17) suggests that it 'can never define an identity; it can only ever disturb one'.

From the above, I take the central analytical task of any use of Queer Theory to be a troubling, a questioning of forms of knowledge and ontology, ostensibly about gender and sexuality, but arguably about other possible identifications. I therefore want to consider how, if at all, this could be related to dementia and in order to begin answering this problematic, it is necessary to explore the complex historicity and social construction of dementia itself. In so doing, the parallels and dissimilarities between Queer Theory and dementia can begin to be addressed theoretically before turning to focus on the more everyday lived experiences of queers living with/caring for others with dementia.

Constructing dementia

In this section of the chapter I want to consider what dementia is and what epis-temological models have been applied to its construction. This will then enable me to consider the experiences of LGB people living with dementia in the following section.

The Alzheimer's Society, one of the UK's leading dementia charities and a source of considerable information and support to people living with dementia, defines the condition on its website as 'a set of symptoms that may include memory loss and difficulties with thinking, problem-solving or language. Dementia is caused when the brain is damaged by diseases, such as Alzheimer's disease or a series of strokes' (Alzheimer's Society, 2014). This definition explicitly references biomedical and psychological conceptions of the disease, or, more accurately, the spectrum of conditions that can be labelled as dementia. What is implicit in this definition is that there are a set of norms, related to cognitive functioning, which are gradually eroded in those people who have dementia. In short, to have dementia, according to biomedical models, means to be ab-normal, or, as Graham (2004) has suggested, to lack cognitive citizenship. It is very easy to understand dementia as loss in this respect. A number of writers have addressed how dementia itself has emerged in this way relatively recently and, in reality, dementia is a more uncertain and questionable entity; indeed, a number of writers have asserted that dementia is itself socially constructed.

Harding and Palfrey (1997) note, for instance, that understandings of dementia in Western Society have their roots in Platonic philosophy, although the medical conception that is now dominant emerged in the late nineteenth and early twentieth centuries. However, it is only really in the past 30 years that dementia has become a serious object of biomedical study and, as such, a whole discourse of dementia has been produced. Dementia is now constructed as a disease, or a cluster of diseases, rather than a natural part of the ageing process. Harding and Palfrey challenge such mechanistic notions of the body as a machine, whose parts 'break down' and need replacement. They also suggest that what is clear from examining this discourse in more detail is that the causes, diagnosis and symptoms of dementia are uncertain and often contradictory. Even with the extended use of computerised tomography or CT scans, some underlying neurological pathologies are only discernable at autopsy and diagnoses are made on the basis of a range of (social) and behavioural factors (Sabat, 2001). Indeed, mirroring the notion of discourse in the social construction of sexuality, a discourse of dementia has emerged that constructs various actions, reactions and behaviours into a syndrome – in effect, once the label of dementia is applied, various characteristics come to be seen as symptoms of pathology and what is unifying is the way that these are represented as negative, degenerative and abnormal; to have dementia is to suffer from a lesser form of self.

One of the key figures to challenge the dominant biomedical model was Tom Kitwood (1997). I cannot in the short space available here do justice to the depth of his critique (for a good overview see Baldwin and Capstick, 2007). Suffice to say that Kitwood took a largely psychosocial and person-centred approach that recognised the significance of social milieu, locating individual neuropathology within a wider social and, above all, biographical context; in effect, a dialectical view of the relationship between body, self and society that changes over time.

Kitwood's views, however, have been joined more recently by other con-structionist approaches. These include intersectionality theory (Hulko, 2004 and in the previous chapter of this volume), which emphasises how people with dementia are always situated at the intersection of many interlocking identities and forms of inequality; thus, it is not simply neuropathology that constructs dementia, but the social situation that those who experience cognitive impair-ments find themselves in. Such circumstances, it is argued, can lead to immense stigma, marginalisation and social exclusion (Bond *et al.*, 2004). Hence, dia-gnoses are applied unevenly and intersect with multiple social factors, such as gender, ethnicity and social class.

Others have pursued more radical forms of social constructionism. Baldwin and Capstick (2007), for example, have examined the expediency of the radical post-structuralist work of Deleuze and Guattari in challenging notions of demen-tia as loss and opening up the possibility for a de-medicalisation of the phenom-enon. They note how others, for example Shabahangi (2005) also adopt this view and suggest that its usefulness lies in allowing 'other ways of being in the world to be fully valued and the uniqueness of persons to be celebrated' (Baldwin and Capstick, 2007: 19).

In effect, what is apparent from this social constructionist work is that demen-tia is a discursive concept that is applied to bodies, behaviours, social interac-tions and existing social inequalities. This is not to deny the very real existence of dementia, as an experience of cognitive difference, but to consider how those differential experiences come to be labelled and understood as dementia in and through society. However, in much of the writing about dementia, issues of sex-uality, particularly sexual identity are obscured or invisible. This is particularly consequential for people whose sexuality is a key vector of identification and social (in)equalities: lesbian, gay and bisexual (LGB) people.

LGB people and dementia

Having briefly outlined and questioned the prevailing biomedical model of dementia in the previous section and explored other approaches, particularly the social constructionist, I want to focus, in this section of the chapter, on studies that take the everyday lived realities of dementia for lesbian, gay and bisexual (LGB) people as their object of study. As such, I will be examining what can be learned from LGB people living with dementia, whether they are caring for those living with dementia or are living with dementia themselves. Doing so, I argue, points towards the need to queer(y) dementia itself, which I will consider in the final section of this chapter.

Sadly, given the recent surge of interest in dementia, there has been scant attention to dementia in the lives of LGB people. In the UK, pioneering work by Elizabeth Price (2008, 2010, 2011, 2012) and Richard Ward *et al.* (2005) has explored the lives of LGB people who are caring for others with dementia, whilst Newman and Price (2012) provide first-hand testimony regarding one older gay man's experiences of advocacy, activism and coping with the vicissitudes of heteronormativity in a dementia context. What is apparent from these works is that queerness affects how dementia is experienced in a number of ways, including: interactions with service providers; imagining a future with dementia; and policy responses.

Interactions with dementia service providers

In their dealings with dementia service providers (such as GPs, psychiatrists, nurses, social workers, support workers and a number of other professionals and specialist service providers), LGB people may adopt a range of strategies concerning how they manage the issue of sexuality in their interactions. Price (2010) has suggested, for instance, that the legacy of stigma associated with their sexuality has led some LGB people to use a range of 'passing' (assuming a heterosexual identity and/or not challenging the assumption of heterosexuality by others) and disclosure practices when interacting with dementia service providers. For instance, whilst some LGB people may remain, as far as possible, completely silent about their sexuality, or that of their partner or friend, others may opt for full disclosure. Price notes that such strategies are highly contextual; they are not, she argues, specifically age-cohort related. In short, those who are older, who we might expect to be more reticent about revealing their sexuality because of earlier life experience (Knauer, 2011; Rosenfeld, 2002), are not necessarily more likely to attempt to pass as heterosexual than those who are younger. Instead, such practices are based on more ad hoc, context-based, situated assessments. Moreover, Price (2008, 2010) also notes that some people's attempts to conceal their sexuality were sometimes disrupted by their own, or their partner's, dementia; a loss of inhibition and/or self-censorship due to dementia affecting a person's ability to pass, conceal or make informed choices about disclosure.

Moreover, some LGB people might find themselves being subjected to heterosexism (the privileging of heterosexuality), whereby they are categorised as heterosexual by professionals, and feel unable to challenge this in a situation where dynamics of care and power are in operation. In my own empirical work, interviewing LGB people over the age of 50 about their life experiences and use of services (Cronin and King, 2010), one gay man referred to a story he had been told by an older lesbian friend who was caring for her mother with dementia. This participant noted:

> she mentioned the fact that her mother had dementia and they [care workers] just immediately assumed that she was a spinster that lived with her mother, and they put her in that category and that was it and erm, she said 'it was just like you know, I didn't exactly want to come out to them but it was just the assumption?' 'Just there, you're in this box.'

Additionally, when service providers do discover the non-heterosexuality of a person who has dementia or their partner or carer, Price (2008) reported stories of people being defined *as* their sexuality; in effect, their sexuality acted as a master identity that overrode all others and determined how they were viewed by health professionals. One example Price gave was of an older gay man with dementia being forced to have an HIV test, even though his dementia was not AIDS-related, and without his partner being consulted. Furthermore, issues about third-party disclosure can also be significant here, there being cases where service providers have disclosed a client's LGB sexuality to other clients or co-workers without their consent.

In the face of such experiences, or more generally in dealing with the experience of dementia, LGB people may turn to others also living with dementia for sources of support. Yet Price's (2010) participants also mentioned that dementia support groups were very heteronormative spaces and participants recounted feeling isolated within them. Indeed, such interactional erasures are recounted in a rich and insightful piece by Newman and Price (2012) where Roger Newman's experiences, as a carer of someone living with dementia, with a range of service providers and support networks are discussed. As an older gay man who cared for his partner who was diagnosed with Alzheimer's disease and who helped to establish a successful UK lesbian, gay, bisexual and trans* (LGBT*) dementia support group, Roger's story is a salutary lesson in the pervasiveness of heteronormativity and its deleterious effects on individual lives and experiences. Aside from misunderstandings and outright discrimination, Roger reported an invisibility of LGBT* lives in healthcare and dementia-specific materials. Such occlusions not only affect interactional aspects of dementia care, as noted above, but the very act of diagnosis of dementia itself: for instance, it is suggested that there is a need to ensure that cognitive/memory tests speak to LGB lives and not to presume a heteronormative life course (Price, 2005, 2008). There is, therefore, a profound need for service providers to understand sexuality and especially the lives and cultures of LGB people. But, perhaps unsurprisingly, as Price's work shows, LGB people express considerable concern about dementia care, either for themselves or significant others. Inevitably, their concerns impact on their imagined futures, their thoughts about possibly ageing with dementia, what that may be like and how they would like it to be.

Imagining future dementia care needs

Participants in Price's (2012) study had few expectations where service providers would take account of their sexuality, with significant numbers expressing a deep concern about a future of living with dementia as an LGB person. This works on two levels: first, fearing an erasure of their sexual identity; second, the need to create a queered space in the future, that is, one that is welcoming and 'LGBT*-friendly', or even the possibility of an 'LGBT*-specific' care home. Whilst the latter may appear to some professionals to be a way of addressing questions of exclusion and diversity, it must be remembered that the wish for in/exclusive LGBT* care facilities may depend on other intersecting factors, such as gender, ethnicity and social class (Heaphy, 2007; O'Connor *et al.*, 2010; Traies, 2012). Price's participants reported making Living Wills (now known as Advanced Decisions or Advanced Directives), or writing detailed 'lists' of preferences as they imagined dementia service futures. Others spoke of the 'dream' of having some form of 'kite mark' system in place, to aid choosing appropriate services, particularly residential care homes. Additionally, as Roger Newman's story illustrates, older LGB people are actively taking matters into their own hands, either through setting up support groups or lobbying for change.

Policy responses – culturally competent services

It has been argued that there needs to be an improvement in the standards of service provision for older LGBT* people (Westwood *et al.*, 2015), particularly that services need to develop cultural competence concerning these people's lives, needs and experiences (McGovern, 2014). Cultural competency means the ability to deliver services to an array of service users, regardless of their social, cultural or ethnic background, yet, in ways, that meet their specific service needs; in short, to equip service providers with an understanding of the lives of their service users. There are, according to McGovern (2014), several forms that cultural competency can take, including: developing LGBT*-affirmative environments; ensuring staff are educated through on-the-job training programmes and qualifications; and developing specialised LGBT* support groups.

Such policy responses may appear to be very appealing and, in the UK, there is a growing range of LGBT* trainers who would be able to upskill frontline workers and managers to undertake their work with LGBT* people in mind. However, cultural competency is subject to a growing body of critique, as is addressed in Chapter 11 in this volume by Sue Westwood and Sally Knocker. As the writing on LGBT* equality and diversity work in local government and its associated service provider partners makes clear, such programmes cannot necessarily overcome more structural factors. For instance, it has been documented that, despite equalities legislation, in the provision of goods and services, as well as equality policies more generally, adherence and enthusiasm for such measures remains variable (Monro, 2006, 2010). In a project exploring LGBT* equalities work in the UK, for instance, it was found that some organisations operated a 'tick-box' approach to such matters; in short, in some locations, training was minimal and cursory (McNulty *et al.*, 2010). Additionally, evidence is beginning to be generated that LGBT* equality work, which includes health and social care sectors where people with dementia are most likely to be found, is affected by austerity measures that have been enacted by central government since the beginning of the latest financial crisis in 2008 (King, 2015). Moreover, for cultural competency to be truly inclusive, it must ensure that a range of voices and experiences are evidenced. If cultural competency means reproducing existing divisions within and between LGBT* people, in terms of gender, class, ethnicity etc, then it really may be little better than a heteronormative model.

Queer(y)ing dementia?

Thus far in this chapter I have introduced Queer Theory, noting how it radically questions and troubles taken-for-granted understandings of sexuality (and indeed other identities, particularly gender) as stable, *a priori*, fixed entities. Instead, Queer Theory posits the view that these are necessary discursive fictions, held together by normative forces. I followed my discussion of this form of queer constructionism with an exposition of dementia that challenges biomedical models. Without denying the very real experiences of cognitive and behavioural change that people with dementia undergo, or how this is felt by those who love and/or care for them, I have nevertheless outlined works that suggest that how we understand dementia is similarly socially constructed. Understandings of cognitive and behavioural change do not exist in a vacuum – they are understood in and through society. Subsequently, I have looked at the small number of studies that explore dementia amongst LGB people. My point in doing this was to emphasise how heteronormativity shapes experiences of dementia for LGB people. In this sense, dementia isn't imposed on LGB people, or LGB selves are not imposed onto dementia, the two are intricately shaped by wider social understandings about the heteronormative and arguably how that interacts with the cognonormative; in short, how sexuality, particularly non-heterosexualities, alongside other intersections, shapes people's experiences of dementia – how they are diagnosed, treated, and supported. In the reminder of this section of the chapter, however, I want to explore, at a more conceptual/theoretical level, the (dis)similarities between Queer Theory and dementia – what I refer to as a queer(y)ing of dementia – before thinking through some implications for policy and practice.

Although Queer Theory is radically deconstructionist and points to the fluidity and (un)becoming of multiple identities, it is nevertheless possible to see that it is largely based on the premise of a rational, acting subject – one who may be constructed through discourse, but who nevertheless acquires agency in this process in an active way. In effect, the definition of *to queer* that I reproduced earlier in this chapter – 'to make strange, to frustrate, to counteract, to delegitimise, to camp up' seems to imply a knowing subject, one who acts, within normative limits. This, therefore, has consequences for the queering of dementia because the latter can gradually erase those things that are taken *as signs* of rational action. I am not suggesting here that people with dementia are irrational, but that cognitive and behavioural changes associated with dementia are sometimes signified as such. In effect, it is possible to see that a queer theoretical ontology can arguably re-inscribe a cognonormative subject; the action in Queer Theory is done by rational actors. This is not to say that an alternative is impossible. Indeed, I think that contained within Butler's work are ways to reposition this debate, so that it becomes possible to challenge who counts as a rational subject, in what ways and when.

In her discussion of transgender and the violence of gender norms (Butler, 2004b) in addition to the legal status of those interred under 'indefinite detention' by the US state (Butler, 2004a), Butler asks the question: under what conditions is a person considered a person with a life worthy of recognition and deemed to be worth living? Through these two examples, Butler reassesses the power of norms to shape existence and the (sovereign) power of the state to suspend legal status and impose conditions of indeterminacy.

In relation to norms, Butler (2004b) argues that norms and the processes by which they operate, normative actions, contain within them all conditions of possibility, that is, there is no outside of norms, nothing is completely socially unintelligible; instead, norms produce and impose a binary logic (the normal and the abnormal), which is in many ways both deterministic, but also illusionary. Those things deemed abnormal are not outside of, but instead they are other and within. If we apply this to dementia, it means seeing dementia not as abnormal but as an-other normal – a different normal. Hence, I think this offers a way of moving beyond the idea of rationality and the binary logic of the rational/irrational. It also ties together with a queer focus on sexuality and the idea that queer is not outside of heterosexuality, but very much central to it, needed by it to maintain the illusion of difference. The question then becomes one of by whom and under what conditions are norms determined and imposed: through what power?

Butler (2004a) borrows and extends the Foucauldian conception of power in modern societies: governmentality; that is, power is not in the hands of one individual or body, but diffused through mechanisms of bureaucracy, administration, and institutions. Foucault sees this as central to the emergence of modern societies, the move from a sovereign regime and form of power, to one that is more mutable. Butler reconsiders the relationship between sovereign and governmental forms of power in contemporary societies, arguing that, in certain circumstances, a sovereign form of power re-emerges, or as she states: 'it might emerge as a reanimated anachronism within the political field unmoored from its traditional anchors' (p. 53). Butler points out that Foucault himself recognised that the two forms of power could co-exist, but he did not attempt to predict under what circumstances. Whilst Butler uses this to call into question US policy on the so-called 'War on Terror' and how those held as prisoners at Guantanamo Bay are conceptualised, I think there is something to be considered in relation to dementia here too. I want to emphasise that I am not suggesting the two are equivalent i.e. dementia and being a so-called 'enemy combatant', who is suspended from judicial law. What I am interested in is how dementia is deemed a condition under which certain rights become impossible and/or unliveable. What is clear from LGB people living with dementia, whether those who have been diagnosed with the condition or those caring for them, is that the intersection of dementia and sexuality can create unliveable conditions, certainly the erasure and problematising of existing forms of queer personhood that I noted in the previous section where heteronorms are forcibly applied to queer lives.

What could, therefore, be done to remedy this situation, not only conceptually but in terms of policy and practice? One possibility is to reconsider the performativity of dementia and to follow Queer Theory in moving away from a single-unified subject. Indeed, it seems to me that there is much to be gained from thinking about the person living with dementia, in whatever guise that might be, and to consider how the contextual instantiation of dementia is accomplished in those circumstances. Whilst there have been calls for more person-centred approaches and the individualising of care in order to retain an enduring sense of self (Fazio, 2008), I think that Queer Theory opens up the possibility for thinking about enduring selves in more open-ended and fractious ways, for instance, by focusing on how people are subjected to different logics, treatments, regimes of living. Again, this is already evident in existing studies, noted above, but could be extended by a focus on the power dynamics inherent in and challengeable through such situations.

Bartlett and O'Connor (2007) have proposed that a citizenship approach to dementia, and its socio-political context, could improve not only the care of, and responses to, people living with dementia, but also the more general place(s) of people with dementia in society. A more rights-based model (see, in this volume, Chapter 15 by Richard Ward) might lead to alternative ways of thinking about dementia 'beyond the realms of medicine and care'. Indeed, Bartlett (2014) has written about the significance of activism and person-centric approaches to the emergent dementia movement, especially how people living with dementia are working together and actively resisting pathological models of disease. She notes that models for activism have come from, amongst other places, the AIDS activist movement. I think there are similarities, but also differences, here in thinking about this activism for LGB people. Thinking this through in terms of normative action and the transgression of norms, it may be possible to see such vital and emergent movements as queer spaces; as spaces in which all cognonorms and heteronorms can be challenged. However, as was evident in Roger Newman's story, some dementia support groups are undoubtedly heteronormative and it should not necessarily be LGB people's responsibility to challenge this. Finding ways to create inclusive spaces for LGB people within dementia activism, and for people living with dementia in LGB activism, remains important.

Conclusion

In this chapter, I have explored the possibilities, and potential limits, of bringing Queer Theory into dialogue with studies of dementia, including studies of lesbian, gay and bisexual people affected by dementia. I have sought to make this dialogue both theoretical/conceptual, but also practical. What is evident from this brief examination is that dementia is both socially constructed and yet challenges existing forms of social construction, that is, Queer Theory. Yet at the same time, I hope to have shown how Queer Theory can provide a conceptual language and ways of thinking that can enable us to re-assess dementia, especially as it is lived and experienced by LGB people. I realise that this dialogue is preliminary and much further work, both theoretical and empirical, remains to be done. However, I contend that there are signs that such a dialogue can bring productive insights to further challenge the prevailing heteronormativity of dementia.

References

Alzheimer's Society (2014) *What is Dementia?* Available at: www.alzheimers.org.uk/site/scripts/documents.php?categoryID=200360.

Baldwin, C. and Capstick, A. (2007) *Tom Kitwood on Dementia*, Maidenhead: Open University Press.

Bartlett R. (2014) The Emergent Modes of Dementia Activism. *Ageing & Society* **34**: 623–644.

Bartlett, R. and O'Connor, D. (2007) From Personhood to Citizenship: Broadening the Lens for Dementia Practice and Research. *Journal of Aging Studies* **21**: 107–118.

Binnie, J. and Klesse, C. (2013) The Politics of Age, Temporality and Intergenerationality in Transnational Lesbian, Gay, Bisexual, Transgender and Queer Activist Networks. *Sociology* **47**: 580–595.

Bond, J., Corner, L. and Graham, R. (2004) Social Science Theory on Dementia Research: Normal Ageing, Cultural Representation and Social Exclusion. In: A. Innes, C. Archibald and C. Murphy (eds) *Dementia and Social Inclusion: Marginalised Groups and Margnalised Areas of Dementia Research, Care and Practice.* London: Jessica Kingsley Publishers, 220–236.

Butler J. (1993) *Bodies that Matter: On the Discursive Limits of Sex*, New York: Routledge.

Butler J. (1999) *Gender Trouble*, London: Routledge.

Butler J. (2004a) *Precarious Life*, London: Verso.

Butler J. (2004b) *Undoing Gender*, London: Routledge.

Cronin, A. and King, A. (2010) Power, Inequality and Identification: Exploring Diversity and Intersectionality amongst Older LGB Adults. *Sociology* **44**: 876–892.

Edelman, L. (2004) *No Future: Queer Theory and the Death Drive*, Durham, NC: Duke University Press.

Fazio, S. (2008) *The Enduring Self in People with Alzheimer's: Getting to the Heart of Individualized Care*, Baltimore: Health Professions Press.

Foucault, M. (1978) *The Will to Knowledge – The History of Sexuality Volume 1*, London: Penguin.

Fuss, D. (1991) Inside/Out. In: D. Fuss (ed.) *Inside/Out: Lesbian Theories, Gay Theories.* London: Routledge, 1–10.

Gamson, J. and Moon, D. (2004) The Sociology of Sexualities: Queer and Beyond. *Annual Review of Sociology* **30**: 47–64.

Giffney, N. (2009) Introduction: The 'Q' Word. In: N. Giffney and M. O'Rourke (eds) *The Ashgate Research Companion to Queer Theory.* Farnham: Ashgate, 1–13.

Graham, R. (2004) Cognitive Citizenship: Access to Hip Surgery for People with Dementia. *Health* **8**: 295–310.

Green, A. I. (2007) Queer Theory and Sociology: Locating the Subject and the Self in Sexuality Studies. *Sociological Theory* **25**: 26–45.

Halberstam, J. (2005) *In a Queer Time and Place: Transgender Bodies, Subcultural Lives*, New York: NYU Press.

Harding, N. and Palfrey, C. (1997) *The Social Construction of Dementia: Confused Professionals?* London: Jessica Kingsley Publishers.

Heaphy, B. (2007) Sexualities, Gender and Ageing: Resources and Social Change. *Current Sociology* **55**: 193–210.

Hulko, W. (2004) Social Science Perspectives on Dementia Research: Intersectionality. In: A. Innes, C. Archibald and C. Murphy (eds) *Dementia and Social Inclusion: Marginalised Groups and Marginalised Areas of Dementia Research, Care and Practice.* London: Jessica Kingsley Publishers, 237–254.

King, A. (2015) Prepare for Impact? Reflecting on Knowledge Exchange Work to Improve Services for Older LGBT People in Times of Austerity. *Social Policy and Society* **14**: 15–27.

Kitwood, T. (1997) *Dementia Reconsidered: When the Person Comes First*, Buckingham: Open University Press.

Knauer, N. J. (2011) *Gay and Lesbian Elders: History, Law and Identity Politics in the United States*, Farnham: Ashgate.

McGovern, J. (2014) The Forgotten: Dementia and the Aging LGBT Community. *Journal of Gerontological Social Work* **57**: 845–857.

McNulty, A., Richardson, D. and Monro, S. (2010) Lesbian, Gay, Bisexual and Trans (LGBT) Equalities and Local Governance: Research Report for Practitioners and Policy Makers. Newcastle: Newcastle University. Available online http://research.ncl.ac.uk/selg/documents/selgreportmarch2010.pdf (accessed 26 June 2013).

Monro, S. (2006) Evaluating Local Government Equalities Work: The Case of Sexualities Initiatives in the UK. *Local Government Studies* **32**: 19–39.

Monro, S. (2010) Sexuality, Space and Intersectionality: The Case of Lesbian, Gay and Bisexual Equalities Initiatives in UK Local Government. *Sociology* **44**: 996–1010.

Newman, R. and Price, E. (2012) Meeting the Needs of LGBT People Affected by Dementia: The Story of the LGBT Dementia Support Group. In: R. Ward, I. Rivers and M. Sunderland (eds) *Lesbian, Gay, Bisexual and Transgender Ageing: Biographical Approaches for Inclusive Care and Support.* London: Jessica Kingsley Publishers, 183–195.

O'Connor, D., Phinney, A. and Hulko, W. (2010) Dementia at the Intersections: A Unique Case Study Exploring Social Location. *Journal of Aging Studies* **24**: 30–39.

Price, E. (2005) All But Invisible: Older Gay Men and Lesbians. *Nursing Older People* **17**: 16–18.

Price, E. (2008) Pride or Prejudice: Gay Men, Lesbians and Dementia. *British Journal of Social Work* **38**: 1337–1352.

Price, E. (2010) Coming Out to Care: Gay and Lesbian Carers' Experiences of Dementia Services. *Health & Social Care in the Community* **18**: 160–168.

Price, E. (2011) Caring for Mum and Dad: Lesbian Women Negotiating Family and Navigating Care. *British Journal of Social Work* **41**: 1–16.

Price, E. (2012) Gay and Lesbian carers: Ageing in the Shadow of Dementia. *Ageing & Society* **32**: 516–532.

Rosenfeld, D. (2002) Identity Careers of Older Gay Men and Lesbians. In: F. Gubrium and J. Holstein (eds) *Ways of Aging.* Oxford: Blackwell, 160–181.

Sabat, S. R. (2001) *The Experience of Alzheimer's Disease: Life Through a Tangled Veil*, Oxford: Blackwell.

Sedgwick, E. K. (1993) Epistemology of the Closet. In: H. Abelove, M. A. Barale and D. M. Halperin (eds) *The Lesbian and Gay Studies Reader.* New York: Routledge, 45–61.

Seidman, S. (1995) Deconstructing Queer Theory or the Undertheorization of the Social and the Ethical. In: L. Nicholson and S. Seidman (eds) *Social Postmodernism: Beyond Identity Politics.* Cambridge: Cambridge University Press, 116–141.

Shabahangi, N. R. (2005) *Redefining Dementia: Between the World of Forgetting and Remembering.* Available at: http://remote.agesongbsp.com/cms/files/nader_dementia.pdf.

Sullivan, N. (2003) *A Critical Introduction to Queer Theory*, Edinburgh: Edinburgh University Press.

Traies, J. (2012) 'Women Like That': Older Lesbians in the UK. In: R. Ward, I. Rivers and M. Sutherland (eds) *Lesbian, Gay, Bisexual and Transgender Ageing: Biographical Approaches for Inclusive Care and Support.* London: Jessica Kingsley Publishers, 67–82.

Ward, R., Vass, A. A., Aggarwal, N., Garfield, C. and Cybyk, B. (2005) A Kiss is Still a Kiss? The Construction of Sexuality in Dementia Care. *Dementia* **4**: 49–72.

Westwood, S., King, A., Almack, K., Suen Y.-T., and Bailey, L. (2015) Good Practice in Health and Social Care Provision for LGBT Older People. In: J. Fish and K. Karban (eds) *Lesbian, Gay, Bisexual and Trans Health Inequalities.* Bristol: Policy Press, 145–158.

5 Reconceptualising dementia

Towards a politics of senility

Richard Ward and Elizabeth Price

Introduction

Our intention for this chapter is to position the study and understanding of dementia in relation to a series of other critical debates and areas of social analysis that focus upon social identity, difference and inequality. As an overarching theme of the chapter, we argue for the benefits of opening up a radical critical space at the margins of mainstream dementia studies.

In many respects, the so-called dementia community has arrived rather belatedly at a debate on rights and citizenship in relation to dementia. Only recently have we begun to witness the emergence of policy and analysis where questions concerning rights, equality and social participation are being explicitly addressed (see the 'Rights' section in this book for examples taken from policy and practice). However, as Ward points out in the final chapter to this book, much can potentially be learned from the campaigns for equality (and the critical response they have engendered) of other interest groups and communities of identity. Indeed, as Ward concludes, a level, or layer, of analysis is largely missing from the field of dementia studies that only becomes clear when we draw comparisons to these other struggles for emancipation. It is this gap, or critical silence, in the field of dementia studies that we wish to address in this chapter. Our intention is to make the case for a more radical critique of the social construction, conditions and politics of dementia. Specifically, we argue for the need to develop a critical commentary in relation to dementia that both mirrors and connects with a radical critique in other fields.

In order to map this territory, we develop a repertoire of ideas that are comparable to, and informed by, key concepts in areas such as sexuality, gender and disability studies, ideas such as performativity, citizenship and, most critically, the contested and sensitive concept of 'senility'. With this goal in mind, we focus upon a selection of key ideas from the fields of sexuality and dementia studies with the aim of drawing out synergies between them. Our intention is to outline the potential for dialogue between these different areas of social analysis; a theme which is developed in greater depth and detail by later chapters in this book.

These efforts are by no means exhaustive, of course, but we hope to show how connections between these divergent critical movements could both shed light on currently overlooked aspects of the debate on dementia and lead to the development of fruitful associations at the level of social action, campaigning and awareness-raising.

Key concepts in sexuality and queer studies

Performativity

We start our explication of key terms and ideas with the notion of performativity, as it sits, for us, centrally, yet steadfastly uncritically, at the core of the experience of dementia as an LGBT* person. The concept of performativity is fundamental in the study of sexuality, yet it is generally not employed as an organising theme in the study of dementia despite the fact that it underpins the ways in which we understand the nature of identity formation and maintenance (key concerns in the context of cognitive loss).

Butler (1993) famously coined the notion of performativity describing it as 'that reiterative power of discourse to produce the phenomena that it regulates and constrains'. That is, identity is generated and constructed through language and action; it is not predetermined or necessarily and un-problematically extant. As King, after Butler (1990), outlines in Chapter 4, our identities are continually linguistically and symbolically constituted and, whilst it is clearly important to 'trouble' the construction and nature of these self (and publicly) imposed identities, there are also very particular questions that arise when considering the notion of performativity in the context of dementia.

A contemporary understanding of dementia is underpinned by a model in which a sense of self (and one's critical identity signifiers such as gender/sexuality etc.) remains intact (though, arguably, inevitably altered in complex and entirely individual ways). Yet, if our sense of self, and the identities that inevitably attach to it, is constituted through both the language and action used to construct and maintain it, then a question must be raised as to how socially constructed and enacted identities pertain when the possibilities for semantic, linguistic and public performance are, at the very least, interrupted or obscured. That is, if the performance of our sexual/gender identity is dependent upon linguistic and symbolic reciprocity, then how might it be possible to maintain a continuing sense of self/identity when one may well be dependent, at least to some degree, on others to assist (and, for some, to fully support) one's identity maintenance.

These questions may become particularly acute in the heteronormative (see below at 'Heteronormativity') environments of residential care, where heterosexuality, its norms, values, associated language and symbolic dominance, constitutes and determines the tenor and rhythm of daily life. These are spaces where language and action (those performative pre-requisites) are governed by, and generated through, a normative heterosexual lens.

In this context, fundamental questions arise around the ways in which LGBT* identities are maintained and whether, in the face of heterosexual domination,

LGBT* identities are particularly vulnerable to the experience of dementia. For trans* people in particular (as pointed out variously in this collection) identity maintenance may be an issue that must be carefully negotiated, by carers and supporters, with exquisite sensitivity, particularly if the person has transitioned and, with dementia, may have lost the capacity to recall the nature and extent of their transition. The work of Witten (Chapter 8 in this volume) suggests that this is a sensitivity that has yet to be realised. Indeed, it may be the case that care providers are yet to even have awareness of its lack.

We might also be cognisant of the fact that the loosening of the customary ties to social convention that can sometimes accompany the experience of dementia might, ironically, constitute a freeing of some of the shackles of identity that bind us increasingly tightly as we age. Instead, then, rather than being required and expected to maintain a particular identity, generated through the use of customary language and taken-for-granted behaviours, preferences and expectations, the experience of dementia may actually generate an emancipatory space in which to explore, hidden, forgotten, or quite new aspects of self and identity in ways that may not previously have been possible (see, for example, Capstick and Clegg, 2013). This is not to deny the negative aspects of the condition, rather, it is simply a recognition that people continue to live (and love) with, rather than just 'suffer from' dementia – it is, after all, a diagnosis for life.

Nonetheless, if indeed identity as an LGBT* person is, at least partly, dependent on the performative collaboration of others, then the construction and maintenance of that identity on a daily basis is fundamentally vulnerable to erasure when the individual in question may no longer adopt an unproblematic and assumed collaborative part in its constitution. Here, then, when considering ways in which identity is maintained when one's cognitive processes are threatened and/or undermined, it is perhaps appropriate to introduce the notion of 'performative asymmetry' (whereby the maintenance of one's chosen/innate identity is intertwined with and relies increasingly upon the conduct and contributions of others). This is in a bid to understand the ways in which LGBT* identities might be particularly vulnerable in the context of a diagnosis of dementia. In this context, 'performative support' is, perhaps, a concept that requires urgent attention from care providers. Again, as the chapters in this book testify, it is a concept yet to receive purposeful critical attention in practice.

Intersectionality

If we are to begin to theorise dementia in a specifically LGBT* context, it is necessary to be able to articulate the ways in which various social locations/categories and positionalities might impact upon our understanding and experience of the condition. The notion of intersectionality, then, is a further key construct which underpins and informs our discussion here. It is an idea that has already been applied in efforts to reconceptualise dementia but is yet to filter into mainstream research or practice, where preoccupation with 'person with dementia' as a stable and unified category of identity still dominates current perspectives.

Wendy Hulko outlines the nature of intersectionality in Chapter 3 in this volume, and has defined it elsewhere as 'a metaphor for the entanglement and interaction of multiple and complex identity categories' (Hulko, 2004: 38). Intersectionality is a notion which poses a challenge to current over-simplistic additive forms of analysis in dementia studies and has the potential to drive a far more inclusive approach within dementia practice, where appreciation of the dynamic nature of social location replaces notions of fixed categories of identity (Cronin *et al.*, 2011). Such an approach would require researchers and practitioners to pay attention to the 'intimate interconnections, mutual constitutions and messiness of everyday identifications and lived experiences' (Taylor *et al.*, 2011: 2). In the context of living with dementia, it is these very connections that can frame the daily lived experience of an LGBT* person – connections which are likely to be invisible threads of experience to those people charged with supporting the person diagnosed.

The proposition in the context of our argument here, however, is that, for LGBT* people, dementia may become the hub around which other intersections of identity inevitably turn. As we note later in this chapter, cognitive ability is perceived to be so fundamental (and largely inalienable and unshifting) to our sense of self and the ways in which we are socially positioned (and position ourselves) that, when cognition is undermined, our new social identity as 'cognitively impaired', effectively trumps all other cognate and socially readable positionalities. For many LGBT* people, who may have generated a range of carefully constructed public and private mechanisms for the management of identity, access to social capital associated with other, perhaps more privileged and valued, social identities may be rendered ineffectual. This shifting social location results not only from the impact of the condition but from others' responses to a person's sexual/gender identity and applies particularly when their lifestyle and choices, post-diagnosis, begin to become publicly visible (Price, 2007). As such, we would suggest that paying attention to the intersection of LGBT* identity and the particularities of living with dementia might help to highlight specific articulations of vulnerability as they apply to LGBT* people.

Heteronormativity

It is in the context of public (and private) visibility that another key concept from queer studies comes to the fore in our efforts to reconceptualise dementia, this being the notion of heteronormativity (the assumption that heterosexuality is the norm). Originally coined in the early 1990s by Michael Warner, it was an idea that marked a step-change in the analysis of socio-sexual relations. We can understand heteronormativity, which built upon earlier ideas of 'compulsory heterosexuality' (Rich, 1980) and the 'heterosexual matrix' (Butler, 1990) as a 'threshold concept' (Meyer and Land, 2003) for queer studies in that it opened the door to a level of social analysis that had previously not existed as an organised set of ideas or line of argument. The concept facilitated thinking that extended beyond existing efforts to identify and challenge forms of direct discrimination and social exclusion on the grounds of sexuality (i.e. hetero-sexism and homophobia) and focused instead upon the more pervasive, but largely hidden and 'unmarked', way in which a certain version of heterosexual-ity had an organising influence across many different realms of everyday experi-ence: politically, socially and culturally. It was an idea that drew particular attention to the ways in which hegemonic heterosexual perspectives and interests are privileged, but in such a way as to be considered natural and hence to remain unseen (Warner, 1991; Seidman, 2005).

The significance of heteronormativity to dementia studies is two-fold. In the still-limited research and debate surrounding sexuality and dementia, some commentators have identified the presence and workings of heteronormativity within dementia care. This is marked, for instance, by assumptions of hetero-sexuality that pervade the delivery of services as well as by an overwhelming emphasis upon the heterosexual life course in discourse. This ranges from casual care-based conversations, brochures for dementia care facilities, and images used by dementia-related charities and campaign groups. It also under-pins how persons with dementia and their supporters are positioned in their relationship to the welfare state through policy and legislation saturated with assumptions regarding the universality of heterosexual biographical mile-stones (Newman and Price, 2012; Price, 2010; Westwood, 2015). In this respect, heteronormativity provides a basis for a critique of dementia care ser-vices that looks beyond questions of discrimination to encompass a more subtle bias that creates a hierarchy of sexualities in the context of providing care and support.

However, we would argue that heteronormativity has even more far-reaching implications for dementia studies. Its pervasive, yet mundane, presence through-out the experience of dementia serves to draw our attention to a further critical silence that exists in relation to a comparable form of analysis surrounding what might be described as 'able-mindedness'. Hence, later in this book, Ward takes as examples the politics of time and space as significant arenas where assump-tions and expectations regarding a certain level of cognitive functioning and capacity have a shaping influence both upon the design and occupation of everyday physical environments as well as the tempo or temporal frame associ-ated with the pace of everyday living. In this way, the notion of heteronormativ-ity invites consideration of what might be an equivalent for dementia studies and for our understanding of the lived experience of dementia and other forms of cognitive and intellectual disability. In light of this insight, we would argue that a cornerstone to any efforts to establish a more radical agenda for dementia studies would be the development of awareness and analysis regarding the pres-ence and experience of this particular, and hitherto largely overlooked, form of normativity.

We turn now to consider examples of key concepts from the field of dementia studies where the introduction of queer and other radical approaches have the potential to contribute to a more critical opening within the field.

Key concepts in dementia studies

Citizenship

While 'personhood' has become an established concept and focus for debate in dementia studies, more recently it has been criticised for an apparent failure to connect the person with dementia to a wider social and structural context. Out of that critique has emerged notions of dementia 'citizenship'. For example, Bartlett and O'Connor (2007) explain that the concept of citizenship can be used 'to promote the status of discriminated groups of people still further, to that of a person with power entitled to the same from life as everyone else' (p. 106). Bartlett and O'Connor go on to explain that citizenship is about status – being a fully included member of society – and about power, that is who is afforded that status and who is not. A citizenship lens, they point out, can be useful in tackling discrimination and social marginalisation, not least in relation to people with dementia. Indeed, dementia citizenship raises and engages with key questions about what it means to be a citizen and how citizenship is not just accorded as a status, but can also be exercised as a set of rights and responsibilities.

While people with dementia should, of course, be accorded citizenship rights, and mobilise those rights through advocacy, activism and engagement in research (Bartlett, 2014), some may find it more difficult to do so because of deteriorating cognitive abilities. Baldwin (2008) responds to the challenges of progressive impairment and associated communication problems by arguing for 'narrative citizenship' which, he argues, operates in three inter-related ways: in how an individual discursively positions themselves in relation to others; in how such narratives are embedded in social relationships and everyday activities; and in collective narratives, for example in social policy, which shape where and how identities can be performed. Central to narrative citizenship, Baldwin argues, is the maintenance of 'narrative agency' (p. 225), that is, being able to produce one's story and get it heard and understood by others. Baldwin differs from Bartlett and O'Connor in arguing that even those with severe cognitive impairment can maintain their narrative citizenship through embodied practices, when sensitively interpreted by attuned others. Hence, embodied practices can be understood as a potential mode of communication in dementia care, drawing upon 'the communicative capacity of the body to enrich our imagination and connect us to the personhood of others' (Kontos and Naglie, 2007: 551).

Narratives, including dementia narratives, can potentially be both empowering and/or disempowering, depending upon how they are produced and whether they are heard. So too can embodied narratives which are themselves embedded in normativities which may not take into account the intersection of 'gender, class, sexuality and ethnicity' (Kontos and Martin, 2013: 297). The silence/silencing of LGBT* dementia narratives in dementia discourse is a good example of this. Indeed, one of the criticisms of the whole notion of citizenship is that it not only defines who is entitled to be considered a citizen, but also who is not, immediately creating both inclusionary and exclusionary spaces. Some of those who are already marginalised in society may, under a citizenship approach, find themselves accorded greater inclusion, but potentially at the cost of pushing others even further to the margins (Richardson, 2005).

Shildrick (2013), writing about sexual citizenship discourse in regard to people with disabilities, rejects the notion that the recognition and regulation of disabled people's sexual citizenship will be somehow liberating for them. Instead, echoing the work of queer/feminist theorists in relation to gender/sexuality, and of crip theorists in relation to disability (McRuer, 2006), Shildrick argues that campaigning for citizenship rights colludes with the inherent ableism (and other normativities) of citizenship by wanting to buy into that discriminatory model rather than seek to develop a new model instead. She proposes that extension of (sexual) citizenship rights to disabled people inadvertently reinforces the underlying idea of the good citizen as a self-sufficient, autonomous actor from which people with embodied and/or cognitive disabilities deviate, having 'special' needs to enable them to make citizenship claims. Shildrick thus proposes a more radical rethinking of how we frame and value people in society, resisting the 'seductive narratives of citizenship' (p. 3607). Instead, she suggests that there are new ethical possibilities in going beyond (normative) citizenship to conceptualise the person in society outwith the binaries of dis/ability. Such a re-visioning might involve an 'ethic of care' (Brannelly, 2011) at its heart, one which recognises our enduring interdependence (as opposed, in the context of dementia, to the presumed and paralysing notion of 'dependence' that is so often the limiting trope that defines debate) and need for reciprocal care and support (Fineman, 2004) as central to the human condition.

Embodiment

The concept and understanding of embodiment is particularly apposite to the argument being developed in this chapter. It has long been a focus for debate in feminist, post-colonial, disability, queer, and transgender studies but has also more recently emerged as a theme to drive critical analysis in dementia studies. As such, there is much potential for bringing these different analyses into dialogue in order to enhance our understanding of embodiment in relation to dementia. At the same time, what we understand of the embodied experience of dementia might also provide the basis for making a critical contribution to these other fields.

In essence, a focus on embodiment brings to the fore an awareness of the lived experience of the body. Anchored within a phenomenological tradition, it has helped to foster debate around the body as the inescapable basis upon which we experience the worlds that we inhabit and, allied to this, an awareness of the 'corporeality of power relations' (Twigg *et al.*, 2011: 178). Attention to embodiment has led to questioning notions of identity and selfhood as discursively constituted. Instead, identities are understood as anchored in the body and our embodied experience of the world. In the context of dementia studies, a recent review of the literature found that embodiment has begun to inform a range of empirical investigations of dementia care as well as efforts to reconceptualise dementia (Kontos and Martin, 2013). In the latter context, Kontos' (2005) notion of embodied selfhood has been central to a critique of interactionist approaches to dementia which have largely overlooked the body and failed to recognise an embodied dimension to personhood.

Kontos argues that aspects of both self- and social-identity reside at a bodily level. In order to recognise the way in which selfhood survives in the context of a condition such as dementia, she suggests that we consider a person's embodied history as well as the 'immediacy of the body' as the primordial basis for experiencing the world. The implications of this approach for how we understand the enduring nature of social identity, and not least the identities of LGBT* individuals living with dementia remains under-developed in Kontos' analysis, but it is here that drawing connections to a wider debate on embodiment may enhance our understanding. We might then begin to think of embodiment and embodied practices as a significant reservoir for different aspects of social identity and our sense of belonging and group membership (Ward *et al.*, 2014).

Writing at the intersection of crip, feminist and queer studies, Kafer's (2013) approach to embodiment also has particular resonance with our discussion here as she seeks to consider some of the more concrete, lived implications of embodied identities. Kafer sets out to identify and promote coalitions between diverse groups based upon their differently embodied experience of the world. With a concern for building what she describes as 'accessible futures', Kafer highlights a series of case studies where aspects of embodied experience of exclusion or regulation provide a basis for coalition, famously using the politics of public toilets to demonstrate that building connections or coalitions is not reserved purely for an abstract realm of theory, but applies in a very direct fashion to how we make sense of the lived experience of the body and the everyday politics that surround it. From this perspective, we can begin to appreciate how a focus on embodiment in dementia studies might similarly hold out the prospect of building fruitful connections, both practically and theoretically, with a wider context of critique and campaigning. Whereas the bodies (and minds) of people with dementia have historically been a basis for their exclusion and marginalisation (Stirling, 1995), commentators such as Kafer reveal how we might understand embodied experience as a point of connection and commonality and as a source of collective affinity with other groups and individuals who have faced comparable conditions.

Senility

In turning to our final key concept, our intention here is to pull together the insights we have highlighted thus far and to consolidate our argument for a more radical critique of the social conditions, politics and construction of dementia. Our argument draws from our readings of the relationship between other critical responses to a rights-oriented discourse in fields such as gender, sexuality, race and disability. For instance, as King explores in this book, the emergence of queer studies created a distinct forum for both challenging and rethinking the discursive organisation of sexuality and gender. In reclaiming a term or label previously used in the 'othering' of sexual and gender dissidents, 'queer' provided the means to step out of or beyond the limiting boundaries of what had until that point been a push for social and political inclusion, or what Richardson (2005) has described as a 'desire for sameness', where new levels of social visibility risked becoming new spaces for control. In light of these arguments, our proposal here is for an equivalent effort to reach beyond the boundaries of a rights-oriented approach to dementia and we suggest that a focus upon the politics of senility might offer such an opportunity.

Senility (Gubrium, 1986) is attractive as an organising focus because it potentially provides a critical space to reflect upon the positioning of people with dementia as part of a wider social, historical and cultural response to debility in later life. Thus, Ballenger (2006) suggests that attention to senility facilitates insight into the 'peculiar dread that dementia generates' (p. 1). In this respect, the politics of senility can be understood as the broader context in which a culturally and historically contingent discourse of dementia has more recently emerged. This wider context provides the basis to critically examine a discourse that is saturated with a medicalised logic of individual deficit, and increasingly cast in a binary relationship to notions of 'healthy ageing' and to an unspecified and unmarked norm of 'able-mindedness'. Like 'queer' and 'crip', 'senile' is a term that historically has facilitated the stigmatising and othering of those perceived or labelled as departing from an unmarked social norm. This process of othering individuals experiencing cognitive and behavioural change in later life is integral to a process of abjection associated with old age (Gilleard and Higgs, 2011). Yet, as Gilleard and Higgs (2011) suggest, abjection and marginalisation are themselves by no means devoid of power or transgressive potential. Rather they can serve as a space for resistance.

Our proposal here draws, in part, from the seminal work of Gubrium (1986) who sought to interrogate what he described as the 'descriptive organisation of senility' that underpinned the medicalisation of dementia and, in particular, emphasised the order and predictability of 'Alzheimer's as a distinct disease entity separate from the varied experiences of normal aging' (p. 3). Gubrium sought to problematise the certainty of medical science as it set out to disentangle ageing and pathology, consequently framing a broader social and cultural understanding of ageing and impairment: 'our analytic interest centres on how the disease entity is used to interpret the thing being described and how alternative realities are guarded against or prevailed upon' (p. 23). This concern for how a discourse of dementia has closed down or circumvented 'alternative realities' is further developed in Cohen's (2006) argument for senility as an opportunity to look beyond the specificity of Alzheimer's disease or vascular dementia: 'To organize our conversations around "senility" [...] as opposed to organizing them around "dementia" is simply not to presume in advance how perception, biology and milieu are related' (p. 1).

Cohen (2006) thereby argues for a more open approach to 'what senility might be becoming' (p. 2) in the context of widespread changes that include growing recognition of the significance of inequalities tied to axes of difference such as gender, race and disability as well as broader structural shifts at the level of economies and institutions. In this context, 'senility' is re-cast as a category of social and cultural analysis that, for Cohen, is the basis for reanimating a relationship with 'creative understanding in the human sciences more broadly, to move beyond the solicitous and welfare-driven categories of contemporary gerontology' (p. 2). From this perspective we can begin to understand senility as a critical space that promotes the interrogation of a series of medicalised assumptions and how they are upheld and reproduced according to the logic of the welfare state.

This concern to establish an alternative critical space is also integral to Katz's (2013) focus upon what he calls the 'long history of memory and the short history of dementia' (p. 304). Through a focus upon an evolving history of memory that he traces back to medieval times, Katz argues for recognition of the way in which a medicalised 'progress narrative' has framed much of the debate on dementia, delimiting the possibilities for how we think about the relationship between memory, senility and ageing. His aim is to promote 'critical curiosity' in relation to the meaning of categories and terms that have been presented as 'inarguable' within a discourse of dementia, but also to reach beyond the limits set by how we currently conceptualise dementia and associated patterns of care: 'Reducing people to their brains and isolating them as sick and marginal in the name of cognitive care harms memory, which is continual, even when forgetful' (p. 311).

In building upon this more critical stance in relation to dementia and the assumptions and expectations it encompasses, we argue for the benefits of reclaiming 'senility' not as a label denoting a particular state or condition, but as a critical space for a debate that rejects the parameters set by the specificity of 'dementia', even according to its various iterations as a biomedical, psychosocial and, latterly, rights-oriented construct. Instead, senility exists as a space 'beyond' dementia and provides a basis for a different scale of social analysis and critique. Hence, a focus upon the politics of senility redirects attention from the struggle for acceptance and inclusion driven by a neoliberal politics of normalisation (Richardson, 2005), and instead embraces a politics of 'anti-normalisation' that has similarly marked the emergence of queer studies, radical feminism and crip studies, all of which have evolved at the margins of an increasingly mainstream discourse of rights and recognition. As Richardson has argued in relation to sexual citizenship:

> The primary focus in the rise of a politics of normalisation is on bringing about social changes so that lesbians and gay men may be regarded as socially valued members of society, rather than attempting to bring about changes in how societies operate in ways that are productive of devalued categories of behaviour, identity and persons.
>
> (2005: 532)

It is this latter concern with wider social and cultural processes of devaluation that marks out the critical space that we are arguing for in relation to dementia. This is a process that many different minoritised groups and communities share experience and understanding of. Hence, an added benefit to such a development is the potential to draw connections with other marginalised perspectives, to identify areas of commonality and to be enriched by the critical and conceptual innovations that have marked these different fields of social analysis.

Reconceptualising dementia: looking ahead

Our argument in this chapter has been two-fold. In light of recent policy developments in relation to a more rights-oriented understanding of dementia, we have advocated opening up a radical critical space at the margins of more mainstream constructions of dementia. Marginality, hooks (1990) suggests, is 'a site of radical possibility, a space of resistance' and a 'central location for the production of a counter-hegemonic discourse that is not just found in words but in habits of being and the way one lives' (p. 206). Our argument here is that such a space is vital to the rapidly evolving debate on dementia. Hence, we have suggested that reorienting ourselves to the politics of senility creates an arena that exists outside of or 'beyond' dementia. Such critical territory could support efforts to deconstruct and reconfigure current thinking and enable a critique of the binary relationship in which dementia has become fixed in regard to notions of 'healthy ageing' and 'able-mindedness'.

In doing this, we have drawn upon similar critical openings in other fields of social analysis, and in particular queer/feminist/disability studies to underline the value of such a development. Hand in hand with such an opening is the potential for a more direct dialogue and marrying of ideas and insights from these other radical spaces, as we have sought to illustrate in this chapter. This is the second 'fold' in our argument and it draws from commentators such as McRuer (2006) and Kafer (2013) who have shed light on the potential for a more integrated analysis. Crucially, Kafer (2013) argues for the need to recognise the 'collective affinities' that exist between 'differently able' groups and individuals, these are both lines of affiliation and potential sources of solidarity that are anchored in our everyday lived (embodied) experience. Kafer's argument is thus for radical forms of coalition that 'trouble the boundaries of the constituencies involved' (p. 151) and lead to questioning of the categories into which people are organised or allotted: 'what is needed then is not only a trenchant critique of ableism but also a desire to think disability otherwise' (p. 153). The parallels here to an agenda for dementia are too compelling to resist. Not only could attention to the politics of senility support efforts to interrogate the 'unseen' and naturalised presence of an able-minded norm in all our lives, but it would enable us to think dementia otherwise. In other words, it could lead to reconceptualising dementia in such a way as to reveal the connections and affinities that exist in efforts to challenge and question hierarchies of difference, and the associated process by which certain categories of behaviour, identity and persons are devalued and ultimately discounted.

References

Baldwin, C. (2008) Narrative, citizenship and dementia: The personal and the political. *Journal of Aging Studies*, **22**(3), 222–228.

Ballenger, J. F. (2006) *Self, senility and Alzheimer's disease in modern America: A history*, Baltimore: Johns Hopkins University Press.

Bartlett, R. (2014) Citizenship in action: The lived experiences of citizens with dementia who campaign for social change. *Disability & Society*, **29**(8), 1291–1304.

Bartlett, R. and O'Connor, D. (2007) From personhood to citizenship: Broadening the lens for dementia practice and research. *Journal of Aging Studies*, **21**(2), 107–118.

Brannelly, T. (2011) That others matter: The moral achievement – care ethics and citizenship in practice with people with dementia. *Ethics and Social Welfare*, **5**(2), 210–216.

Butler, J. (1990) *Gender trouble: Feminism and the subversion of identity*, London: Routledge.

Butler, J. (1993) *Bodies that matter: On the discursive limits of sex*, London: Routledge.

Capstick, A. and Clegg, D. (2013) Behind the stiff upper lip: War narratives of older men with dementia. *War and Culture Studies*, **6**(3), 239–254.

Cohen, L. (2006) Introduction: Thinking about dementia. In A. Leibing and L. Cohen (eds) *Thinking about dementia: Culture, loss and the anthropology of senility*, New Jersey: Rutgers.

Conaghan, J. and Grabham, E. (2007) Sexuality and the citizen carer. *Northern Ireland Legal Quarterly*, **58**, 325–341.

Cronin, A., Ward, R., Pugh, S., King, A. and Price, E. (2011) Categories and their consequences: Understanding and supporting the caring relationships of older lesbian, gay and bisexual people. *International Social Work*, **54**(3), 421–435.

Fineman, M. (2004) *The autonomy myth*, New York: The New Press.

Gilleard, C. and Higgs, P. (2011) Ageing, abjection and embodiment in the fourth age. *Journal of Aging Studies*, **25**(2), 135–142.

Gubrium, J. F. (1986) *Old timers and Alzheimer's: The descriptive organization of senility*, Greenwich, CT: JAI Press.

Harding, R. (2011) *Regulating Sexuality: Legal consciousness in lesbian and gay lives*, Abingdon: Routledge.

hooks, b. (1990) *Yearning: Race, gender and cultural politics*, New York: South End Press.

hooks, b. (1990) *Yearning: Race, gender and cultural politics*. New York: South End Press.

Hulko, W. (2004) Social science perspectives on dementia research: Intersectionality. In A. Innes, C. Archibald and C. Murphy (eds) *Dementia and social inclusion*, pp. 237–254. London: Jessica Kingsley Publishers.

Kafer, A. (2013) *Feminist, queer, crip*, Bloomington: Indiana University Press.

Katz, S. (2013) Dementia, personhood and embodiment: What can we learn from the medieval history of memory? *Dementia*, **12**(3), 303–314.

Kontos, P. C. (2005) Embodied selfhood in Alzheimer's disease: Rethinking person-centred care. *Dementia: International Journal of Social Research and Practice*, 553–571.

Kontos, P. C. and Martin, W. (2013) Embodiment and dementia: Exploring critical narratives of selfhood, surveillance, and dementia care. *Dementia*, **12**(3), 288–302.

Kontos, P. C. and Naglie, G. (2007) Bridging theory and practice: Imagination, the body, and person-centred dementia care. *Dementia*, **6**(4), 549–569.

McRuer, R. (2006) *Crip theory: Cultural signs of queerness and disability*, New York: NYU press, 2006. Kindle Edition.

Meyer, J. and Land, R. (2003) *Threshold concepts and troublesome knowledge: Linkages to ways of thinking and practicing within the disciplines*, Edinburgh: University of Edinburgh, www.etl.tla.ed.ac.uk//docs/ETLreport4.pdf [accessed 4 August 2015].

Newman, R. and Price, E. (2012) Meeting the needs of LGBT people affected by dementia. In R. Ward, I. Rivers and M. Sutherland (eds), *Lesbian, gay, bisexual and transgender ageing: Biographical approaches for inclusive care and support*, pp. 183–195. London: Jessica Kingsley Publishers.

Price, E. (2007) Pride or prejudice: Gay men, lesbians and dementia. *British Journal of Social Work.* Advance Access. [Online]. Available: http://bjsw.oxfordjournals.org/cgi/reprint/bcm027v1.pdf.

Price, E. (2010) Coming out to care: Gay and lesbian carers' experiences of dementia. *Health and Social Care in the Community*, **18**(2), 160–168.

Rich, A. (1980) Compulsory heterosexuality and lesbian existence. *Women: Sex and Sexuality*, **5**(4), 631–660.

Richardson, D. (2005) Desiring sameness? The rise of a neoliberal politics of normalisation. *Antipode*, **37**(3), 515–535.

Seidman, S. (2005) From polluted homosexual to the normal gay: Changing patterns of sexual regulation in America. In C. Ingraham (ed.) *Thinking straight: New work in critical heterosexuality studies*, pp. 39–62. New York: Routledge.

Shildrick, M. (2013) Sexual citizenship, governance and disability: From Foucault to Deleuze. In S. Roseneil (ed.) *Beyond citizenship?: Feminism and the transformation of belonging*, pp. 138–159. Palgrave Macmillan. Kindle version.

Stirling, J. (1995) Dementia, discourse, difference and denial: 'Who did I become?' *Law Text Culture*, **2**, 147–159. http://ro.uow.edu.au/ltc/vol.2/iss1/7 [accessed 4 August 2015].

Taylor, Y., Hines, S. and Casey, M. (2011) Introduction. In Y. Taylor, S. Hines and M. E. Casey (eds) *Theorizing intersectionality and sexuality*, pp. 1–12. Basingstoke: Palgrave Macmillan.

Twigg, J., Wolkowitz, C., Cohen, R. L. and Nettleton, S. (2011) Conceptualising body work in health and social care. *Sociology of Health and Illness*, **33**(2), 171–188.

Ward, R., Campbell, S. and Keady, J. (2014) 'Once I had money in my pocket, I was every colour under the sun': Using 'appearance biographies' to explore the meanings of appearance for people with dementia. *Journal of Aging Studies*, **30**, 64–72.

Warner, M. (1991) Introduction: Fear of a queer planet. *Social Text*, **29**, 3–17.

Westwood, S. (2015) Complicating kinship and inheritance: Older lesbians' and gay men's will-writing in England. *Feminist Legal Studies*, **23**(2), 181–197.

Part II
Practice

Introduction to Part II

Sue Westwood and Elizabeth Price

This section addresses a range of practice issues relating to the provision of health and social care services to LGBT* people living with dementia. In Chapter 6, Mark Hughes explores the ways in which health and social care providers should recognise and address the needs and wishes of LGBT* people living with dementia. In Chapter 7, Catherine Barrett and colleagues explore the experiences of lesbian, gay and trans* people living with dementia and, in particular, the challenges they have faced in engaging with specialist services which are under-prepared to meet their needs. Chapters 8 and 9 address issues relating to trans* people with dementia. In Chapter 8, 'Trans* people anticipating dementia care: findings from the Transgender MetLife Survey', Tarynn Witten describes the findings from a recent USA survey which explored trans people's fears and concerns about dementia care provision. In Chapter 9, 'Dementia care and trans* people: practice implications', Chryssy Hunter, Jenny-Anne Bishop and Sue Westwood explore the implications of dementia for trans* identities and trans* dementia care

In Chapter 10, Elizabeth Price considers the position of LGBT* carers of people with dementia, who may or may not be LGBT* individuals. She reflects upon the invisibilisation and marginalisation of LGBT* carers, the consequent lack of appropriate support they receive, and how this might be addressed. In the final chapter in this section, Chapter 11, Sue Westwood and Sally Knocker critically consider the benefits of one-day staff training interventions to raise awareness of, and improve services for, LGBT* people, arguing for the need for more comprehensive interventions to support enduring organisational change.

All six chapters highlight the complexities of LGBT* experiences of dementia and the challenges – both actual and anticipated – people face with regard to health and social care provision. The chapters also serve to highlight the challenges faced by health and social care providers in developing services which are equipped to meet the needs of LGBT* people with dementia. In offering the narratives of LGBT* people themselves, the chapters demonstrate the significance of the lived experiences of LGBT* people affected by dementia, and current inequalities associated with those lived experiences. They demonstrate how a lack of appropriate services to support LGBT* people with dementia, their families, friends and carers not only adds to the stresses which can be associated with dementia but can also exacerbate symptoms and increase the risk of carer breakdown.

The chapters offer useful insights for commissioners, policy makers and providers of health and care services for people with dementia, as well as signposting possible pathways to develop services which are more responsive to the needs of LGBT* people living with dementia. They also offer concrete examples of why and how gender, sexuality/sexual identity and gender identity inform the experiences of dementia and dementia services, and why and how policy makers, commissioners and providers must take these issues into account when developing and delivering responsive services for people with dementia.

6   Providing responsive services to LGBT* individuals with dementia

Mark Hughes

Introduction

Like many people, LGBT* individuals express concerns about memory loss and dementia as they grow older. In a survey of 443 LGBT* people in Queensland, Australia, nearly 40 per cent said one of their top three health concerns was a decline in mental health and cognitive ability (including dementia) (Queensland Association for Healthy Communities (QAHC), 2008). And, for many LGBT* people with dementia, their needs will be the same as any other person with this condition: staying independent, setting up practical and emotional supports, and maintaining a meaningful lifestyle and sense of self. However, the diverse lives and experiences of LGBT* people generally indicate that, for LGBT* people with dementia, there are likely to be additional issues and specific challenges that need to be addressed (Birch, 2009). The origin of, and responsibility for, many of these lie not so much with the LGBT* individual with dementia, but with our service systems' failure to recognise and respond effectively to sexuality, gender and gender identity diversity. This chapter examines some of the challenges facing agencies in responding to the needs of LGBT* people with dementia, such as negotiating privacy and acknowledging the impact of discrimination. It also explores the opportunities for developing more responsive services both at organisational levels and in worker-client relationships.

Challenges in providing responsive services

Acknowledging the complexities of gender, gender identity and sexuality diversity

One challenge facing service providers in responding to the needs of LGBT* individuals with dementia is acknowledging and engaging with the complexities of how people relate to and experience their gender, gender identity and sexuality. Sexuality is commonly understood in terms of the gender of people we are sexually attracted to, although it is argued that this is a product of scientific discourse in the nineteenth century (Sedgwick, 1990). Gender is a cultural construction of normative assumptions about how people born with particular sexual or reproductive organs should behave. The terms 'sexual identity' 'gender' and 'gender identity' refer to labels that people ascribe to themselves or connect to wider groups. While people may relate to being lesbian, gay, bisexual or trans* as personal identities, these have also been constructed as collective identities (e.g. through social movement campaigns) to advance political interests and human rights (Gamson, 1995). Yet, there is evidence that these normative boundaries may be being stretched, for example by gender/sexuality fluid and/or trans* people (some of whom may call themselves queer) who eschew identity binaries such as male/female, straight/gay etc. Many people feel sympathy with the queer perspective that questions the 'unity, stability, viability, and political utility' of identities (Gamson, 1995: 397), while others acknowledge their limitations but consider them 'necessary fictions' (Weeks, 1995: 99).

Thus gender, gender identity and sexuality comprise various dimensions that may be experienced differently by different people. This adds another layer of complexity when working with LGBT* people with dementia, especially because people may lose memories of how their sexuality or gender has shifted over time (e.g. a trans* person not remembering they have had gender affirmation medical procedures carried out) (Alzheimer's Australia, 2014; Witten, 2014). Some of the dimensions of gender, gender identity and sexuality include:

- Gendered and sexual behaviour: the activities we engage in (perform) to express our gender, gender identity and sexuality.
- Feelings of gender identification and sexual attraction: how our gender, gender identity and sexuality evoke feelings and emotions, including sexual desire.
- Community/group affiliation: feelings of connection with others who share the same or similar gender history and/or gender identity and/or sexual identity.
- Sense of self as emerging across the lifespan: the way in which gender, gender identity and sexuality are connected to our sense of who we are at different points in the lifespan.

As examined in Chapter 3 in its discussion of intersectionality, invariably there is a complex interplay between sexuality, gender and gender identity in each of these dimensions, which are also impacted by other personal or social characteristics, such as age, ethnicity and socio-economic status. In some contexts, such as an employment setting, it may be the denigration of older age and being a woman, rather than her sexuality, that mainly impacts on an older lesbian's social standing (Hughes and Kentlyn, 2015). For some older gay men, the importance of projecting an idealised masculine image may change across the lifecourse, with it being less a priority in an aged care environment, where women may outnumber men. For some transwomen, the ageing of the body (e.g. wrinkles, difficulty walking in high heels) may provide additional challenges in presenting one's gender identity publicly (Siverskog, 2015).

The implication for service providers is to not make assumptions about sexuality, gender and gender identity and to be open to the diverse ways in which people might relate to these aspects of their lives. Clearly there is a need to not assume people are heterosexual and to recognise LGBT* identities, but there is also a need to not assume that all LGBT* people relate to the LGBT* labels in the same way (Cronin *et al.*, 2012), and that the experiences of lesbians, gay men, bisexual people and trans* people may all be quite different from each other. For example, a woman who has presented publicly as heterosexual throughout most of her life, may come out in later life as having a fluid or undefinable sexuality. Some people, including those identifying as bisexual, may chart unconventional life paths, which resist typical 'landmarks' such as getting married and having children (Jones, 2012). And, while some trans* people may feel a connection with LGB people based on a shared experience of marginalisation, not all do (Simmons and White, 2014). Indeed, some trans* people may relate not so much to the idea of being trans* as to being recognised for their internal gender identity – that is, male or female. For gender/sexuality fluid and/or trans* people the challenge may be in resisting binary definitions and identity labels imposed by others (including LGBT* people) and by society (Budge *et al.*, 2014).

Negotiating privacy

One of the common challenges identified in responding to the needs of LGBT* people is negotiating privacy (Harrison, 2001). The idea that sexuality, in particular sexual identity, is a private matter is well established in western societies. Indeed, the framing of privacy as a legal right provided the basis for the decriminalisation of homosexuality in many parts of the world (Waites, 2013). Yet the gay liberation and lesbian feminist movements of the 1970s decried the treatment of homosexuality as private and sought to represent it as an attribute to be celebrated publicly (Rosenfeld, 2010). Some older people (particularly those who came out in the mid rather than latter twentieth century) may feel that it is important that their sexuality is kept private; although the extent to which this is due to a moral position or fear of reprisal and discrimination is debatable (Rosenfeld, 2010).

For trans* people, being private about one's trans status can be very important because 'most of us would like to be seen in a way that is congruent with our internal identity' (Reynolds and Goldstein, 2014: 136). For some older trans* people it is essential that their trans history is not 'outed' and thus a range of strategies can be employed to ensure this does not happen (Siverskog, 2015). However, this privacy is frequently breached because social and organisational practices assume two distinct genders that conform to specific biological characteristics and that are static across the lifespan. Public toilets, birth certificates, passport applications, and information kept online may all invoke infringement of privacy for trans* people. Indeed, in the UK, trans* people are required to disclose their gender history prior to entering a marriage or civil partnership, which arguably breaches the European Convention on Human Rights (Sharpe, 2012).

The way LGBT* people with dementia relate to their sexuality, gender and gender identity inevitably impacts on how private they consider these aspects of their lives to be. For example, those who may consider their sexuality to relate only to sexual behaviour and not their sense of self or community affiliation may be less likely than others to want service providers to openly acknowledge their sexuality. For some people, keeping their sexuality, gender or gender identity history private may be seen as important to protect them from discrimination or simply because they may feel that these parts of their life are not relevant to the service that is being provided (Hughes, 2007). Some bisexual people living in opposite-sex relationships may prefer to hide this aspect of their identity from partners or children (McCormack *et al.*, 2014). And some trans* people may 'feel tired or bored of talking about gender, or … discover that it is no longer as important to highlight as it had once been' (Reynolds and Goldstein, 2014: 136).

The experience of dementia may pose additional complications. Previously held positons on privacy may break down as they are forgotten. Birch (2009) noted that a person with dementia may inadvertently reveal their own sexuality or their partner's in contexts where such information would previously have been treated as private. According to Birch,

> in the early stages of dementia, some lesbians and gay men with dementia may become concerned and frustrated when trying to remember how much they have revealed to a service provider. Remembering the fictions that may have been created to prevent being identified as lesbian or gay becomes harder.
>
> (2009: 17)

A similar concern may be raised with trans* people who may not remember the extent to which one's transitioning experience has been disclosed to different service providers.

The challenge for service providers is to ensure people have the opportunity to disclose these aspects of their gender, gender identity and sexuality in the manner and circumstances of their own choosing, which may include the expression of a non-binary identity, or a rejection of the notion that these parts of their life reflect a stable identity at all. And the key barrier to this is service providers' own attitudes. If they assume sexuality, gender and gender identity to be private, then LGBT* people with dementia become invisible in the delivery of services. Thus, there is a danger that assumptions of heterosexuality and normalised male/female categories take hold and LGBT* people go unrecognised. In a survey of residential aged care facilities in Western Australia, 86 per cent of 83 senior staff respondents were unaware or unsure of having LGBT* residents in their facility and 79 per cent said that residents' sexuality was not the concern of staff (Horner, 2012). As Ward *et al.* (2005: 53) argued, '[a]ny decision taken at an individual level [by an LGB person] not to be open regarding sexual orientation must be understood as distinct from the processes by which care settings draw a veil over the sexualities of residents.'

The impact of discrimination

Understanding LGBT* people's experience of discrimination is also a key challenge for service providers. Many LGBT* people with dementia, because of their age, are likely to have been subject to discrimination across their lifespan (Ward *et al.*, 2005). For example, in countries such as the UK and Australia, consensual sex between men was criminalised for significant periods of the lifetime of LGBT* seniors. For other LGBT* people, discrimination has manifested in other ways, including being required to attend psychiatric and psychological treatment (Hughes, 2007). Discriminatory attitudes have been particularly directed towards those who do not conform to binary gender roles (Budge *et al.*, 2014), such as gay men who may appear to be more stereotypically 'feminine', which denigrates both women and gay men. In a study of lesbian and gay people's experiences accessing health and aged care services, people reported being subject to abuse and discrimination in their workplace, harassment and ostracisation from family members, and violence on the street (Hughes, 2007). For bisexual people, discrimination can be experienced both from heterosexuals and from gay and lesbian people who may question the legitimacy of a bisexual identity and treat bisexual people as being unable to commit to a lesbian or gay identity (McCormack *et al.*, 2014). For trans* people, in particular, there are concerns that institutionalised discrimination continues. For example, in the recent iteration of the Diagnostic and Statistical Manual (DSM-5), gender variance is still classified as a mental disorder, albeit termed gender dysphoria rather than the previous categorisation as gender identity disorder (Lev, 2013). As discussed earlier, the experience of discrimination may also be mediated by other personal or social characteristics such as age and ethnicity.

The significance of past experiences of discrimination – both the distant and recent past – is that they potentially impact on current and future service use. In the QAHC survey, approximately 65 per cent said that they were concerned that their sexuality or gender identity may affect the quality of services provided to them in later life (QAHC, 2008). And there is evidence that fears of discrimination do translate into delays in seeking assistance and treatment (Hash and Netting, 2009; Williams and Freeman, 2007). This is particularly a concern for trans* people who may have had negative experiences receiving medical treatment and may subsequently avoid routine screening and preventative health care (Alzheimer's Australia, 2014). For people accessing services in their own home or who are being admitted to residential care, the concern may be how to hide their sexuality or gender history in order to avoid discrimination. In Price's (2012) UK research, gay and lesbian carers of people with dementia expressed concerns about how they might access services in the future based on current experience of community and residential providers.

Given such concerns and the widely held expectation of discrimination, it is unsurprising then that LGBT* people overwhelmingly want mainstream community and residential aged care services to become more LGBT*-friendly and inclusive (Hughes, 2007). Others want LGBT*-specific services, with the notion of an LGBT*-specific residential home much debated (Price, 2012). Some men have expressed a fear that such a facility could become a 'gay ghetto' (Hughes, 2007); while some lesbians would much prefer a lesbian-only space (Hughes and Kentlyn, 2015). Others feel that they would prefer a person who identifies in the same way as them to provide them with personal care or to be their general practitioner (Hughes, 2007). In the survey of health and wellbeing noted earlier, a number of participants felt that it was their responsibility, as members of LGBT* communities, to set up services and supports for LGBT* seniors. One respondent said: 'I tend to think it is much more preferable that we do this for ourselves than have programmes set up for us, particularly if the model for straight people is used and adapted' (Hughes and Kentlyn, 2014: 40).

Understanding diverse support and care networks

The perspective of some LGBT* people wanting to create their own support systems in later life highlights the ways LGBT* people's support networks may differ from other people's networks. The concept of 'families of choice' has emerged to reflect the idea that some LGBT* people create their own meaningful supports from among a friendship network that may replace or enhance a biological family network (Heaphy *et al.*, 2004). In a survey of the support LGBT* Queenslanders expect to receive in later life, about 58 per cent said they expect to be supported emotionally by LGBT* friends, compared to 24 per cent and 16 per cent expecting to be supported emotionally by siblings and children respectively (QAHC, 2008). This contrasts with non-LGBT* people, for whom the sources of expected support are, overwhelmingly, spouses and children (Lin and Wu, 2014).

While expectations of support from friends are valuable, there remain questions about how this support can be mobilised into care when a person with dementia needs it. That is, how a support network can transform into a care network (Hughes and Kentlyn, 2011). For example, with expectations to provide care for members of their own biological families, which can be considerable not only for non-LGBT* people but also LGBT* people (Brotman *et al.*, 2007), the availability of friends to provide the degree of care required is unclear. Birch (2009) argued that sometimes, with the onset of dementia and the need for care, previously estranged biological family members may become more involved with the person's life, creating additional pressures for partners and friends.

For LGBT* people, partners are also clearly an important source of support. In the QAHC study, 54 per cent expected to receive emotional support from their partners, while 52 per cent expected to receive practical or physical support from partners (QAHC, 2008). The challenge for service providers is that same-sex partners are not always recognised in the delivery of services, especially if sexuality or gender identity is treated as private. In the qualitative research on lesbian and gay people's experience of service use, one man reported being ignored by a surgeon treating his partner and a woman, who had been in hospital receiving treatment for breast cancer, did not disclose that the 'friend' visiting her was actually her partner, for fear of staff reaction (Hughes, 2008b). Additionally, for people with dementia, it is possible that a current same-sex partner may be forgotten, but previous heterosexual partners remembered, making the current partner 'feel totally rejected and alone' (Birch, 2009: 17).

Opportunities in providing responsive services

Culture change within aged care agencies

As suggested by the concerns of LGBT* people, a key challenge lies in improving mainstream agencies' responsiveness to LGBT* people with dementia and their carers. Many organisations and their staff are eager to improve their services because of their professional and organisational values, such as valuing diversity and social justice. Alzheimer's societies in the UK and Australia, for example, have developed strategies to facilitate LGBT* inclusion (Alzheimer's Australia, 2014; Alzheimer's Society, 2013). Unfortunately, there are also organisations and staff that may be ambivalent or hostile to becoming more LGBT* inclusive. For example, when the Australian Government announced plans to make it unlawful for all aged care providers to discriminate against LGBT* people, Anglicare Sydney argued not only that they should be free to discriminate against people because of their 'sexual orientation', marital status and gender identity, but also that this 'freedom of religion' should be extended to other areas (Anglicare Sydney, 2012).

In the desire (or requirement) to become more inclusive of diverse identities and communities, mainstream organisations are confronted with the question of how to avoid tokenism. That is, how is change to be achieved in a meaningful and lasting way? Sensitivity-training programmes, as discussed by Westwood and Knocker in Chapter 11, have been important and have demonstrated some success in increasing participants' knowledge of and attitudes towards working with LGBT* seniors (e.g. Leyva *et al.*, 2014). However, the extent to which they can lead to lasting change and actually improve the experience of LGBT* people with dementia has yet to be established. Understandably, there are concerns about what may happen when these providers who have been trained move on.

How then to achieve more lasting change? There seems to be an opportunity here for a 'whole of organisation' change process that moves organisations from a culture of heteronormativity – that is, the implicit assumption of stereotypical sexuality and gender norms – towards one that embraces sexuality and gender diversity, including non-binary gender and sexual identities (e.g. gender/sexuality fluid and/or trans* people). While many non-LGBT* staff and clients may feel very strong connections with these norms, it is possible that other non-LGBT* people may feel liberated by not having to continually relate to the gender and sexual ideals of what it means to be a 'good man' or a 'good woman' (Seidman, 2001). This is particularly likely for those older people who may feel alienated by the youth-oriented and reproductive-centric basis of these norms (Ward *et al.*, 2005).

This change strategy would ideally involve all members of the organisation; modelled by the CEO and the managers/leaders of specific aged care services. Critically it should involve employees and volunteers at all other levels. Initially this may involve participation in sensitivity training, but it may also go much further. For example, staff may be involved in auditing the sexuality and gender inclusivity of client records, forms, written documentation, websites and promotional material (Birch, 2009). This could lead to the introduction of a third gender option in recording client details, or providing people with the opportunity to use the gender neutral pronouns, zie (for s/he) and hir (for him/her) (Budge *et al.*, 2014). They could evaluate the physical environment and the extent to which it promotes diversity (e.g. are there gender neutral toilets?). It may also involve assessing the nature of activities to ensure that these do not make heteronormative assumptions (e.g. making sure that group discussions are inclusive of diverse relationships).

There are other activities that could also assist in enabling clients, staff and volunteers to be more comfortable with and open about diverse expressions of gender, gender identity and sexuality. In the human resource management literature, 'new voice mechanisms' are promoted as helping people from minority groups to link with others and access needed resources. Bell *et al.* (2011) highlighted four dimensions of voice that human resource managers should promote for LGBT* employees, but which could equally apply to LGBT* clients and volunteers:

- Articulation of individual dissatisfaction, such as effective complaints and advocacy processes.
- Expression of collective organisation, for example through union representation involving LGBT* employees.
- Contribution to management decision making, including the allocating of funds to support equality strategies.
- Mutuality, such as forming collaborations with LGBT* community organisations to promote equality internally and externally to the organisation.

Each of these strategies demonstrates an active and authentic commitment to gender, gender identity and sexuality diversity that may be recognised by people inside the organisation, as well as outside it. This can assist a mainstream agency to become known as an ally and partner with LGBT* people.

Promoting legal rights, including advance care planning

For people with dementia, and those involved in their care, a key concern is what will happen when the person's ability to make decisions reduces, and who will be there to assist them in future decision making. If those providing formal care are not aware of their client's sexuality or gender history, then heteronormative assumptions can lead to significant people – such as same-sex partners and LGBT* friends – being ignored or excluded from decision-making processes.

Or, of even more concern, care providers or biological family members may deliberately act in discriminatory ways to exclude these significant people. A key concern is that people with dementia may be less able than they had in the past to advocate for who they want to have involved or consulted in their care (Birch, 2009).

However, health and aged care organisations may not have to act as barriers to the needs of LGBT* people with dementia and their carers; they may indeed be uniquely positioned to advance the rights of LGBT* people in some specific ways. Of particular significance to LGBT* people with dementia is the range of legal options available that may ensure that their wishes are protected, in the event of their decision-making ability reducing (Knauer, 2010). What options are available vary between jurisdictions, but may involve enduring power of attorney (management of finances), enduring guardianship (management of life-style and health issues) and advance care directives (a plan that sets out the person's wishes in the event of the loss of decision-making ability (Hughes and Cartwright, 2014).

Unfortunately, reflecting patterns within the general population (Jackson *et al.*, 2009), there is not a widespread take up or even knowledge of these options among LGBT* people. In a survey of 305 LGBT* people in New South Wales (NSW), 87 per cent of those who answered the question said that they had heard of enduring power of attorney, 59 per cent had heard of enduring guardian, 52 per cent of person responsible, and 38 per cent of advance care directive (Hughes and Cartwright, 2014). In this study, 76 per cent of respondents said they would be comfortable with their health provider raising these issues with them. Thus, there is substantial scope for health and aged care providers to actively promote these legal options to their LGBT* clients, including to people with dementia (before they lose legal decision-making capacity) and their carers. This will help ensure that the decision-making arrangements LGBT* people with dementia want in place are enacted when the time comes for this to be necessary.

Conversational and narrative approaches to providing support

Conversations about gender, sexuality, identities and needs are at the centre of providing responsive services to LGBT* individuals with dementia. Part of this involves providing a welcoming, safe and supportive environment where these conversations can take place (McGovern, 2014). That is, people are given the opportunity to talk about their gender, gender identity and sexuality and to explain what significance these have in the way that services should be delivered. Critically, this should allow for diverse expressions of sexuality, gender identity and of non-binary identity, rather than be limited to rigid versions of what it means to be LGBT*. This welcoming environment begins to be constructed the moment the person has first contact with the organisation: the first phone call, the first time in the reception area, the first few minutes of the first interview. This requires an appropriate physical environment; that is, signals (such as posters, flyers, etc.) that LGBT* people are welcome in this space (Birch, 2009).

Other modes of communication, including the verbal and non-verbal behaviour of staff and volunteers, are also significant.

The initial contact interview, in particular, is likely to be important, as this provides cues about what the organisation and its staff are open to discussing and, in turn, what the client feels comfortable discussing. Open language – such as talking about partners rather than husbands or wives – is clearly important. McGovern (2014) suggested open questions, such as 'who are you closest to?'. In researching social workers' views on how sexuality should be discussed in assessment interviews (Hughes, 2008a), there was a view that the availability of resources (particularly time) is critical in providing the opportunity for the in-depth and meaningful interviews that are likely to facilitate disclosure:

> It's part of a holistic conversation that takes time to set up, time to create, time to enrich, time to engage; [it] is a whole process that needs respect and time and trust. And I just don't think that at this stage our service providers are in a position to offer that apart from doing the tick boxes as they quickly scoot from person to person.
>
> (Quoted in Hughes, 2008a: 8)

One practice strategy that can be used to facilitate this kind of conversation is enabling narratives; that is, encouraging people to tell stories about their life (Ward, 2012). In counselling and social work, narrative work is becoming increasingly popular (Roscoe *et al.*, 2011), just as it is seen as more significant in work with people with dementia (Baldwin and Bradford Dementia Group, 2008). A narrative approach values an individual's personal 'truth' as reflected in the stories they tell about their life (Plummer, 1995). Narratives are typically constructed in a way that conveys a significant message between the narrator and the audience. They are particularly suited to expressions of identity and how people want their identity acknowledged by others (Hughes, 2008b). However, rather than being a static process, this act – of articulating identity through story telling – is inevitably interactive, iterative and reflexive. Czarniawska (1997: 49) argued that identity narratives involve the narrator and the audience 'in formulating, editing, applauding, and refusing various elements of the ever-produced narrative'. Thus it is important to be conscious of how the service provider, as audience, may be involved in co-constructing the narrative.

There remains a concern, however, about how LGBT* people with dementia can express their narratives. A common discourse about dementia is the 'loss of self' that is perceived to be a product of cognitive decline. Within this discourse the capacity of people with dementia to narrate their lives – by drawing on memories of their past experiences – is called into question (Brock, 1993, cited in Baldwin and Bradford Dementia Group, 2008: 224). According to McGovern (2014: 847–848), 'because [dementia] transforms the self by collapsing the foundations of identity, the lived experience of dementia for persons who identify as LGBT* is different from that of living with other chronic illnesses'. For Baldwin and the Bradford Dementia Group (2008: 224), however, it is this very discourse that undermines people's narrative capacity and, through this process, the stories of people with dementia become marginalised. Given identity and life history are so significant to many LGBT* people, denial of narrative capacity because of dementia would be particularly problematic. As with other people with dementia, this would not only reflect a denial of selfhood, but also citizenship (Baldwin and Bradford Dementia Group, 2008: 226).

This suggests that there remains considerable potential in enabling LGBT* people with dementia to express narratives of significance to them and their life histories. And, in terms of the expression of citizenship, this may not only relate to narratives conveyed within the context of service delivery, it may also involve conveying narratives in public forums to influence politics and policy making. Baldwin and the Bradford Dementia Group (2008: 225, 226) noted some of the advocacy strategies that are increasingly drawing upon the voice of people with dementia, as well as the need for policy makers to create spaces to facilitate the narratives of people with dementia. Where people lose some communication abilities, other opportunities for narrative expression, or agency, are possible: including through dance, music and artistic expression (Baldwin and Bradford Dementia Group, 2008: 225). Narrative agency may also be facilitated through joint authorship of narratives, that is, people with dementia being engaged in co-constructing narratives, as well as by acknowledging the contribution of people with dementia in others' narratives (Baldwin and Bradfgord Demetia Group, 2008: 225).

Conclusion

Dementia is a significant feature in the lives of lesbian, gay, bisexual and trans* (LGBT*) people as they age, just as it is for the general population. Nonetheless, there are some important considerations that service providers may take into account so they are responsive to the needs of LGBT* people with dementia. These include understanding LGBT* people's experiences of discrimination, their diverse support networks, and their complex expression of gender, gender identity and sexuality. Service providers are also well positioned to promote the rights of LGBT* people with dementia, for example through facilitating access to advance care planning options. Responsiveness also requires a capacity to listen to people's narratives and give recognition to the way they discuss their sexuality, gender and gender identity and the implications of this for service provision. At a wider level, while the development of training for health and social care practitioners in LGBT* issues is needed, for mainstream agencies to become fully responsive to LGBT* people with dementia what is needed is a 'whole of organisation' change process.

References

Alzheimer's Australia (2014) *Dementia, transgender and intersex people: do service providers really know what their needs are?* [online] Canberra: Alzheimer's Australia. Available at: https://fightdementia.org.au/about-dementia-and-memory-loss/glbtiq-communities [accessed 21 November 2014].

Alzheimer's Society (2013) *Supporting lesbian, gay and bisexual people with dementia.* [online] London: Alzheimer's Society. Available at: www.alzheimers.org.uk/site/scripts/documents_info.php?documentID=1100 [accessed 21 November 2014].

Anglicare Sydney (2012) *Submission to the Attorney-General's Department in response to consolidation of Commonwealth anti-discrimination laws: discussion paper.* Parramatta: Anglicare Sydney.

Baldwin, C. and Bradford Dementia Group (2008) Narrative(,) citizenship and dementia: the personal and the political. *Journal of Aging Studies*, **22**: 222–228.

Bell, M. P., Ozbilgin, M. F., Beauregard, T. A. and Surgevil, O. (2011) Voice, silence, and diversity in 21st century organizations: strategies for inclusion of gay, lesbian, bisexual and transgender employees. *Human Resource Management*, **50**(1): 131–146.

Birch, H. (2009) *Dementia, lesbians and gay men.* Melbourne: Alzheimer's Australia.

Brotman, S., Ryan, B., Collins, S., Chamberland, L., Cormier, R., Julien, D., Meyer, E., Peterkin, A. and Richard, B. (2007) Coming out to care: caregivers of gay and lesbian seniors in Canada. *The Gerontologist*, **47**(4): 490–503.

Budge, S. L., Rossman, H. K. and Howard, K. A. S. (2014) Coping and psychological distress among genderqueer individuals: the moderating effect of social support. *Journal of Issues in Counseling*, **8**: 95–117.

Cronin, A., Ward, R., Pugh., S, King., A. and Price, E. (2012) Categories and their consequences: understanding and supporting the caring relationships of older lesbian, gay and bisexual people. In R. Ward, I. Rivers and M. Sutherland, eds. *Lesbian, gay, bisexual and transgender ageing: biographical approaches for inclusive care and support,* pp. 102–113. London: Jessica Kingsley Publishers.

Czarniawska, B. (1997) *Narrating the organization: dramas of institutional identity.* Chicago: The University of Chicago Press.

Gamson, J. (1995) Must identity movements self-destruct? A queer dilemma. *Social Problems*, **42**: 390–407.

Harrison, J. (2001) 'It's none of my business': gay and lesbian invisibility in aged care. *Australian Occupational Therapy Journal*, **48**: 142–145.

Hash, K. M. and Netting, F. E. (2009) It takes a community: older lesbians meeting social and care needs. *Journal of Gay and Lesbian Social Services*, **21**: 326–42.

Heaphy, B., Yip, A. K. T. and Thompson, D. (2004) Ageing in a non-heterosexual context. *Ageing and Society*, **24**: 881–902.

Horner, B. (2012) How prepared is the retirement and residential aged care sector in Western Australia for older non-heterosexual people? *Quality in Primary Care*, **20**: 263–274.

Hughes, M. (2007) Older lesbians and gays accessing health and aged care services. *Australian Social Work*, **60**(2): 197–209.

Hughes, M. (2008a) Information placed in trust: social workers and older gay men on talking about sexual identity. *Geriaction*, **26**(1): 15–20.

Hughes, M. (2008b) Imagined futures and communities: older lesbian and gay people's narratives on health and aged care. *Journal of Gay and Lesbian Social Services*, **20**(1/2): 167–86.

Hughes, M. and Cartwright, C. (2014) LGBT people's knowledge of and preparedness to discuss end-of-life care planning options. *Health and Social Care in the Community*, **22**(5): 545–552.

Hughes, M. and Kentlyn, S. (2011) Older LGBT people's care networks and communities of practice: a brief note. *International Social Work*, **54**(3): 436–444.

Hughes, M. and Kentlyn, S. (2014) *Report of the survey of the health and wellbeing of lesbian, gay, bisexual, transgender and intersex (LGBTI) older people in NSW, 2013–2014.* West Gosford and Bilinga: Evergreen Life Care and Southern Cross University.

Hughes, M. and Kentlyn, S. (2015) Older lesbians and work in the Australian health and aged care sector. *Journal of Lesbian Studies*, **19**: 62–72.

Jackson J. M., Rolnick S. J., Asche, S. E. and Heinrich, R. L. (2009) Knowledge, attitudes, and preferences regarding advance directives among patients of a managed care organization. *American Journal of Managed Care*, **15**: 177–186.

Jones, R. (2012) Imaging the unimaginable: bisexual roadmaps for ageing. In R. Ward, I. Rivers and M. Sutherland, eds. *Lesbian, gay, bisexual and transgender ageing: biographical approaches for inclusive care and support*, pp. 21–38. London: Jessica Kingsley Publishers.

Knauer N. J. (2010) Gay and lesbian elders: estate planning and end-of-life decision making. *Florida Coastal Law Review*, **12**: 163–216.

Lev, A. L. (2013) Gender dysphoria: two steps forward, one step back. *Clincial Social Work Journal*, **41**: 288–296.

Leyva, V. L., Breshears, E. M. and Ringstad, R. (2014) Assessing the efficacy of LGBT cultural competency training for aging services providers in California's central valley. *Journal of Gerontological Social Work*, **57**(2–4): 335–348.

Lin, I. and Wu, H. (2014) Intergenerational exchange and expected support among the young-old. *Journal of Marriage and Family*, **76**: 261–271.

McCormack, M., Anderson, E. and Adams, A. (2014) Cohort effect on the coming out of bisexual men. *Sociology*, **48**: 1207–1223.

McGovern, J. (2014) The forgotten: dementia and the aging LGBT community. *Journal of Gerontological Social Work*, **57**(8): 845–857.

Plummer, K. (1995) *Telling sexual stories: power, change and social worlds*. London: Routledge.

Price, E. (2012) Gay and lesbian carers: ageing in the shadow of dementia. *Ageing and Society*, **32**: 516–532.

Queensland Association for Healthy Communities (2008) *The young, the ageing and the restless: understanding the experiences and expectations of ageing and caring in the Qld LGBT* community*. Brisbane: QAHC.

Reynolds, H. M. and Goldstein, Z. G. (2014) Social transition. In L. Erickson-Schroth, ed. *Trans bodies, trans selves: a resource for the transgender community*, pp. 124–154. New York: Oxford University Press.

Roscoe, K. D., Carson, A. M. and Madoc-Jones, L. (2011) Narrative social work: conversations between theory and practice. *Journal of Social Work Practice*, **25**(1): 47–61.

Rosenfeld, D. (2010) Lesbian, gay, bisexual, and trandgender ageing: shattering myths, capturing lives. In D. Dannefer and C. Phillipson, eds. *The SAGE handbook of social gerontology*, pp. 226–238. London: Sage.

Sedgwick, E. K. (1990) *Epistemology of the closet*. Berkeley: University of California Press.

Seidman, S. (2001) From identity to queer politics: shifts in normative heterosexuality and the meaning of citizenship. *Citizenship Studies*, **5**: 321–328.

Sharpe, A. (2012) Transgender marriage and the legal obligation to disclose gender history. *The Modern Law Review*, **75**(1):33–53.

Simmons, H. and White, F. (2014) Our many selves. In L. Erickson-Schroth, ed. *Trans bodies, trans selves: a resource for the transgender community*, pp. 3–23. New York: Oxford University Press.

Siverskog, A. (2015) Ageing bodies that matter: age, gender and embodiment in older transgender people's life stories. *NORA: Nordic Journal of Feminist and Gender Research*, **23**: 4–19.

Waites, M. (2013) United Kingdom: confronting criminal histories and theorising decriminalisation as citizenship and governmentality. In C. Lennox and M. Waite, eds. *Human rights, sexual orientation and gender identity in the Commonwealth*, pp. 145–181. London: Human Rights Consortium.

Ward, R. (2012) Conclusion: making space for LGBT lives in health and social care. In R. Ward, I. Rivers and M. Sutherland, eds. *Lesbian, gay, bisexual and transgender ageing: biographical approaches for inclusive care and support*, pp. 196–209. London: Jessica Kingsley Publishers.

Ward, R., Vas, A. A., Aggarwai, N., Garfield, C. and Cybyk, B. (2005) A kiss is still a kiss? The construction of sexuality in dementia care. *Dementia*, **4**(1): 49–72.

Weeks, J. (1995) *Invented moralities – sexual values in an age of uncertainty*. Cambridge: Polity Press.

Williams, M. E. and Freeman, P. A. (2007) Transgender health: implications for aging and caregiving. *Journal of Gay and Lesbian Social Services*, **18**(3/4): 93–108.

Witten, T. M. (2014) It's not all darkness: robustness, resilience, and successful transgender aging. *LGBT Health*, **1**(1): 24–33.

7 Person-centred care and cultural safety

The perspectives of lesbian, gay and trans* (LGT*) people and their partners on living with dementia

Catherine Barrett, Pauline Crameri, J. R. Latham, Carolyn Whyte and Sally Lambourne

Introduction

In this chapter we explore research that documents the perspectives of lesbian, gay and trans* (LGT*) people and their partners on living with dementia. While there is an emerging body of literature on the needs of LGT* people living with dementia, few publications have documented the perspectives of LGT* people and their partners. The lack of evidence here could be attributed to the relative invisibility of older LGT* people. Many older LGT* people have never known a time it was safe to disclose their sexual orientation or gender identity (Barrett *et al.*, 2014a; Barrett, 2008) and they therefore may not be willing to disclose in order to participate in research. Compounding this challenge is the difficulty inherent in finding ways to ensure that people living with dementia participate meaningfully in research. However, while research in this area is challenging, it is critical to seek the perspectives of LGT* clients in understanding how services should be developed to meet their needs (Barrett *et al.*, 2013; Barrett and Stephens, 2011). This chapter outlines the experiences and needs of LGT* people living with dementia and presents a model for ensuring person-centred and culturally safe services.

Method

The chapter draws on two small qualitative studies conducted in Australia. The first study, *Understanding and Meeting the Needs of LGBTI People Living with Dementia* (*The LGBTI Dementia Project*) was a collaboration with Alzheimer's Australia to document the experiences and needs of LGBTI people living with dementia (Crameri *et al.*, 2015). This chapter draws on interviews with the four same-sex couples: three gay and one lesbian. No bisexual, trans* or intersex participants were recruited.

The second study, the *Trans Ageing and Aged Care Project*, was a collaboration with the Gender Centre, Transgender Victoria and FTM Shed to document older trans* people's experiences of ageing and service use (Latham and Barrett, 2015). The chapter draws on interviews with ten trans* women as well as one interview with service providers regarding a trans* client with dementia.

Both projects were approved by the Human Research Ethics Committee at La Trobe University. Recruitment occurred through LGBTI organisations in Australia and prospective participants were provided with information sheets and consent forms. Interviews were semi structured and sought to document participants' historical experiences, needs, service use and suggestions for the development of inclusive aged care services. Interviews were taped, transcribed and returned to participants for verification and de-identification.

Data from the two studies was pooled and analysed using the five stages of 'Framework': familiarisation; application of a framework; indexing; mapping and interpretation (Ritchie and Spencer, 1994). A core theme was the challenges to achieving person-centred and culturally safe services. Three particular challenges were identified. The first relates to disclosure of sexual orientation and gender identity and the stress that accompanies a reduced capacity to manage disclosure following the diagnosis of dementia. The second involves the importance of spaces where LGT* people's sexual orientation and gender identity is valued and affirmed and where they feel supported to 'be themselves'. The third relates to the effects of dementia on sexual orientation and gender identity and the constraining influences of families of origin.

This chapter outlines these three subthemes and then presents a framework for cultural safety that adapts principles of a person-centred approach to the needs of LGT* people living with dementia.

The management of disclosure

The impacts of dementia on the lives of LGT* people included a reduced capacity to control who they disclosed their sexuality or trans* status to. For many, hiding their sexuality or trans* status was the only protection against the widespread discrimination that characterised their youth and middle years. Disclosure could result in arrest and imprisonment, psychiatric incarceration, enforced 'cures' and the loss of family, friends and employment (Barrett *et al.*, 2014b). While significant legislative reforms have occurred in their later years, many older LGT* people continue to keep private their sexuality or trans* status. However, in our studies, we found that this was increasingly difficult for LGT* people living with dementia and their partners as the symptoms of dementia progressed.

All the same-sex couples interviewed for the *LGBTI Dementia Project* (Crameri *et al.*, 2015) described the importance of being discrete about their sexual orientation. For example, Kevin, a 75-year-old gay man, described how he and his 77-year-old partner Greg:

> have never been the type to flaunt our sexuality ... when I see people that do I would think I'd say to myself, I'm glad I'm not them.... I am glad because I don't want myself exploited, I don't exhibit myself ... when you flaunt you are embarrassing yourself.
>
> (Kevin, 75, gay man)

Kevin and others noted that hiding sexual orientation was considered essential to avoid negative stereotypes about gay men as sexually perverse and predatory. Similarly, Nick, a 54-year-old gay man, described how he and his 63-year-old partner, George, were 'lucky' they were not 'outrageously gay' because this enabled them to avoid discrimination:

> I think George and I have been lucky because we are not outrageously gay ... we're not really outrageous and not very camp in our actions.... There's a lot of people that are and they are the ones that are going to find a lot of discrimination I think ... George and I are pretty straight gays if you know what I mean, not flamboyant or you're not kind of putting it in people's faces ... I think that's why we fit into a lot of the norm. If George was a bit more camp ... someone would probably says 'are you one of those poofters?'
>
> (Nick, 54, gay man)

Nick added that because older people were often presumed to be exclusively heterosexual, gay men who were not flamboyant could pass as heterosexual and escape homophobic discrimination. The importance of not upsetting others was also shared by Anne, a 60-year-old lesbian, who noted that she and her 64-year-old partner, Edie, were not 'provocatively confronting' with their sexuality. Rather, Anne noted that they:

> make it easier for people, you know, not to consider it too much of an issue ... a person who doesn't draw too much attention to themselves is not going to be as upsetting as a lesbian who ... has an obvious male look about them.
>
> (Anne, 60, lesbian)

Despite significant historical reforms in legislation and human rights, some older lesbians and gay men still feel an onus of responsibility to conform to heteronormative values (Barrett *et al.*, 2014b). The perceived need to be discrete is also reinforced by the knowledge that disclosure can result in discrimination in aged care services (Barrett, 2008).

While the experiences of older trans* people differed from those of older lesbians and gay men there were also a number of parallels. Several trans* participants withheld their gender history, fearing transphobic discrimination (Latham and Barrett, 2015). Others who identified only as male or female, rather than as 'trans', chose not to disclose their gender history because they wanted their affirmed gender to be recognised and respected.

While maintaining privacy around sexual orientation and gender identity was considered important, some LGT* people with dementia experienced changes that made it difficult to do so. The primary change related to diminishing cognitive function; a significant level of cognitive function is required to prevent disclosure of sexual orientation or transgender identity. This difficulty was highlighted by Kevin (the 75-year-old gay man partnered to Greg, 77) who described the cognitive decline of his partner and how, as a consequence, their relationship was inadvertently disclosed at a Service Club of which they are both members. While the disclosure had no adverse effects on their friendships within the Club, Kevin described a sense of anxiety around not being able to manage disclosure in ways that were important to them. Inadvertent disclosure can create additional stress for older same-sex couples who have negotiated an agreed level of disclosure that works for them both (Barrett *et al.*, 2014a).

A number of participants also expressed concern about their same-sex relationship being revealed if residential aged care services were required. These concerns were also documented in an Australian study involving interviews with older LGBTI people accessing aged care (Barrett, 2008).

Safe and supportive spaces

Given the historical need to hide sexual orientation or trans* status, it is not surprising that a high value was placed on safe and supportive spaces where LGT* people felt they could be themselves. The *LGBTI Dementia Project* highlighted that intimate partners were a critical source of social support. For example, Anne described how her partner's diagnosis of dementia was a 'nightmare' but:

> The way we've faced it has been through just total trust and commitment to each other. And that's why in many respects we have a better life. Not that we want dementia to be a part of it, but it is a part of it and we can't change that, but we know our roles.
>
> (Anne, 60, lesbian)

Partners valued and affirmed sexual orientation (Barrett *et al.*, 2014a) and gender identity (Barrett, 2008) and provided safe and supportive spaces where LGT* people could be themselves. For some, being with other lesbians or gay men created a sense of safety and affirmation. Kevin noted that he and his partner,

> have quite a few lesbian neighbours ... we look after them and they look after us ... I think it's important because, again, you can freely be yourself. Like me saying we don't flaunt our sexuality ... but when you are mixing with your own type, if you like, you speak freer.
>
> (Kevin, 75, gay man)

The absence of likeminded friends was lamented by Nick, the 54-year-old gay man, who noted that, in caring for his partner with dementia, 'the biggest thing is kind of really isolation from the gay community'. Nick added that, 'it would be really nice to get some real gay friends as well in the same sort of situation ... somebody that you can really discuss things with and see how you are going'. The unique experiences of same-sex couples was highlighted by Nick's 63-year-old partner, George, who attended Planned Activity Groups in a local community centre and noted the predominantly heterosexual participants:

[they've] ... got their family ... and they've got their children and grand-children for support and everything, and whereas we have nothing ... we don't have that in our lives. And that can make it quite difficult, because we have to rely on each other ... we've got some good friends but I'm a bit of a stubborn person, I don't like to burden other people.

(George, 63, gay man)

Others agreed that the worsening symptoms of dementia meant that they were more socially isolated. Anne, who referred to dementia as a 'double stigma' for a lesbian, particularly highlighted that:

there's stigma associated with dementia and you know that's an issue in itself but you know Edie and I grew up when – in a time where there was certainly stigma associated with being lesbian and gay ... there are many people who have a reserve or a cautiousness or they don't understand us, a discomfort, that's not expressed ... it's a double whammy.

(Anne, 60, lesbian)

Anne illustrated the point by comparing the support she and her partner received with that offered to a friend who had cancer. She noted her friend received 'incredible support, you know, of people always dropping round meals and contacting them ... but we don't get that; dementia is a terminal illness but we don't get that level of support'. In reflecting on why this was the case Anne suggested:

You can't do what you used to be able to do and a lot of people can't cope with that, so our social life is very, very limited now and it evolves around close family. Some ... close friends and some people are just extraordinary. You know, the ones that you've got left are so important to you but a lot of people ... drift away and I haven't got the time or the energy – you know, you've got to put time and energy into relationships, I don't have that time and energy.

(Anne, 60, lesbian)

While other LGT* people were a key source of support, Anne found significant support in a mainstream carers' support group. She noted that in the group there was:

a real warmth and comradery amongst these people because ... you all have an understanding of what each other's lives are like ... they make no judge-ments; they're all very comfortable ... with us because, you know, we're all in the same team in a sense. We're all battling the same thing and so you're just trying to keep your head afloat.... There's an acceptance and a genuine warmth.... That seems to transcend sexuality, you know.

(Anne, 60, lesbian)

Others reported feeling that their experiences were poorly understood and were not valued in carers' support groups, where the focus was predominately on the experiences of heterosexual carers. For example, Graham (55, gay) described how he accessed a support service and 'felt like a fish out of water ... because a lot of them were heterosexual couples'. The belief that carer support services are heteronormative can contribute to a reluctance to access such services (Brotman *et al.*, 2007).

Still gay (lesbian, trans*) – renegotiating with families of origin

The impacts of dementia on sexual orientation and gender identity were explored, to challenge the belief held by some service providers that gay and lesbian people 'become straight' and trans*gender people 'revert to their birth sex' as a symptom of dementia. Participants were invited to respond to this notion.

Lesbian and gay participants unequivocally and expressively refuted that their sexual orientation was 'lost' with dementia. For example, Greg (the 77-year-old gay man with dementia) laughed at the suggestion he would 'become straight' and added that he was 'naturally' still gay. Greg's partner Kevin (aged 75) noted that in his view being gay 'is part of your makeup ... we can't make it disappear because you've got dementia, it's there in front of you'. Similarly, Anne (60, lesbian) reported that the idea that her partner would become heterosexual because she had dementia was as crazy as saying that 'hippopotamuses turn pink when they get to age 70'. She added that sexual orientation is not 'a rinse colour that you put through your hair. It's fundamental ... to who you are and how you relate to people'. Anne was confident that her partner would not 'turn away from what she's been all her life and who she's been with most of her life and go to something a [heterosexual relationship] that was unnatural for her'. She added that while 'people with dementia disconnect' they would not disconnect from something as fundamental as sexual orientation.

While sexuality/sexual identity remained a constant among this sample, recognition and expression of sexuality/sexual identity and gender identity could be adversely affected by the interventions of homophobic and transphobic family members. The escalating symptoms of dementia and loss of independence meant some LGT* people needed to renegotiate relations with their family of origin. The historical context of these negotiations and relationships with families of origin could profoundly impact LGT* people's experiences of declining health.

Many older LGT* people were coming of age at a time when their sexual orientation or transgender identity was viewed as an illness from which they could be cured (Barrett *et al.*, 2014b). This pervading view was often endorsed by family members – some LGT* people were disowned, disinherited, physically attacked, committed to a psychiatric institution, prohibited from accessing their children and accused of bringing shame to their family (Barrett *et al.*, 2014b). Unsurprisingly, experiences of rejection by family had a detrimental impact on mental wellbeing and some older LGT* people survived by creating new families or surrounding themselves with people that valued and affirmed their sexual orientation or transgender identity (Barrett *et al.*, 2014a).

As autonomous adults, some older LGT* people were able to renegotiate relationships with their family, without compromising their sense of personhood. However, the increasing symptoms of dementia meant the loss of capacity to make decisions and, for some, this meant they were once again vulnerable to the values and beliefs of homophobic and transphobic family members.

In one such example, Graham, a 55-year-old gay man, described how he applied for legal power to make financial and medical decisions on behalf of his 74-year-old partner, Rick, who had dementia. The application was challenged by Rick's 80-year-old cousin, whom Graham described as 'conservative, small-minded, pious, and very religious'. In a letter written to the organisation reviewing the application, Rick's cousin made reference to his homosexuality and added that she was 'only grateful that my children are of an appropriate sexual orientation'. Graham described how the experience 'was stressful ... I would wake up, it was constantly on my mind'. While same-sex relationships are legally recognised in Australia, Graham felt that this challenge to his legal rights as a partner was evidence that Rick's cousin didn't recognise or value their (homosexual) relationship. While Graham was able to successfully advocate for recognition of their relationship, the homophobic remarks made by Rick's cousin created additional stress for him.

The challenges renegotiating with family of origin were also identified in the *Trans Ageing and Aged Care project*. Service providers in a residential aged care facility shared in an interview the story of Edna, an 80-year-old woman who was admitted following an acute illness. Edna had transitioned to female 40 years earlier. Prior to her admission, Edna was given an ultimatum by her son to present as male or never see her grandchildren again. As the service providers recounted, Edna's family said: 'If you embarrass us and you don't dress like a man, you won't see any grandchildren.' Edna complied and it was not until staff assisted her to shower that they became aware that she was a transgender woman.

Edna was reliant on service providers to advocate on her behalf, and they were not sure how to do so. In their interview, the service providers empathised that 'this poor man who can't be who he wants to be ... he's living as he's been told he needs to ... he's the one that's had to suffer more, for the sake of the family'. The staff referred to Edna as a male, but acknowledged that it would be difficult for Edna to live as a male because 'he has sort of lived his life as female for so long before coming here'. However, they were unsure how to challenge Edna's family and were concerned that doing so would jeopardise her access to her grandchildren. As a consequence of her dementia, Edna lost the capacity to educate staff about her needs, and was more vulnerable to the transphobic demands of her family. She was dependent on others who did not sufficiently understand her transgender needs and she was incapable of self-advocacy. Edna's dementia symptoms escalated rapidly after her admission to the aged care service.

Edna's story highlights how trans* people who transition later in life may be more vulnerable to rejection by adult children, adversely affecting their ability to live in their self-ascribed gender (Latham and Barrett, 2015). Edna's presentation as a male could be misread as an indication that her trans* status was lost because she had dementia. But this was not the case. Rather, dementia provided an opportunity for family members to reassert their own transphobic beliefs, with devastating consequences.

In order to achieve a person-centred approach to the care of LGT* people living with dementia, service providers need to understand the experiences, needs and values of their LGT* clients and ensure these are central to decision making. This can create challenges, particularly where family members are not supportive of sexual orientation or trans* gender. However, it is critical that service providers advocate for the rights of LGT* people with dementia and provide culturally safe services.

Culturally safe services

Cultural safety is an important consideration in the delivery of person-centred services for LGT* people with dementia. In this section we draw on the Nursing Council of New Zealand's *Guidelines for Cultural Safety in Nursing Education and Practice* (2005) and the literature relating to person-centred care for people living with dementia to present a framework for culturally safe services. The framework builds on the experiences of LGT* people outlined in this chapter and encompasses cultural awareness, or understanding culture, as well as understanding history and its impacts, power in relationships and the impact of staff values and beliefs on the services provided.

Understanding culture

Unhelpful stereotypes about LGT* people include the beliefs that sexual orientation is just about choice of sexual partner and gender is just about choice of clothing. These stereotypes can be underpinned by the view that these 'choices' should not be permitted or are no longer important to older people (Barrett, 2008). The consequences of this poor understanding of culture and the need to be LGT* inclusive results in reduced capacity to access safe and supportive spaces. Service providers need to develop a robust awareness of the cultural needs of older LGT* people in order to understand how dementia may impact on sexuality or gender identity and to provide a context for understanding the unique needs of individual LGT* people living with dementia.

Understanding history

Many LGT* people living with dementia have endured extraordinary historical experiences of discrimination. In this chapter, we have highlighted how some LGT* people were rejected by family members and have never known a time when it was safe to be open about their sexuality or trans* gender. We described how some continue to be estranged from their family of origin and feel the need to conceal their sexual orientation, same-sex relationship or trans* status in order to be safe from discrimination – particularly when accessing services.

This history needs to be understood by service providers who may believe they don't have any LGT* clients because no clients have disclosed this information to them (GRAI, 2010). Understanding history in this way can enable service providers to better understand the experiences and perceptions that LGT* clients bring to their encounter with services. Hearing older LGT* people's narratives can highlight the historical context of inequality and oppression and is an important component of person-centred approaches (Cronin *et al.*, 2010).

However, while this general history needs to be understood, strategies for gathering this information need to be carefully negotiated. In dementia services, common approaches to person-centred care involve understanding each client's unique perspective on life, their feelings, wants and needs in order to individualise care (Røsvik *et al.*, 2011). Implementing this approach often involves constructing life histories or participating in memory or reminiscence groups and this approach can be an empowering activity for a person with dementia (Alzheimer's Society UK, undated). The approach assumes that people feel safe sharing their history and that their history is a positive one. However, for some LGT* people with dementia, being asked about their experiences growing up, their family and early relationships precipitates anxiety and may be re-traumatising. People with dementia who have encountered early trauma may rework the trauma at each new phase of their life (Gordon, 2010). It can take enormous energy to cover up trauma in order to live a 'normal life' and dementia can expose the person, leaving them vulnerable and scared to relive the memories or feelings associated with past trauma (Williams, 2010).

These factors need to be carefully considered in the gathering of life histories from LGT* people with dementia. Asking questions about historical experiences without understanding the context in the lives of older LGT* people risks missing opportunities to support older LGT* clients and communicate the message that their sexuality, gender, history and life stories are valued and respected.

Understanding power imbalances

Historically, health services have exercised considerable control over the lives and autonomy of older LGT* people (Barrett *et al.*, 2014a). Being identified as LGT* could result in being committed to a psychiatric facility for shock therapy and other attempts to cure sexual orientation or transgenderism. These historical experiences can have significant impacts on LGT* people's perceptions and experiences of power in relationships with services providers. It can also result in delays accessing services.

There is also concern about the risk of discrimination from other clients in residential services. The dynamic between clients in residential services needs to be understood and addressed if services are to be culturally safe for LGT* people living with dementia. Some service providers fail to understand the impact of the imbalance of power and their responsibility to protect LGT* people from discrimination (Barrett *et al.*, 2009). Service providers are also well positioned to utilise their power to advocate for the needs of LGT* people with dementia – particularly where family members compromise the expression of sexuality or gender. Service providers could encourage LGT* people to document advance care directives to ensure that care continues to be centred around the client's wishes if they lose the capacity to make decisions. Advance care planning is widely considered good practice in the provision of quality, mainstream dementia care (Department of Health, Victoria, 2010), but its value in ensuring person-centred care for LGT* people with dementia is only just beginning to be understood.

It is important that service providers understand the reticence of LGT* people with dementia to disclose their sexual orientation or trans* status. They also need to understand what it means for older lesbians and gay men to have their sexuality disregarded (Cronin *et al.*, 2010) and their gender dismissed. By doing so, they will better understand how they hold privileged positions of power and can improve access to services by sending the message to LGT* people with dementia that they are valued, respected and safe.

Understanding staff values and beliefs

The final principle of cultural safety is ensuring that service providers understand their own values and beliefs and how these impact on a person-centred approach. Across the interviews reported in this chapter, LGT* people described how they believed that individual staff members would discriminate against them or provide a lesser standard of care if they knew their client was lesbian, gay or trans*. However, given the relative invisibility of older LGT* people, many aged care services do not have policies on LGT* inclusiveness and therefore staff may be guided by their own values and beliefs (Barrett *et al.*, 2013). In order to deliver culturally safe services for LGT* people with dementia, services could, for example, conduct surveys of staff to identify attitudes and beliefs that threaten the cultural safety of LGT* clients. This information could assist organisations to understand what support and education staff need.

Lesbian, gay and trans* people living with dementia have the right to culturally safe services. The onus of responsibility for education to achieve this does not rest with LGT* clients and their partners. Rather, it is the responsibility of all services providers to ensure they deliver cultural awareness education that addresses history, power imbalances and the influence of personal values and beliefs on person-centred approaches. Such a shift requires more than a one-off education session. It necessitates ongoing education and the development of organisational policies that send a clear message to staff about the importance of cultural safety. Service providers who are culturally aware, and who are providing culturally safe services, are well placed to engage, understand and meet the needs of LGT* people living with dementia.

Discussion

This chapter has explored the experiences and needs of a small number of LGT* Australians living with dementia. Their stories refute the idea that LGT* people with dementia 'become straight' because they have dementia. Rather, it demonstrated vulnerability to the reassertion of control by homophobic and transphobic family members, which compromised expression of sexuality or gender.

The chapter also highlighted the importance of being socially connected and supported by people who were valuing and affirming of sexual orientation and gender identity. These connections provided safe and supportive spaces where LGT* people could be themselves. Older LGT* people rely most heavily on their partner and friends as they age (Fredriksen-Goldsen, 2011). While these supports are a unique strength (Brotman *et al.*, 2007) a heavy reliance on partners may be problematic (Barrett *et al.*, 2014a) given the adverse impacts on health and wellbeing (Cummins *et al.*, 2007). The importance and nature of these safe and supportive spaces need to be understood so that they can be maintained and expanded for LGT* people living with dementia.

We also considered the implications for dementia services and emphasised the importance of service providers engaging LGT* clients on their own terms. This means being cognisant that accessing services can result in private lives becoming public (Price, 2010) and increased levels of anxiety and stress (Price, 2008). It also entails being mindful that some LGT* people may conceal their sexual orientation or trans* status or history in order to maintain their own sense of safety. Dementia services need to send the message to LGT* clients that they are valued and safe. While clients do not feel safe sharing the realities of their relationships or bodies, it is difficult to see how a person-centred approach to care can be achieved.

Conclusion

This chapter examined a small body of data in Australia where significant reforms recognising the rights of older LGT* people have taken place in the last few years. Further research is needed to understand the experiences and needs of bisexual (Dworkin, 2006) and intersex people living with dementia and to further expand on the understanding from the current studies. There is also a need to document the experiences of LGBTI people living with dementia who do not have a partner to advocate on their behalf. How can we ensure that their needs are understood and that their rights are not violated? This chapter highlighted the importance of advocacy for LGT* people living with dementia and raises questions about the experiences of LGT* people with dementia in countries where there are no rights or access to advocates.

In order to achieve a person-centred approach to the care of LGT* people living with dementia, service providers need to understand the experiences, needs and values of their LGT* clients and ensure these are central to decision making. This can create challenges, particularly where family members are not supportive of sexual orientation or trans* gender. However, it is critical that service providers advocate for the rights of LGT* people with dementia and provide culturally safe services.

Acknowledgement

The authors would like to acknowledge that this research was funded by the Australian Government Department of Social Services.

References

Alzheimer's Society UK (undated) *Remembering together: Making a life history book.* Alzheimer's Society UK. Available from: www.alzheimers.org.uk.

Barrett, C. (2008) *My people: Exploring the experiences of gay, lesbian, bisexual, transgender and intersex seniors in aged care services.* Melbourne, Matrix Guild Victoria Inc and Vintage Men Inc.

Barrett, C. and Stephens, K. (2012) *Beyond: 'We treat everyone the same'. A report on the 2010–2011 program: How2 create a gay, lesbian, bisexual, transgender and intersex inclusive service.* Gay and Lesbian Health Victoria, Melbourne Australia.

Barrett, C., Harrison, J. and Kent, J. (2009) *Permission to speak. Towards the development of gay, lesbian, bisexual, transgender and intersex friendly aged care services.* Melbourne, Matrix Guild Victoria Inc and Vintage Men Inc.

Barrett, C., Turner, L. and Leonard, L. (2013) *Beyond a rainbow sticker. A report on How2 create a gay, lesbian, bisexual, transgender and intersex (GLBTI) inclusive service 2012–2013.* Gay and Lesbian Health Victoria, Melbourne Australia.

Barrett, C., Whyte, C., Comfort, J., Lyons, A. and Crameri, P. (2014a) 'Social connection, relationships and older lesbian and gay people' [Special Issue]. *Sexual and Relationship Therapy.*

Barrett, C., Whyte, C., Leonard, W. and Comfort, J. (2014b) *No need to straighten up: Discrimination, depression and anxiety in older lesbian, gay, bisexual, transgender and intersex Australians.* Australian Research Centre in Sex, Health and Society La Trobe University, Melbourne Australia.

Brotman, S., Ryan, B., Collins, S., Chamberland, L., Cormier, R., Julien, D., Meyer, E., Peterkin, A. and Richard, B. (2007) 'Coming out to care: Caregivers of gay and lesbian seniors in Canada'. *The Gerontologist,* **47**: 490–503.

Crameri, P., Barrett, C., Whyte, C. and Lambourne, S. (2015) *The Dementia Project: Understanding and meeting the needs of LGBTI Australians living with dementia.* Australian Research Centre in Sex, Health and Society, La Trobe University.

Cronin, A., Ward, R., Pugh, S., King, A. and Price, E. (2010) 'Categories and their consequences: Understanding and supporting the caring relationships of older lesbian, gay and bisexual people'. *International Social Work,* **54**(3): 421–435.

Cummins, R., Hughes, J., Tomyn, A., Gibson, A., Woerner, J. and Lair, L. (2007) *The wellbeing of Australians-carer health and wellbeing.* Australian Centre on Quality of Life. Deakin University Melbourne.

Department of Health, Victoria (2010) *Advanced care planning, good practice for quality dementia care.* Department of Health, Melbourne.

Dworkin, S. H. (2006) Aging bisexual: The invisible of the invisible minority. In D. Kimmel, T. Rose and S. David (eds), *Lesbian, gay, bisexual and transgender aging: Research and clinical perspectives*, pp. 36–52. New York: Columbia University Press.

Fredriksen-Goldsen, K. I. (2011) Resilience and disparities among lesbian, gay, bisexual, and transgender older adults. In R. B. Hudson (ed.) *Integrating lesbian, gay, bisexual, and transgender older adults into aging policy and practice*, pp. 3–7. Public Policy & Aging Report series. Washington: National Academy on an Aging Society. Available from: http://bit.ly/1IeevFv.

Gordon, R. (2010) *The passage through life. Ageing, dementia and adult survivors of childhood sexual assault.* ACSSA Aware (24). Australian Institute of Family Studies.

GRAI (2010) *We don't have any of those people here: Retirement accommodation and aged care issues for non-heterosexual populations.* Perth, Western Australia: GRAI (GLBTI Retirement Association Inc) and Curtin Health Innovation Research Institute, Curtin University.

Latham, J. R. and Barrett, C. (2015) *Understanding the experiences and needs of older trans people in Australia (from the 'Trans Ageing and Aged Care Projects').* Australian Research Centre in Sex, Health and Society, La Trobe University.

Nursing Council of New Zealand (2005) *Guidelines for cultural safety, the Treaty of Waitangi and Maori health in nursing education and practice.* Available from www.nursingcouncil.org.nz.

Price, E. (2008) 'Pride or prejudice? Gay men, lesbians and dementia'. *British Journal of Social Work*, **38**: 1337–1352.

Price, E. (2010) 'Coming out to care: Gay and lesbian carers' experiences of dementia services'. *Health and Social Care in the Community*, **18**(2): 160–168.

Ritchie, J. and Spencer, L. (1994) 'Qualitative data analysis for applied policy research'. In A. Bryman. and R. Burgess (eds) *Analyzing qualitative data.* London, Routledge.

Røsvik, J., Kirkevold, M., Engedal, K., Brooker, D. and Kirkevold, Ø. (2011) 'A model for using the VIPS framework for person-centred care for persons with dementia in nursing homes: A qualitative evaluative study'. *International Journal of Older People Nursing*, **6**: 227–236.

Williams, A. (2010) *Dementia and survivors of childhood sexual abuse. Ageing, dementia and adult survivors of childhood sexual assault.* ACSSA Aware (24). Australian Institute of Family Studies.

8 Trans* people anticipating dementia care

Findings from the Transgender MetLife Survey

Tarynn M. Witten

Prologue

When I offered to write a chapter on dementia and trans* ident[...]
it would be a fairly straightforward effort. After all, I have been a gerontologist
for over 40 years now and have written numerous papers and book chapters on
various aspects of ageing in the trans* communities. Digging into the current
complex literature on dementia and its care has shown me how shallow my original thoughts about dementia were. For example, the literature on sexuality in
nursing homes shows significant challenges for the lesbian and gay community
members, their caregivers and their families. Homophobia, lack of training in
LGBT healthcare, and even denial of care, are all part of the challenges for older
lesbian and gay people in nursing homes. Moreover, my literature research
demonstrated that, while there are articles that address gender self-perceptions/
presentation in relation to dementia (Campbell, 2012; Twigg and Buse, 2013;
Buse and Twigg, 2014) there have been only a very small number that have
focused on trans* individuals and dementia (McGovern, 2014; Withall, 2014;
Marshall *et al.*, 2015).

We do know, however, that there is a fundamental fear of care facilities for
older people among the trans* population. For example, one respondent in the
Transgender MetLife Survey (TMLS) (Witten, 2014a) said,

> My worst fear is being physically mistreated or neglected, ridiculed, dis-
> counted, marginalized, ignored.
>
> (TMLS Respondent, Witten, 2014a, original data)

Both trans* individuals and people with dementia have been constructed as
deviants within medical models. The concept of dementia itself has been
described as an example of the 'medicalization of deviance' (Fazio, 2013: 17)
while being gender variant is still considered deviance (mental illness) in many
areas, as it is still an entry in the *The Diagnostic and Statistical Manual of
Mental Disorders, Fifth Edition* (*DSM V*) and in the *International Statistical
Classification of Diseases and Related Health Problems 10th Edition* (*ICD-10*),
a medical classification list by the World Health Organization (WHO). Abuse,

denial of care and even violence at the hands of healthcare workers is now an unfortunate part of the trans* healthcare literature (e.g. Witten, 2008; Finkenauer *et al.*, 2012; Fredriksen-Goldsen *et al.*, 2014b; Shukla *et al.*, 2014). This history has created a significant fear, among transgender-identified persons, around accessing any form of healthcare (Redman, 2011; Shulka *et al.*, 2014). It is easy, then, to hypothesize that this history of discrimination and abuse could lead to a variety of negative dynamics for older trans* people and, more specifically, for those with dementia (Finkenauer *et al.*, 2012; Witten, 2014a).

In this chapter I will explore the potential challenges that dementia poses for members of the trans* community, and for dementia care providers. I will identify a series of research questions and policy challenges in need of urgent attention. I shall be drawing upon data from the Transgender MetLife Survey (TMLS) which I conducted (Witten, 2014a). This 83-question survey was conducted with 1963 participants aged over 18 who identified as one of the following: transsexual, transgender, intersex, DSD (disorders of sexual development), cross-dresser, gender variant, gender queer-identified, First Nations and Non-Western gender identities. The majority (81 per cent) of the participants came from the USA, with the remainder (19 per cent) coming from other countries, which included Canada, Australia, Sweden and the United Kingdom. Full details of the methodology is described in detail in Witten (2014a).[1] The studies I have conducted, as reported in this paper, have received ethical approval from: the University of Michigan Ann Arbor, the University of Texas Health Science Center at San Antonio and/or the Virginia Commonwealth University.

Prevalence

Until recently, older people among trans* populations have been invisible (Persson, 2009). Given the constant ebb and flow of gender descriptors in the trans* community, it is difficult to provide an accurate estimate for both the US and the global number of gender nonconforming people. However, we can make some reasonable estimates. Using 1999 census data and an estimate of 1 per cent to 3 per cent transgender population prevalence, I previously estimated (Witten, 2003) that there were approximately 347,000 to 1,041,000 transgender-identified persons in the United States over 65 years of age. Similarly, I estimated that the worldwide population, for the same group, was 4,097,020 to 12,291,060 individuals (Witten, 2003). Based upon more recent 2010 population estimates, I have argued (Witten, 2015a) that the US population estimates should be revised to be between 1.2 million and 2.8 million transgender-identified individuals over 65 years of age. Other researchers have presented different demographics for identifying the gender non-conforming population (Winter and Conway, 2011; Meier and Labuski, 2013). The sparse data available makes estimates of the overall trans* population unreliable. It also makes it extremely difficult to estimate how many trans* people are affected by dementia.

Currently, there are many unanswered questions regarding risk factors. Health risks may be associated with long-term exposure to hormone therapy and gender reassignment surgeries (Cook-Daniels, 2006, 2011). High levels of oestrogen may be linked to a greater risk of developing dementia (Whitmer *et al.*, 2011). This raises the question of whether or not male-to-female transsexuals on oestrogen or female-to-male transsexuals, who were on oestrogen, are at greater risk of dementia than their cisgender peers. Female sex is also a risk factor. This raises the question of how testosterone may or may not mediate dementia risk factors. Additionally, cis-women are at greater risk of dementia as they live longer than cis-men (Alzheimer's Disease International, 2015). What are the implications for male-to-female and female-to-male transsexual people who have taken cross hormones and/or had gender reassignment surgery?

In terms of other risk factors, the data on the impact of smoking on dementia risk are conflicting (Rusanen, 2011). If smoking is relevant to dementia, given the trans* population is known to smoke significantly more than the cisgender population (Fredriksen-Goldsen *et al.*, 2014a), then there might be an increased risk of dementia among trans* people. The impact of drug and alcohol use on dementia risk is also open to debate (Panza *et al.*, 2012). The LGBT* population's level of drug and alcohol use is significantly higher than that of the non-LGBT* population (Burkhalter *et al.*, 2009; Clarke and Coughlin, 2012), and that of trans* people greater than cisgender LGB people (Fredriksen-Goldsen *et al.*, 2011). Again, if there is a link between drug and alcohol use and dementia, it may be that the trans*-identified population is more likely to be at increased risk of later-life dementia. Depression is now recognized to be linked to dementia (Saczynski *et al.*, 2010; Byers and Yaffe, 2011; Kessing, 2012). The LGBT* population is at increased risk of depression compared with the non-LGBT* population (Fredriksen-Goldsen *et al.*, 2013, 2014a), and trans* people experience higher rates of depression compared with cisgender LGB people (Fredriksen-Goldsen *et al.*, 2011). This suggests that trans* people may also be at heightened risk of dementia associated with depression.

Trans* people's fears about ageing and dementia

While many aspects of dementia are similarly experienced by the trans* identified and cisgender population, trans* identities bring additional complexities to dementia and, in particular, to healthcare dynamics. This was highlighted in the responses to the Transgender MetLife Survey (TMLS) (Witten, 2014a). For many trans*-identified people, dementia is one of the most feared ageing-related challenges:

> Like many, I have a fear about dementia-related illnesses.
> (TMLS survey respondent, Witten 2014a, original data)

Trans* people's fears about dementia relate to two concerns: (1) the intersectionality of stigmas around ageing and mental illness (Chapman *et al.*, 2006: 7) and (2) the implications of memory loss for trans* identities. For any human being, the potential loss of a sense of self is crucial. For the trans* population, loss of the sense of a self and the changes and losses in the experience of the self ('I am not as I was', Dalby *et al.*, 2011: 75) which has been navigated against imposed gendered norms and expectations is particularly fear-provoking.

> It's not really about being queer, but I'm terrified of dementia. I guess it relates to losing my sense of identity.
>
> (TMLS Respondent, Witten 2014a, original data)

> I am concerned that I will be unable to maintain my identity.
>
> (TMLS Respondent, Witten 2014a, original data)

This question of identity is central to fears about dementia for trans* people, particularly those who have transitioned.

> I am worried that I will develop dementia and will not remember that I have transitioned.
>
> (TMLS Respondent, Witten 2014a, original data)

Some older trans women and men may have transitioned when they were younger, others in later life, and the different ages and stages when they transitioned will influence how they experience ageing (Bailey, 2012) and associated physical and mental health problems (Fredriksen-Goldsen *et al.*, 2014b), including dementia. While some trans* people mobilize fluid notions of gender identity which may be more compatible with the fluidities which may be associated with dementia, others, particularly transsexual individuals, may mobilize a more binary discourse. For such individuals, memory and loss and identity changes associated with dementia (Fazio, 2013) can pose challenges to the idea of the true self. It can also provoke considerable anxieties among those individuals who have transitioned, who may have fought long and hard to achieve a congruent sense of a binary gendered self, and who perceive dementia as posing a threat to that sense of congruence. Marshall and colleagues have recently described a transsexual woman with dementia who was very confused about her gender identity:

> When Jamie was transferred to a long-term care facility, the staff noted she was confused as to whether she was male or female, asking, 'What am I?' She frequently looked down at her breasts and asked, 'Where did these come from?' At times she expressed a desire to dress and be addressed as a female, and at other times as a male.
>
> (Marshall *et al.*, 2015: 113–114)

The greatest fear among trans women and men who have transitioned is that dementia may take them back to assuming they must present a gender identity congruent with their birth-assigned sex, even though for most, if not all, of their lives, they have felt that such a gender identity does not reflect their true selves.

The fear of loss of self, and associated loss of memory, is also linked to the fear of a lack of support,

> I am worried that I will not be able to support myself and that there will be no one to take care of me. I am already becoming so forgetful and unable to concentrate at 55 years of age that I worry I will not be able to hold or keep a job at some point within the next five years or longer. I worry that I will not have the resolve to kill myself when I cannot support myself any longer. I worry that I will become a 'bag lady' living on the street, unable to afford or access testosterone.
>
> (TMLS Respondent, Witten 2014a, original data)

While there is a literature on gender and caregiving (Chappell *et al.*, 2014), we know next to nothing about caregiving networks (Koehly *et al.*, 2014) in the trans* community (Grossman *et al.*, 2000) or the well-being of those individuals who care for trans* people with dementia (Chappell *et al.*, 2014). Wolff and Spillman (2014: S65) point out that family caregivers provide the overwhelming majority of disability-related assistance to adults. In the TMLS, respondents were asked who is likely to be a person's primary caregiver in the event of a major illness or when the need arises. Respondents were given a set of choices and asked to pick only one response. Thirty percent of the respondents stated that they were not sure who would take care of them (Witten, 2014a: 9–10). Many trans* people experience rejection from their families because of their gender nonconformity and/or after they have transitioned. The lack of informal support increases the likelihood that they will need formal healthcare support.

Trans* people's fears about dementia care

While there has been an increase in the number of nursing homes in the USA that have a 'special unit for people with dementia' (Jalbert *et al.*, 2008: 25), currently only 20 per cent of nursing homes in the USA have such a unit, and there is no known unit specializing in the complex care of trans*-identifying people with dementia. As noted above, trans* people are fearful of any sort of caregiving environment:

> I know with pretty fair certainty I don't ever want to be in a position where I am dependent on medical staff for my care. I have been asked to leave doctors' offices because I am trans. They plead ignorance over minor issues related to my care and I've been treated like an animal in the zoo. My old gyn [ecologist] asked whether or not she could show me to staff. Also, even minor problems like muscle pulls get blamed on my 'situation'.
>
> (TMLS Respondent, Witten 2014a, original data)

> I do not want to be institutionalized. I don't want to die in a hospital either. I hate hospitals. I've been treated so badly in them because of my gender....

They get so scared and freaked out by trans people, that they can't handle the conditions I'm there for.

(TMLS Respondent, Witten 2014a, original data)

The experience of abuse by some trans* people at the hands of the healthcare system makes it exceptionally difficult for those individuals to feel safe in care facilities for older people, and this is heightened for those whose bodies are not in alignment with their gender identities.

> I do not want to rely on strangers in the medical field that have little to no experience helping people with bodies like mine.
>
> (TMLS Respondent, quoted in Witten, 2014a: 18)

> My partner and I are both male-to-female trannies [transsexuals]. Neither of us could afford the genital realignment surgery we both so desperately desire. My deepest fear is how the world will see us when we come to a point where we need assisted living care or when one of us dies. God forbid they put together that our lesbian relationship is between two women who have penises.
>
> (TMLS Respondent, Witten, 2014a, original data)

It is easy to see that these fears revolve around anticipated healthcare workers' perceptions of the patient's physical identity as well as the patient's gender presentation. Vulnerability, abuse, violence, denial of appropriate care and denial of identity are among the many things that older trans* people fear in relation to dementia (Withall, 2014). Because dementia is a progressively worsening condition, individuals will need increasing levels of caregiving, often eventually involving 24-hour support. This caregiving can occur in the home, in assisted living facilities but is most likely to end in some form of nursing home or other 24-hour nursing facility (Jalbert *et al.*, 2008). As we have already seen, trans* individuals are fearful of any sort of caregiving environment, much heightened in the context of dementia care.

> I am a woman with a penis. What will they do to me in a nursing home? What will happen if I cannot defend myself because of dementia?
>
> (TMLS Respondent, quoted in Witten, 2015b: 79)

> I worry that I will become incapacitated and not be able to communicate my history as a trans* person [medical, surgical history] before requiring care. I worry that caregivers will not be experienced in dealing with trans* bodies and health issues and I will at best not get the care I need and at worst be ridiculed, mocked or ignored because of the state of my body.
>
> (TMLS Respondent, Witten 2014a, original data)

Will I be treated with dignity? Will I be respected? Will I be in a defence-less situation at the mercy of those that do not or are unwilling to understand me being trans?

(TMLS Respondent, quoted in Witten 2014a: 19)

As can be seen, trans* people perceive dementia care needs as increasing their vulnerability to a system which is already ill-equipped to meet their needs.

Practice issues

Maslow (2013) points out that 'patient-centered care is one of the six major aims in redesigning the United States' healthcare system' (p. 8) and that patient-centered and person-centered are often used equivalently. However, when it comes to dementia, Doyle and Rubinstein (2013) explain that 'person-centered care (PCC) represents a shift in focus away from a traditional, biomedical, approach toward a more holistic and individualized model of elder care' (p. 952). They go on to highlight that a biomedical approach focuses on mental pathology and thereby compromises the personhood of people with dementia (Kitwood, 1997) and reinforces the negativity of the biomedical approach by pointing out that it 'did not fully consider the psychological, social, and cultural complexities of the person with dementia' (Doyle and Rubinstein, 2013: 952).

Critical to a person-centered approach to dementia for trans* individuals is: focusing on the trans* individual with dementia; developing ways the trans* individual can connect with a care environment which respects and validates how that person identifies; developing ways for the individual to have meaning-ful inclusion in their respective residential environments; and developing trans*-focused methods for life review and reminiscence. Development of methods to include the family, no matter how it is defined legally or by choice, is important, along with the encouragement of active participation by all family members.

Given the large number of trans* people who state that they are living alone and have no children, it is clear that institutional support for those with dementia must be developed (FORGE, 2011; Lambda Legal, 2013; Hyndal *et al.*, 2014). This could be the development of specialized homes for trans* people or through cul-tural sensitivity training in already available geriatric care units. The complex iden-tity constructions for trans* people demand that good person-centered care means finding ways to support the 'self' in everyday care, particularly as the sense of self evolves under the effects of the disease dynamics. Care environments need to focus on assisting the individual with dementia to connect with others. Support staff need to bring the world in and need to develop mutual understanding with the client and to allow the client to have as meaningful a contribution to their lives as is possible. Patients with dementia need to be helped to reminisce as much as possible, and this includes trans* individuals with dementia.

Care staff should be prepared to deal with the uncertainties and ethical dilem-mas which may be posed (Marshall *et al.*, 2015). For example, how does one manage sexuality with a gender variant person who has body parts that are inconsistent with their gender expression and who may want to be in a non-heterosexual relationship or a heterosexual relationship? How does a staff member address the needs of a transsexual person who no longer remembers that they have transitioned? How should staff members deal with situations when other residents and/or family members are not accepting or supportive of the trans* person's gender identity? Which gender identity (past or present) should be recognized and validated? The identity flow of a trans* person with dementia can be particularly complex and lead to potentially uncomfortable situations and staff should be equipped to deal with those situations.

End-of-life issues

The end of life can come in various settings: nursing homes, assisted living or other residential care facilities or in individual homes. However, for those who are trans*, end-of-life care can be particularly complex. In a series of articles (Witten and Whittle, 2004; Witten, 2009, 2014a) I have discussed later and end-of-life challenges for trans* people. It is essential that legal paperwork be executed to ensure the wishes of the trans* person are respected should they lose capacity and/or when they die. However, as I have documented (Witten, 2014b), there was a lack of later-life legal protection in the trans* participants in the TMLS. For example, I found that, in the TMLS, only 14.1 per cent of the respondents had completed a legal will, 13.1 per cent had completed a living will, 10.7 per cent had completed a durable power of attorney, 1.1 per cent had completed an ethical will, 3.3 per cent had completed pre-arranged funeral/cremation or other end-of-life ceremony plans, and 3.9 per cent had completed informal caregiving arrangements. These low numbers demonstrate the great legal vulnerability that the participants have when it comes to later and end-of-life decision-making, particularly when it involves an older trans* person who has dementia.

Such vulnerabilities can also be present after death, as is evident in two recent cases: one, where a trans woman died and was presented by her family (who did not respect her gender identity) as a man in her casket (Rothaus, 2014); and another where a trans man Dave (who had undergone some gender affirmation surgery in his sixties and lived as a man since then) was rejected by his adult daughters who had nothing to do with him for the last 20 years of his life, and eventually buried Dave, when he died aged 80, as their mother 'Lucy', ignoring how Dave had identified his gender for the previous 20 years (Withall, 2014).

The intersection of trans* identity and faith-based organizations in the USA is often problematic or outwardly discriminatory (Kidd and Witten, 2007). Faith-based hospitals in the USA may make it clear that certain aspects of advanced directives will not be honoured due to faith-based conflicts. This may be especially problematic when the physical body does not necessarily align with the patient's stated gender identity. The literature on the importance of religion, spirituality and faith in the general geriatric population is large and continues to grow (Lawler-Row and Elliott, 2009; Stuckey, 2003; Suri, 2010). More recently, a number of research papers address the role and importance of spirituality, religion and faith in the trans* population (Porter *et al.*, 2013). Despite this importance, trans* people in the USA often face exclusion, penalties or other deleterious behaviours on the part of spiritual organizations due to beliefs that being trans* is a sin (Kidd and Witten, 2007). Trans* people have spoken of being denied funereal ceremony rights, being denied burial rights in the church graveyard, being denied marriage ceremonies, being denied last rights, and even being denied access to spiritual counselling when needed because they were trans* people (Witten and Whittle, 2004; Witten, 2009). For couples in which one or both of the partners are trans* people, legal marriage may not be realized, according to the legal context of where a couple is living. Consequently the remaining partner may not have access to the appropriate support services that come with legal marriage, and may be denied the appropriate opportunities to mourn. The complexities of mourning for the person with dementia, which may occur both before and after the person has died (Michel *et al.*, 2002) is made even more complicated at their intersection with trans* identities.

Trans* people, with their respective families (including 'families of choice', Weston 1991, Weeks *et al.*, 2001) need to make formal advance directives, specifying their wishes for end-of-life care and/or designating someone (either biological family or 'family of choice' member) as their surrogate decision-maker in the event that they become incapacitated. This is particularly important where the trans* person does become incapacitated. Family members need to be aware of this document and be insistent that it be implemented when patients face a healthcare crisis, as the dementia advances (Haley *et al.*, 2002).

Research questions and policy issues

The domain of trans* dementia is unstudied and nearly any question is likely to have very limited scholarly literature available. We need estimates of the size of the older trans* population to make accurate projections of the dynamics of this cohort and we need information on levels of dementia in this population. There are numerous biomedical questions around the interaction of cross-gender hormones and environment with the onset, progression and type of dementia occurring in this population.

Traditional caregiver-related questions are also important. Assessment of caregiver burden, well-being and resilience are all important to understand. Gendered interactions of the caregiver with the care recipient are of interest (Robinson *et al.*, 2014). Interactions of 'self-management' programmes (Toms *et al.*, 2015) with caregiving and the trans* person remain unstudied. Religion, spirituality and faith in the caregiving, residential and dementia environments are also unstudied. Moreover, the development of trans*-focused measuring instruments in ageing remain marginal and are crucial to the effective understanding of later and end-of-life challenges for older trans* people. There are also specific questions to be addressed at the intersection of gender identity and dementia, each potentially offering useful insights on the other, as Marshall and colleagues have observed,

What is the basis of gender identity? Is gender something that can be 'forgotten' in the course of dementia? Future research about the relation between memory and gender identity is needed, as it may have more far reaching implications, for example, on the understanding of the development of gender identity and the role of cognitive abilities (and impairments) as part of that.

(Marshall *et al.*, 2015: 117)

Because the current and upcoming older trans* population may be at greater risk due to the age-related factors associated with dementia, this population should be specifically targeted as a priority in addressing all modifiable factors associated with the risk of dementia. There is an urgent need for good practice guidance on the provision of care and support to trans* people with dementia. I continue to argue for the need to include trans* and intersex identities when collecting national and international population health data, including dementia status.

Post haec

When dealing with a loved one who is trans* and who also has dementia, the intersectionality of the trans* identity with the numerous later and end-of-life factors can create significant tension in already difficult conditions. In the end, it is about helping the loved one leave this world with grace and a sense of self. May we all have that type of support from our friends, families, allies, healthcare workers and our other loved ones.

Acknowledgements

I am in debt to many colleagues and friends who have, over the years, supported my efforts to understand the various processes involved in ageing within the global trans* population. Your support has been essential. However, I want to acknowledge the 1,963 respondents to my recent research survey, as well as the nearly 1000 respondents from past surveys. Your honesty and willingness to share your deepest feelings and concerns honours me greatly and I am humbled and deeply moved by your words. Without you, I would not have the power to write everything that I have written in hopes of effecting change.

Editors' note

Many thanks to Jenny-Anne Bishop and Chryssy Hunter, for their editorial input on this chapter.

Note

1 Quotations already quoted in other publications are marked as such. Quotations from the original data, not previously quoted elsewhere, are also indicated.

References

Alzheimer's Disease International (2015) *Women and dementia: A global research review*. London: Alzheimer's Disease International.

Bailey, L. (2012) Trans ageing: thoughts on a life course approach in order to better understand trans lives. In R. Ward, I. Rivers and M. Sutherland (eds) *Lesbian, gay, bisexual and transgender ageing: Biographical approaches for inclusive care and support*, pp. 51–66. London and Philadelphia, PA: Jessica Kingsley Publishers.

Burkhalter, J. E., Warren, B., Shuk, E., Primavent, L. and Ostroff, J. S. (2009) 'Intention to quit smoking among lesbian, gay, bisexual and transgender smokers'. *Nicotine and Tobacco Research*, **11**(11), 1312–1320.

Buse, C. and Twigg, J. (2014) 'Women with dementia and their handbags: Negotiating identity, privacy and "home" through material culture'. *Journal of Ageing Studies*, **30**, 14–22.

Byers, A. L. and Yaffe, K. (2011) 'Depression and risk of developing dementia'. *Nature Reviews Neurology*, **7**(6), 323–331.

Campbell, S. (2012) 'A close shave: Masculinity and bodywork in dementia care'. *Graduate Journal of Social Science*, **9**(3), 87–95.

Chapman, D. P., Williams, S. M., Strine, T. W., Anda, R. F. and Moore, M. J. (2006) 'Dementia and its implications for public health'. *Preventing Chronic Disease* **3**(2), A34.

Chappell, N. L., Dujela, C. and Smith, A. (2014) 'Caregiver well-being: Intersections of relationship and gender'. *Research on Ageing*. DOI: 10.1177/0164027514549258.

Clark, M. P. and Coughlin, J. R. (2012) 'Prevalence of smoking among the lesbian, gay, bisexual, transsexual, transgender and queer (LGBTTQ) subpopulations in Toronto – the Toronto Rainbow Tobacco Survey (TRTS)'. *Canadian Journal of Public Health*, **103**(2), 132–136.

Cook-Daniels, L. (2006) Trans ageing. In D. Kimmel, T. Rose and S. David (eds) *Lesbian, Gay, Bisexual and Transgender Ageing*, pp. 20–35. New York: Columbia University Press.

Cook-Daniels, L. (2011) 'Growing older transgender'. Available from: https://forge-forward.org/2011/06/growing-old-transgender/ [downloaded 16 June 2015].

Dalby, P., Sperlinger, D. J. and Boddington, S. (2011) 'The lived experience of spirituality and dementia in older people with mild to moderate dementia'. *Dementia*, **11**(1), 75–94. DOI: 10.1177/1471301211416608.

Doyle, P. J. and Rubinstein, R. L. (2013) 'Person-centered dementia care and the cultural matrix of othering'. *The Gerontologist*, **54**(6), 952–963. DOI: 10.1093/geront/gnt081.

Fazio, S. (2013) 'The individual is the core – and key – to person-centered care'. *Generations: Journal of the American Society on Ageing*, **37**(3), 16–21.

Finkenauer, S., Sherrat, J., Marlow, J. and Brodey, A. (2012) 'When injustice gets old: A systematic review of trans ageing'. *Journal of Gay and Lesbian Social Services*, **24**, 311–330.

FORGE (2011) *Quick tips for caregivers of transgender clients*. Available from: https://forge-forward.org/2011/06/quick-tips-for-caregivers-of-transgender-clients/ [downloaded 16 June 2015].

Fredriksen-Goldsen, K. I., Kim, H.-J., Emlet, C. A., Muraco, A., Erosheva, E. A., Hoy-Ellis, C. P., Goldsen J. and Petry, H. (2011) *The aging and health report: Disparities and resilience among lesbian, gay, bisexual, and transgender older adults*. Seattle, WA: Institute for Multigenerational Health. https://depts.washington.edu/agepride/

wordpress/wp-content/uploads/2012/10/factsheet-keyfindings10-25-12.pdf [downloaded 16 June 2015].

Fredriksen-Goldsen, K. I., Kim, H.-J., Barkan, S. E., Muraco, A. and Hoy-Ellis, C. P. (2013) 'Health disparities among lesbian, gay, and bisexual older adults: Results from a population-based study'. *American Journal of Public Health*, **103**(10), 1802–1809.

Fredriksen-Goldsen, K. I., Hoy-Ellis, C. P., Goldsen, J., Emlet, C. A. and Hooyman, N. R. (2014a) 'Creating a vision for the future: Key competencies and strategies for culturally competent practice with lesbian, gay, bisexual, and transgender (LGBT) older adults in the health and human services'. *Journal of Gerontological Social Work*. Advanced on-line access. DOI: 10.1080/01634372.2014.890690.

Fredriksen-Goldsen, K. I., Cook-Daniels, L., Kim, H.-J., Erosheva, E. A., Emlet, C. A., Hoy-Ellis, C. P., Goldsen, J. and Muraco, A. (2014b) 'Physical and mental health of transgender older adults: An at-risk and underserved population', *The Gerontologist* **54**(3), 488–500.

Grossman, A. H., D'Augelli, A. R. and Hershberger, S. L. (2000) 'Social support networks of lesbian, gay and bisexual adults 60 years of age and older'. *Journal of Gerontology: Psychological Sciences*, **55B**(3), P171–179.

Haley, W. E., Allen, R. S., Reynolds, S., Chen, H., Burton, A. and Gallagher-Thompson, D. (2002) 'Family issues in end-of-life decision making and end-of-life care'. *American Behavioral Scientist*, **46**(2), 284–298.

Hyndal, P., Yates, J., Rutherford, S., Stanley, S., Sweeney, L., Lindsay, C., Savigny, J. and Green, J. (2014) *Navigating diversity: Information for transgender, intersex and diverse communities and service providers*. Ainslie, Australia: A Gender Agenda. Available from: http://genderrights.org.au/sites/default/files/u9/AGA%20InfoPack%20 2014.pdf [accessed 16th July 2015].

Jalbert, J. J., Daiello, L. A. and Lapane, K. L. (2008) 'Dementia of the Alzheimer type'. *Epidemiologic Reviews*, 30: 15–34. DOI: /10.1093/epirev/mxn008.

Kessing, L. V. (2012) 'Depression and the risk for dementia'. *Current Opinion in Psychiatry*, **25**(6), 457–461.

Kidd, J. D. and Witten, T. M. (2007) 'Assessing spirituality, religiosity and faith in the transgender community: A case study in violence and abuse – implications for the ageing transgender community and for Gerontological Research'. *Journal of Religious Gerontology*, **20**(1–2), 29–62.

Kitwood, T. (1997) *Dementia reconsidered: The person comes first*. Buckingham, UK: Open University Press.

Koehly, L. M., Ashida, S., Schafer, E. J. and Ludden, A. (2014) 'Caregiving networks – using a network approach to identify missed opportunities'. *Journals of Gerontology, Series B: Psychological Sciences and Social Sciences*, DOI: 10.1093/gerontb/gbu111.

Lambda Legal (2013) *Creating equal access to quality health care for transgender patients: Transgender-affirming hospital policies*. New York: Lambda Legal. Available at www.lgbtagingcenter.org/resources/resource.cfm?r=625#sthash.I8VkGiwq.dpuf [downloaded 16 June 2015].

Lawler-Row, K. A. and Elliott, J. (2009) 'The role of religious activity and spirituality in the health and well-being of older adults'. *Journal of Health Psychology*, **14**(1), 43–52. DOI: 10.1177/1359105308097944.

Marshall, J., Cooper, M. and Rudnick, A. (2015) 'Gender dysphoria and dementia: A case report'. *Journal of Gay & Lesbian Mental Health*, **19**(1), 112–117.

Maslow, K. (2013) 'Person-centered care for people with dementia: Opportunities and challenges'. *Generations: Journal of the American Society on Ageing*, **37**(3), 8–15.

McGovern, J. (2014) 'The forgotten: Dementia and the aging LGBT community'. *Journal of Gerontological Social Work*, **57**(8), 845–857.

Meier, S. C. and Labuski, C. M. (2013) The demographics of the transgender population. In A. K. Baumle (ed.) *International handbook on the demography of sexuality*, pp. 289–327. Springer Netherlands, DOI 10.1007/9978-94-007-5512-3_16, 289–327.

Michel, J.-P., Pautex, S., Zekry, D., Zulian, G. and Gold, G. (2002) 'End-of-life care of persons with dementia'. *Journal of Gerontology Medical Sciences*, **57A**(10), M640–M644.

Panza, F., Frisardi, V., Seripa, D., Logroscino, G., Santamato, A., Imbimbo, B. P., Scafato, E., Pilotto, A. and Solfrizzi, V. (2012) 'Alcohol consumption in mild cognitive impairment and dementia: Harmful or neuroprotective?' *International Journal of Geriatric Psychiatry*, **27**(12), 1218–1238.

Persson, D. I. (2009) 'Unique challenges of transgender aging: Implications from the literature'. *Journal of Gerontological Social Work*, **52**(6), 633–646.

Porter, K. E., Oala, C. R. and Witten, T. M. (2013) 'Transgender spirituality, religion & successful ageing: Findings from the Trans MetLife Survey'. *Journal of Religion, Spirituality and Ageing*, **25**(2), 112–138.

Redman, D. (2011) 'Fear, discrimination and abuse: Transgender elders and the perils of long-term care'. *Ageing Today*, **XXXII** (2), 1–2.

Robinson, C. A., Bottorff, J. L., Pesuit, B., Oliffe, J. L. and Tomlinson, J. (2014) 'The male face of caregiving: A scoping review of men caring for a person with dementia'. *American Journal of Men's Health*, **8**(5), 409–426. DOI: 10.1177/1557988313519671.

Rothaus, S. (2014) 'Transgender woman dies suddenly, presented at funeral in open casket as a man'; www.miamiherald.com/news/local/community/gay-south-florida/article4055600.html#/tabPane=tabs-30a8a142-1.

Rusanen, M., Kivipelto, M., Quesenberry, C. P., Jr, Zhou, J., and Whitmer, R. A. (2011) 'Heavy smoking in midlife and long-term risk of Alzheimer disease and vascular dementia'. *Archives of Internal Medicine*, **171**(4), 333–339.

Saczynski, J. S., Beiser, A., Seshadri, S., Auerbach, S., Wolf, P. A., and Au, R. (2010) 'Depressive symptoms and risk of dementia The Framingham Heart Study'. *Neurology*, **75**(1), 35–41.

Shukla, V., Asp, A., Dwyer, M., Georgescu, C. and Duggan, J. (2014) 'Barriers to healthcare in the transgender community: A case report'. *LGBT Health*, **1**(3), 229–232.

Stuckey, J. C. (2003) 'Faith, ageing and dementia. Experiences of Christian, Jewish and non-religious spousal caregivers and older adults'. *Dementia*, **2**(3), 337–352.

Suri, R. (2010) 'Working with the elderly: An existential-humanistic approach'. *Journal of Humanistic Psychology*, **50**(2), 175–186. DOI: 10.1177/0022167809335687.

Toms, G. R., Quinn, C., Anderson, D. E. and Clare, L. (2015) 'Help yourself: Perspectives on self-management from people with dementia and their caregivers'. *Qualitative Health Research*, **25**(10), 87–98.

Twigg, J. and Buse, C. (2013) 'Dress, dementia and the embodiment of identity'. *Dementia*, **12** (3), 326–336.

Weeks, J., Heaphy, B. and Donovan, C. (2001) *Same sex intimacies: Families of choice and other life experiments*. London: Routledge.

Weston, K. (1991) *Families we choose*. New York: Columbia University Press.

Whitmer, R. A., Quesenberry, C. P., Zhou, J. and Yaffe, K. (2011) 'Timing of hormone therapy and dementia: The critical window theory revisited'. *Annals of Neurology*, **69**(1), 163–169.

Winter, S. and Conway, L. (2011) *How many trans* people are there? A 2011 update incorporating new data.* www.transgenderasia.org/paper-how-many-trans-people-are-there.htm [accessed 9 August 2015].

Withall, L. (2014) *Dementia, transgender and intersex people: Do service providers really know what their needs are?* Melbourne: Alzheimer's Australia.

Witten, T. M. (2003) 'Transgender ageing: An emerging population and an emerging need'. *Review Sexologies*, **XII**(4), 15–20.

Witten, T. M. (2008) Transgender bodies, identities, and healthcare: Effects of perceived and actual violence and abuse. In J. J. Kronenfeld (ed.) *Research in the sociology of healthcare: Inequalities and disparities in health care and health – concerns of patients.* v. 25, pp. 225–249. Oxford, England: Elsevier JAI.

Witten, T. M. (2009) 'Graceful exits: III. Intersections of ageing, transgender identities and the family/Community'. *Journal GLBT Family Studies*, **5**, 36–63. Online DOI: 10.1080/15504280802595378.

Witten, T. M. (2014a) 'End of life, chronic illness, and trans-identities'. *Journal of Social Work in End-of-Life & Palliative Care*, **10**(1), 34–58.

Witten, T. M. (2014b) 'It's not all darkness: Resilience, robustness and successful aging in the trans-community'. *LGBT Health*, **1**(1), 24–33.

Witten, T. M. (2015a) Transgender ageing. In A. Goldberg (ed.) *The SAGE encyclopedia of LGBT Studies*. London: Sage.

Witten, T. M. (2015b) 'Elder transgender lesbians: Exploring the intersection of age, lesbian sexual identity, and transgender identity'. *Journal of Lesbian Studies*, **19**(1), 73–89.

Witten, T. M. and Whittle, S. P. (2004) 'TransPanthers: The graying of transgender and the law'. *The Deakin Law Review*, **9**(2), 503–522.

Wolff, J. L. and Spillman, B. (2014) 'Older adults receiving assistance with physician visits and prescribed medications and their family caregivers: Prevalence, characteristics and hours of care'. *Journals of Gerontology Series B: Psychological Sciences and Social Sciences*, **69**(7), S65–S72. DOI: 10.1093/geronb/gbu119.

9 The complexity of trans*/gender identities

Implications for dementia care

Chryssy Hunter, Jenny-Anne Bishop and Sue Westwood

Introduction

In this chapter, we will discuss the complexity and fluidity of trans* identities. We contrast these with mainstream understandings of trans* lives and discuss the implications for later life care for trans* people with dementia. We will situate our discussion in the context of the increased visibility and confidence of trans* populations in the United Kingdom (UK) in the early twenty-first century. This is a time when limited legal recognition and protections have now been enacted in the UK, and when trans* issues are increasingly part of mainstream discussion. This is also a time when public health and social care systems are under increasing pressure to respond to issues of diversity in dementia care while also having to deal with constraints upon resources. We identify some core good practice guidelines in working with trans* people with dementia. Recognising the lack of UK-specific research in this field to date, we also begin a conversation which explores potential directions for future research to inform policy and practice.

Problems with conceptualising trans* issues

Persson has observed that 'transgender elders are both underserved and understudied. Neither the aetiology nor prevalence of transgender is well understood' (Persson, 2009: 633). This quote captures part of the reason why there is so little information on older transgender people in general and therefore the subset of trans* people with dementia. We do not know how many trans* people there are (Meier and Labuski, 2013), including in the UK (Reed *et al.*, 2009; GIRES, 2011), and in a very real way it is difficult to say what or who should be counted under the trans* umbrella, especially as the understanding of what trans* is or can be continues to evolve (Stryker and Whittle, 2006).

Trans* is an umbrella term which covers the sex/gender identity spectrum: transgender, transsexual, transvestite, genderqueer, genderfluid, non-binary, genderless, agender, non-gendered, third gender, two-spirit, bigender and other sex/gender non-conformity (Tompkins, 2014). However, the term is limited in that not all the individuals clustered under the umbrella would identify with it and that it engages with binary notions of sex/gender (even when describing those people who reject them) which many 'trans*' individuals would refute (Currah, 2006). There are an increasing number of people who identify as non-binary or gender fluid (Reed *et al.*, 2009), which is to say they do not identify themselves as having a primary sex/gender identity of exclusively female or male, or even of *either* female or male. That said it is also important to acknowledge that there are many trans* people who do identify very strongly within the binary, that is as either male or female. Some transsexual individuals who have transitioned[1] understand their transitions as processes of alignment with their 'inner' selves, and at the perceived conclusion of their transitions to have completed a journey to either female or male congruence of embodiment and expression with identity. There are ongoing contestations within trans* discourses, particularly about the ontological implications of those who transition. It is crucial to uphold and recognise the validity of individual self-identification. In discussing care issues it is important to approach the broad range of trans* possibilities as equally valid and deserving of respect and understanding.

This diversity of identity within trans* populations also means understanding that, while there is a growing trans* political movement, not all trans* people identify with it. This is particularly the case for those individuals with binary identities who have transitioned. Post-transition, once they have achieved social and/or physical alignment, many are comfortable to get on with their lives and do not wish to engage with the trans* movement. Their experiences are further differentiated between those who transition earlier in their lives, and those who do so later in life (Cook-Daniels, 2006; Bailey, 2012). Trans* people also engage with all possibilities of sexualities and sexual identity, both fixed and fluid, including lesbian, gay, bisexual and heterosexual as well as asexual (people with a lack of/no sexual attraction/desire) and pansexual (sexual/romantic attraction to people across the gender/sexuality spectrums).

Because of this diversity, rather than thinking of a unified trans* community, it is more useful to understand different groups of trans* people as constituting a collection of sub-communities, with some shared characteristics but with many and significant differences, including a variety of different socio-political and medical aims.

UK legal context

The Gender Recognition Act (GRA) 2004 and the Equality Act (EQA) 2010 are the two key pieces of legislation that offer legal recognition and protection for trans* people in the UK. Under the GRA, an individual can obtain a new birth certificate for the gender with which they identify providing they have lived as that gender for two years previously and have a diagnosis of 'gender dysphoria' (Sharpe, 2007). The most radical aspect of the GRA when it was passed is that, contrary to some other jurisdictions, hormone treatment and/or surgery are not prerequisites for the granting of a new birth certificate. However, importantly, trans* and sex/gender non-conforming people whose identities and expressions are non-binary receive no recognition under the GRA. 'Gender Reassignment' is the protected characteristic under the EQA, affording protections from discrimination, harassment and victimisation:

> (1) A person has the protected characteristic of gender reassignment if the person is proposing to undergo, is undergoing or has undergone a process (or part of a process) for the purpose of reassigning the person's sex by changing physiological or other attributes of sex.
>
> (Equality Act 2010 c. 15 Part 2 Chapter 1 Section 7)

However, again, there is no current protection offered for people who assert their identities and present as gender neutral, genderqueer or any other identity marker that takes them outside of the binary sex/gender system. The point we are making here is that UK legislation still reinforces a gender binary system, that is, either male or female, rather than one which can accommodate gender fluidity and/or non-binary gender identities (Sharpe, 2007).

Implications of the complexities for dementia care practices with trans* people

Providing support, and particularly personal care, to trans* individuals whose bodies may not wholly or partly be congruent with their gender identity can be extremely challenging for care staff (Witten, 2014). This is in no small part because some of these individuals do not conform with the expected male/female sex/gender binary presentation and/or expressed identification. This may be further complicated by memory loss. In Chapter 2 of this volume, Sue Westwood refers to a recent article by Marshall *et al.* (2015) in which the case of Jamie, a trans* woman diagnosed with dementia, is discussed. After admission to a nursing facility, when her hormone treatment was abruptly stopped (for no apparent clinical reason) Jamie was apparently confused about her gender identity, questioning 'What am I?' and showing ambivalence about a wish to wear feminine or masculine clothing. The other residents ostracised her and her daughter discounted Jamie's prior gender transitioning, saying she was still a man. The care team were faced with a very difficult situation in finding a way to support Jamie's expression of gender without also being marginalised by other residents and Jamie's family.

Recognising how challenging this was for the team only goes to emphasise the limited extent to which trans* identities are understood and accommodated in dementia/other health and social care contexts. As Westwood observes 'the most obvious solution, that they should respond to Jamie's presentation at any given moment in time, and not try to get Jamie to conform to "either/or" binary notions of gender, does not appear to have been considered' (Westwood, Chapter 2, this volume). This gives clear and significant indications that more radical non-binary approaches to sex/gender issues were not conceptually available to the caregivers involved. Had Jamie not died, this would undoubtedly have affected the treatment Jamie received and the quality of Jamie's life. If Jamie had a Gender Recognition Certificate (GRC) this would have further compli-cated the situation for the care givers.

Good practice guidelines

Fredriksen-Goldsen *et al.* (2014b), writing about the physical and mental health of older trans* people, have called them 'an at-risk and underserved population' (p. 488). Health and social care teams working with trans* people often lack the necessary knowledge and expertise required to provide those individuals with appropriate care and support (Siverskog, 2014), especially in the context of dementia (McGovern, 2014; Withall, 2014). As a result, trans* people are very fearful about needing health and social care provision in later life, even more so in the context of dementia (Witten, 2014; see also this volume, Chapter 8). There is a growing number of good practice guidelines, both generic (in relation to older lesbian, gay, bisexual and trans* people) and specific (in relation to trans* people). Westwood *et al.* (2015), in the UK, reviewing various good practice guidelines in relation to older LGBT people, identified seven areas underpinning such guidance: inclusive consultation in service design and delivery; appropriate equality and diversity *and* LGBT-specific policies; creating a safe working and living environment for service users and staff; a robust staff training strategy; teaching appropriate language and cultural representation; person-centred assess-ment and care planning; and setting and auditing standards. Fredriksen-Goldsen *et al.* (2014a), in the USA, have identified ten core competencies for educators and providers working with older LGBT* people:

1   Critically analyse personal and professional attitudes toward sexual ori-
    entation, gender identity, and age, and understand how factors such as
    culture, religion, media, and health and human service systems influ-
    ence attitudes and ethical decision-making.

(p. 84)

2   Understand and articulate the ways that larger social and cultural con-
    texts may have negatively impacted LGBT older adults as a historically
    disadvantaged population.

(p. 85)

3   Distinguish similarities and differences within the subgroups of LGBT
    older adults, as well as their intersecting identities (such as age, gender,
    race, and health status) to develop tailored and responsive health strategies.

(p. 87)

4   Apply theories of aging and social and health perspectives and the most
    up-to-date knowledge available to engage in culturally competent prac-
    tice with LGBT older adults.

(p. 88)

5 When conducting a comprehensive biopsychosocial assessment, attend to the ways that the larger social context and structural and environmental risks and resources may impact LGBT older adults.

(p. 89)

6 When using empathy and sensitive interviewing skills during assessment and intervention, ensure the use of language is appropriate for working with LGBT older adults to establish and build rapport.

(p. 91)

7 Understand and articulate the ways in which agency, program, and service policies do or do not marginalize and discriminate against LGBT older adults.

(p. 93)

8 Understand and articulate the ways that local, state, and federal laws negatively and positively impact LGBT older adults, to advocate on their behalf.

(p. 94)

9 Provide sensitive and appropriate outreach to LGBT older adults, their families, caregivers and other supports to identify and address service gaps, fragmentation, and barriers that impact LGBT older adults.

(p. 96)

10 Enhance the capacity of LGBT older adults and their families, caregivers, and other supports to navigate aging, social, and health services.

(p. 97)

With regard to specific guidance, the World Professional Association for Transgender Health (WPATH) has established detailed *Standards of Care for the Health of Transsexual, Transgender, and Gender-Nonconforming People* (Coleman *et al.*, 2012). Unfortunately, the Standards make no reference to dementia care. They do caution against 'the abrupt withdrawal of hormones' (Coleman *et al.*, 2012: 207) when a transsexual person enters an institution as there is a 'high likelihood of negative outcomes such as surgical self-treatment by autocastration, depressed mood, dysphoria, and/or suicidality' (p. 207).

Other trans*-specific good practice guidelines in relation to health and social care indicate that all providers should have policies and documentation which are trans* inclusive, and developed in consultation with trans* people (Department of Health, 2008; FORGE, 2011; Lambda Legal, 2013; National LGBT Center, 2013; Hyndal *et al.*, 2014). The following is a brief outline of good practice guidance with regard to specific aspects of care, drawn from a range of documents from across the world.

Use of appropriate language

It is vital to use the right language both with, and when referring to, a trans* individual: 'Show respect for the transgender person's right to self-determination by … using the terms they use to refer to their body, life, relationships, or identity' (FORGE, 2011: 1). Sometimes, when first meeting someone, it is not clear how they identify:

> It is not always possible to know someone's gender based on their name or how they look or sound. This is the case for all people, not just transgender people. When addressing patients we don't know, we can accidentally call them by the wrong gender, causing embarrassment. One way to prevent this mistake is by addressing people without using any terms that indicate a gender. For example, instead of asking 'How may I help you, sir?' you can simply ask, 'How may I help you?' You can also avoid using 'Mr./Mrs./Miss/Ms.' by calling someone by their first name (if this is an acceptable practice in your organization) or by using their first and last name together. You can also avoid using a person's name by tapping the person on the shoulder and saying, for example, 'Excuse me, we're ready for you now. Please come this way.' (National LGBT Center 2013: 6) [NB: we would add that a first name should only be used if acceptable to the client, which should be checked out immediately 'Hi Jane, is it OK if I use your first name?'].

Such cautious use of language applies not only when communicating directly with an individual but also when communicating within teams:

> It is also important to avoid gender terms when talking to others about a patient. For example, rather than saying 'he is here for his appointment', or 'she needs a follow-up appointment', you can say 'the patient is here in the waiting room', or 'Dr. Reed's 11:30 patient is here'. You can also use 'they' instead of 'she' or 'he'. For example, you can say: 'they are here for their 3 o'clock appointment'. Never, however, refer to a person as 'it'.
>
> (National LGBT Center, 2013: 6)

Sometimes a person's preferred name and pronoun (he/she/they) will be clear from their records. Other times this may not be clear. When in doubt, ask the person. 'If a person's gender identity is unclear, staff should 'discreetly and politely ask the [person] for [their] preferred pronoun and name' (Lambda Legal, 2013: 8). Sometimes, mistakes happen. They can be easily dealt with by a simple apology and moving on: 'I apologize for using the wrong pronoun/name. I did not mean to disrespect you' (National LGBT Center, 2013: 8).

If a person's gender identity is fluid and changeable, a person-centred approach involves responding to how the person is presenting themselves in each particular moment. If a trans* person does not consistently identify with a particular name or gender, but wishes to be addressed differently at different times, staff should go with what the person is comfortable with at any given moment in time. Similarly, people who cross-dress and/or transvestites (who do not usually change their basic gender identification but do sometimes temporarily change their gender expression/presentation) may also prefer to be addressed differently at times. This may involve staff shifting back and forth, but it is the only way to offer attuned, person-centred care, when the person at the centre of that care is shifting in their gender identification and/or gender expression/presentation.

A culture of respect

Trans* people should, obviously, be treated with respect at all times. Sadly, this has not always been their experience in care contexts, particularly with regard to mental health concerns (Witten, 2008; McNeil *et al.*, 2012). Respect is multi-faceted:

> For transgender individuals, respect must be shown for their identity and history, for their personal style (clothes, accessories, etc.), for their bodily configuration, and for their name and pronoun. Respect extends beyond direct interactions to include what you say and how you behave even outside of their presence.
>
> (FORGE, 2011: 1)

Creating a culture of respect extends beyond immediate interactions with a trans* individual to being mindful about how they are spoken about in general: 'Try to not show surprise, shock, dismay or concern when you are either told or inadvertently discover that a person is transgender' (FORGE, 2011: 1).

Care teams need to be mindful about their own cultural representations of trans* people within their teams:

> *Do not gossip or joke about transgender people*: Gossiping about someone's transition, or making fun of a person's efforts to change their gender expression, for example, should not be tolerated. In addition, only discuss a patient's transgender identity with those who need to know for providing appropriate and sensitive care. This is consistent with policies concerning discussion of all patients.
>
> *Continue to use a patient's preferred name and pronoun, even when they are not present*: This will help maintain respect for the patient and help other staff members learn the patient's preferences.
>
> *Create an environment of accountability*: Don't be afraid to politely correct your colleagues if they use the wrong names and pronouns, or if they make insensitive comments. Creating an environment of accountability and respect requires everyone to work together.
>
> (National LGBT Center, 2013: 7)

It is also essential to demonstrate the importance of remembering and understanding the patient's preferences and to discourage general and specific gossip about patients among staff. GIRES (2011) offers these basic principles in providing respectful care environments to trans* individuals:

- Trans people are a wide and very varied group of people: care should not be presumed but should be agreed with the individual
- People should be accommodated according to their presentation: the way they dress, and their current names and pronouns
- This may not always accord with the sex appearance of the chest or genitalia
- It does not depend upon their having a gender recognition certificate (GRC) or legal name change
- Privacy, confidentiality, dignity and respect are of the utmost importance
- Health records should protect the confidentiality of trans people's gender history while flagging for appropriate screening, diagnosis and treatment.

(GIRES, 2011: 1)

Person-centred care

Person-centred care involves seeing the whole person in context, not just one aspect of someone's identity. Trans* people are 'not just trans' (Department of Health, 2008: 46): they are complex individuals from a wide range of intersecting social backgrounds, with their own wants, needs, interests, likes and dislikes. Trans* individuals are, first and foremost, *people*. Person-centred care for trans* people involves being sensitive to their historical experiences of discrimination and how this may inform their anxieties when in receipt of care, especially dementia care, when they may be less well orientated to time and place: 'Transgender people report very high rates of being discriminated against.... Recognise that their hesitance in accepting help may be related to prior discrimination, not what they think about you' (FORGE, 2011: 1). Trans* people with dementia may have had previous traumatic experiences in health and social care services and they may find institutional care, and surveillance, potentially highly triggering of those previous traumas and associated feelings. Care providers need to be attuned to this and to the fact that trans* individuals may be very worried that carers will be shocked, amused, embarrassed and/or disrespectful, especially when personal care is involved. Thinking outside the box can also make a huge difference to providing care,

> Sometimes small choices can make a big difference. For example, if a trans man in a nursing home has feet that are too small for men's slippers, rather than buying women's slippers, service providers should purchase boy's slippers instead.

(AGE UK, 2011: 24)

Links should be supported and/or facilitated for trans* people with dementia to have connections with other trans* individuals: 'Help the transgender person you care for remain connected with their friends and support groups, and try to establish such ties if they do not exist' (FORGE, 2011: 1).

At the same time, care teams need to recognise that there can be tensions with some biological family members who do not accept that a person has transitioned (Witten, 2009). GIRES offers this guidance: 'views of family members may not accord with the trans person's wishes, in which case, the trans person's view takes priority' (GIRES, 2015).

Affirmative care

Care providers need to be more than simply non-discriminatory. It is not enough to not pathologise a trans* person or their gender identity. Instead, care should be provided that is both positive and affirmative, with staff demonstrating that they either fully appreciate the health and social care needs and concerns of gender variant people or are at least open to learning about them. Local trans* groups should be involved and included in consultations about the provision of care. Services should be proactive in making it clear that they welcome transgender clients/patients/services users. Premises should have, as an option, for example, single-use, gender neutral, toilet facilities.

Alzheimer's Society (UK) (2013), writing about LGB dementia care, also recommends that dementia health and social care providers review their publicity material and policy documents to ensure that the language used is inclusive. They also have this advice to staff about how to respond to disclosures:

> If the person with dementia or their carer feels able to come out to you, your first and immediate reaction will be very significant. If you feel embarrassed or surprised you might change the subject or avoid direct acknowledgement of what the person has shared with you. This might stop the person feeling comfortable with you and opening up further. Find ways to acknowledge the person ... and give reassurance that you are not prejudiced – for example, 'Thank you for telling me. It must be hard having different professionals coming in to your house, not knowing what their attitudes are', or, 'Let me know if there are any particular things we need to consider about services for you, which might make you feel more comfortable'.
>
> (Alzheimer's Society, 2013: 3)

Dementia care organisations should also ensure that all of their staff are trained annually in providing care to trans* individuals. It can be helpful to assign a member of staff to take responsibility for championing trans* issues. There should also be 'procedures in place that hold staff accountable for making negative or discriminatory comments or actions against transgender people' (National LGBT Center, 2013: 13). Staff should also be provided with guidance and support in regard to challenging prejudice and discrimination on the part of other service users, their families and friends.

Making decisions for a future self

It is important that we cultivate an environment in which trans* issues are better understood and policies that reflect this understanding are developed and enforced. It is also important that trans* individuals make their health and social care, and end-of-life, preferences known ahead of time, using legal means such as advance directives, advance decisions, living wills, Powers of Attorney, and so on (Knauer, 2009). This is essential in order to ensure that a trans* person's wishes are not overruled by family members who may not respect their trans* identity. However, a complicated and sensitive issue is how much a trans* person should make decisions for their future self in regard to gender identity. Many trans* people who have had to struggle long and hard to reach a place where they are living with the gender expressions they are comfortable with, are fearful that they will be treated as the 'wrong' gender by health and social care staff (Witten, 2014, and this volume, Chapter 8). They are also worried that they will, with dementia, 'forget' the truth of their hard-fought gender identities (National LGB&T Partnership, 2012). This can cause some advocates to encourage trans* individuals to try and lock in their future self (with dementia) to their gender identity in the present day, by the use of advance directives, etc. (e.g. Prachniak, 2014). This can potentially create both ethical dilemmas and practical problems.

The issue of identity, personhood and dementia has been, and continues to be, the subject of considerable debate (O'Connor *et al.*, 2007). Part of that debate involves whether and, if so, how, a core self endures with the general memory loss and cognitive decline associated with dementia (Caddell and Clare, 2010), and also the personality changes associated with particular kinds of dementia, for example frontotemporal dementia (Alzheimer's Society, 2013). Tied in with this is the extent to which a person could or should make moral judgements (Mendez *et al.*, 2005) on behalf of a future self with dementia, when that future self may be very different from the present one. Should, for example, a married individual with a history of monogamy be able to insist that a still-married future self with dementia not be allowed to be non-monogamous when in a care home (Bauer *et al.*, 2014)?

An extended version of this ethical issue relates to whether one could or should choose the gender identity of a future self, particularly given that that gender identity can be fluid. Not only can gender identity shift and change for some trans* people across time, individuals who have identified as cisgender for most of their lives may also seek to express greater gender fluidity which they have previously suppressed. The practical problem is in relation to what it would mean for a trans* person with dementia to have a gender identity imposed on them (by their historical self) if they no longer wanted to identify with it. A person-centred approach, we would suggest, would necessitate responding to the trans* person with dementia (or anyone who expresses gender fluidity) as they identify at any given point in time, rather than forcing them to align with their historical self/selves. This does, of course, throw up huge challenges for many trans* people and their carers in relation to identity, and notions of a core gender identity, for some, which dementia may undermine. The sensitive use of life story work (McKeown *et al.*, 2010) can help to validate the life history of a trans* person with dementia whilst also responding to their gender expression in the moment, even if it is at variance with that history.

Conclusion

This chapter has considered the complexity of trans* identities and the implications for the care of trans* people with dementia. We have placed our discussion in the context of the increased visibility and confidence of trans* populations in the UK. We have identified some core good practice guidelines in working with trans* people with dementia, focusing on the use of appropriate language, creating cultures of respect, delivering person-centred and affirmative care. There is a need for comprehensive guidelines on good standards of care specifically in relation to trans* individuals with dementia, and for rigorous auditing of the extent to which dementia care organisations comply with them. Such compliance is not only an issue of good practice, but also of compliance with the law, particularly, in the UK, the Gender Recognition Act 2004 and the Equality Act 2010.

There is a paucity of research on the experiences of trans* individuals affected by dementia and on delivering services to such individuals (McGovern, 2014). As a result, there is an urgent need to both include trans* individuals in mainstream dementia research and to conduct research which specifically focuses on the experiences of trans* people. Research is also urgently needed to understand how best to support individuals with dementia who have gender identity issues, which may include people who have not previously identified as trans*.

The issue of advocacy is important for all older people who lack capacity, and, for LGBT* people in particular, who are more likely to be marginalised in dementia care. Advocacy is paramount for trans* people affected by dementia, because of the unique combination of issues which affect them, and their care, and which can raise particular rights issues. Yet, non-statutory advocacy for people with dementia in general, never mind LGBT* people, is thin on the ground. This raises the very real possibility that trans* individuals' rights in dementia care contexts may not be upheld, when they lack capacity and they do not have affirming social networks, and/or appointed attorneys to represent them. Putting legal arrangements in place to ensure people are there to speak on their behalf, in the way the trans* person would wish, is of vital importance. At the same time, as the previous section has demonstrated, a trans* person's arrangements for their future should allow flexibility for their future self to determine how they wish to identify and present themselves.

With a growing number of openly trans* individuals and a rapidly expanding number of people choosing to transition, many more trans* people with, or developing, dementia are likely to be presenting to dementia services. It is essential that dementia services and dementia care teams educate themselves about trans* individuals affected by dementia. They should be ready to meet the needs of trans* individuals with dementia before they are confronted with those needs, rather than playing catch-up while trying to support the person and their friends/ family at the same time. Developing services which can respond to the complexity, individuality and non-conformity of trans* lives will enhance those services, not only in relation to trans* people with dementia, but also in terms of providing truly person-centred care. As the needs and concerns of trans* people demonstrate, the only way to work in a person-centred manner is to meet the individual on their own terms, responding to what is important to that person at any given moment in time. Learning about meeting the needs of trans* people with dementia will expand our wider understanding of providing individualised, personalised, care for all.

Note

1 Transitioning is the process whereby people whose gender and biological sex do not line up take steps to achieve greater alignment through how they identify and/or present themselves. Some seek medical treatment to do so, some do not.

References

Age UK (2011) *Transgender Issues in Later Life*. London: Age UK.
Alzheimer's Society (2013) *What is Frontotemporal Dementia?* Factsheet 404. London: Alzheimer's Society.
Bailey, L. (2012) Trans ageing: thoughts on a life course approach in order to better understand trans lives. In R. Ward, I. Rivers and M. Sutherland (eds) *Lesbian, Gay, Bisexual and Transgender Ageing: Biographical Approaches for Inclusive Care and Support*, pp. 51–66. London and Philadelphia, PA: Jessica Kingsley Publishers.
Bauer, M., Nay, R., Tarzia, L. and Fetherstonhaugh, D. (2014) 'We need to know what's going on': views of family members toward the sexual expression of people with dementia in residential aged care. *Dementia*, **13**(5), 571–585.
Caddell, L. S. and Clare, L. (2010) The impact of dementia on self and identity: A systematic review. *Clinical Psychology Review*, **30**(1), 113–126.
Coleman, E., Bockting, W., Botzer, M., Cohen-Kettenis, P., DeCuypere, G., Feldman, J. and Zucker, K. (2012) Standards of care for the health of transsexual, transgender, and gender-nonconforming people, version 7. *International Journal of Transgenderism*, **13**(4), 165–232.
Cook-Daniels, L. (2006) Trans ageing. In D. Kimmel, T. Rose and S. David, S. (eds) *Lesbian, Gay, Bisexual and Transgender Ageing*, pp. 20–35. New York: Columbia University Press.
Currah, P. (2006) Gender pluralisms under the transgender umbrella. In P. Currah, R. M. Juang and S. P. Minter (eds) *Transgender Rights*, pp. 3–31. Minneapolis: University of Minnesota Press.

Department of Health (2008) *Trans: A Practical Guide for the NHS.* London: Department of Health.

FORGE (2011) *Quick Tips for Caregivers of Transgender Clients.* Available from: https://forge-forward.org/2011/06/quick-tips-for-caregivers-of-transgender-clients/ [downloaded 16 June 2015].

Fredriksen-Goldsen, K. I., Hoy-Ellis, C. P., Goldsen, J., Emlet, C. A., and Hooyman, N. R. (2014a) Creating a vision for the future: key competencies and strategies for culturally competent practice with lesbian, gay, bisexual, and transgender (LGBT) older adults in the health and human services. *Journal of Gerontological Social Work.* Advanced online access. DOI: 10.1080/01634372.2014.890690.

Fredriksen-Goldsen, K. I., Cook-Daniels, L., Kim, H.-J., Erosheva, E. A., Emlet, C. A. Hoy-Ellis, C. P., Goldsen, J. and Muraco, A. (2014b) Physical and mental health of transgender older adults: an at-risk and underserved population. *The Gerontologist*, **54**(3), 488–500.

Gender Identity Research and Education Society (GIRES) (2011) *The Number of Gender Variant People in the UK – Update 2011*, Available from: www.gires.org.uk/assets/Research-Assets/Prevalence2011.pdf [downloaded 23 September 2015].

Gender Identity Research and Education Society (GIRES) (2015) *Hospital Accommodation of Trans People and Gender Variant Children.* Available from: www.gires.org.uk/health/hospital-accommodation-of-trans-people-and-gender-variant-children [downloaded 23 September 2015].

Hyndal, P., Yates, J., Rutherford, S., Stanley, S., Sweeney, L., Lindsay, C., Savigny, J. and Green, J. (2014) *Navigating Diversity: Information for Transgender, Intersex and Diverse Communities and Service Providers.* Ainslie, Australia: A Gender Agenda. Available from: http://genderrights.org.au/sites/default/files/u9/AGA%20InfoPack%20 2014.pdf [downloaded 16 July 2015].

Knauer, N. (2009) LGBT elder law: toward equity in aging. *Harvard Journal of Law and Gender*, 32, 301–358.

Lambda Legal (2013) *Creating Equal Access to Quality Health Care for Transgender Patients: Transgender-Affirming Hospital Policies.* New York: Lambda Legal. Available at www.lgbtagingcenter.org/resources/resource.cfm?r=625#sthash.I8VkGiwq.dpuf [downloaded 16 June 2015].

Marshall, J., Cooper, M. and Rudnick, A. (2015). Gender dysphoria and dementia: a case report. *Journal of Gay & Lesbian Mental Health*, **19**(1), 112–117.

McGovern, J. (2014) The forgotten: dementia and the aging LGBT community. *Journal of Gerontological Social Work*, **57**(8), 845-857.

McKeown, J., Clarke, A., Ingleton, C., Ryan, T. and Repper, J. (2010) The use of life story work with people with dementia to enhance person-centred care. *International Journal of Older People Nursing*, **5**(2), 148–158.

McNeil, J., Bailey, L., Ellis, S., Morton, J. and Regan, M. (2012) *Trans Mental Health and Emotional Wellbeing Study 2012.* Edinburgh: The Scottish Transgender Alliance.

Meier, S. C. and Labuski, C. M. (2013) The demographics of the transgender population. In A. K. Baumle (ed.) *International Handbook on the Demography of Sexuality*, pp. 289–327. Springer: Netherlands. DOI 10.1007/9978-94-007-5512-3_16, 289-327.

Mendez, M. F., Anderson, E. and Shapira, J. S. (2005) An investigation of moral judgement in frontotemporal dementia. *Cognitive and behavioral neurology*, **18**(4), 193–197.

National LGB&T Partnership (2012) *Trans Health Factsheet on Ageing – Rising to the challenge.* https://nationallgbtpartnershipdotorg.files.wordpress.com/2012/07/np-trans-health-factsheet-ageing-final.pdf [downloaded 23 September 2015].

National LGBT Center (2013) *Affirmative Care for Transgender and Gender Non-Conforming People: Best Practices for Front-line Health Care Staff.* Boston, MA: Fenway Institute. www.lgbthealtheducation.org/wp-content/uploads/13-017_TransBest-PracticesforFrontlineStaff_v6_02-19-13_FINAL.pdf [downloaded 23 September 2015].

O'Connor, D., Phinney, A., Smith, A., Small, J., Purves, B., Perry, J. and Beattie, L. (2007) Personhood in dementia care. Developing a research agenda for broadening the vision. *Dementia*, **6**(1), 121–142.

Persson, D. I. (2009) Unique challenges of transgender aging: implications from the literature. *Journal of Gerontological Social Work*, **52**(6), 633–646.

Prachniak, C. (2014) *Creating End-of-Life Documents for Trans Individuals: An Advocate's Guide.* New York: The National Resource Center on LGBT Aging & Whitman Walker Health.

Reed, B., Rhodes, S., Schofield, P. and Wylie, K. (2009) *Gender Variance in the UK: Prevalence, Incidence, Growth and Geographic Distribution.* Ashstead, Surrey: Gender Identity Research and Education Society (GIRES). Available from: http://xa.yimg.com/kq/groups/17851560/542410794/name/GenderVarianceUK-report.pdf [downloaded 23 September 2015].

Sharpe, A. N. (2007) Endless sex: The Gender Recognition Act 2004 and the persistence of a legal category. *Feminist Legal Studies*, **15**(1), 57–84.

Siverskog, A. (2014) 'They just don't have a clue': Transgender aging and implications for Social Work. *Journal of Gerontological Social Work*, **57**(2–4), 386–406.

Stryker, S. and Whittle, S. (eds) (2006) *The Transgender Studies Reader.* New York: Routledge.

Tompkins, A. (2014) Asterisk. *TSQ: Transgender Studies Quarterly*, **1**(1–2), 26–27.

Westwood, S., King, A., Almack, K. and Suen, Y.-T. (2015) Good practice in health and social care provision for older LGBT people. In J. Fish and K. Karban (eds) *Social Work and Lesbian, Gay, Bisexual and Trans Health Inequalities: International Perspectives*, pp. 145–159. Bristol: Policy Press.

Withall, L. (2014) *Dementia, Transgender and Intersex People: Do Service Providers Really Know What Their Needs Are?* Melbourne: Alzheimer's Australia. https://sa.fight-dementia.org.au/sites/default/files/130739_LGBTI%20Discussion%20Paper.2-21.pdf.

Witten, T. M. (2008) Transgender bodies, identities, and healthcare: effects of perceived and actual violence and abuse. In J. J. Kronenfeld (ed.) *Research in the Sociology of Healthcare: Inequalities and Disparities in Health Care and Health – Concerns of Patients*. v. 25, pp. 225–249. Oxford, England: Elsevier JAI.

Witten, T. M. (2009) Graceful exits: intersection of aging, transgender identities, and the family/community. *Journal of GLBT Family Studies*, **5**, 36–62.

Witten, T. M. (2014) End of life, chronic illness, and trans-identities. *Journal of Social Work in End-of-Life & Palliative Care*, **10**(1), 34–58.

10 Looking back whilst moving forward

LGBT* carers' perspectives

Elizabeth Price

Introduction

As we have noted elsewhere in the book, this volume represents a significant step forward in the mapping and understanding of diverse experiences of dementia. The book is, of course, timely, yet there is also a sense that a consideration of the ideas, issues and very personal experiences presented here might reasonably be perceived as a somewhat tardy appearance in the context of the study of dementia more broadly. Nonetheless, for many readers, I'm sure, this book will be a first opportunity to situate the experience of dementia in LGBT* people's lives (and vice versa). For me, however, the book and, in particular, this chapter also represents something of an ironic dénouement.

A number of years ago, as a social worker working with people diagnosed with dementia, I had a chance conversation with a colleague who expressed genuine surprise when I commented that the world of dementia appeared to have a significant absence – LGBT* people's experiences of the condition. His surprise was centred on the notion that dementia does not discriminate, that a person's sexuality should have no bearing on their cognitive function nor their subsequent experiences. His genuine question, 'why is it different for them?' pre-empted an exploratory journey that has spanned the past 15 years and which has witnessed a growing, if long overdue, interest in person-centred approaches to dementia in which an LGBT* perspective has a legitimate voice.

The work which was the outcome of my early explorations has been variously published elsewhere (Price, 2005, 2006, 2008, 2010, 2011a, 2011b; Manthorpe and Price, 2003, 2006) and, inevitably, the data on which the work is based is demonstrating signs of increasing empirical age. Reading my colleagues' work for this volume, however, has very much persuaded me that, whilst our theoretical perspective on LGBT* people's experiences of dementia is developing swiftly and our attempts to communicate the complexities of life as an LGBT* person with dementia to those who are tasked with supporting them are increasingly welcome, it would seem that applying the principles of genuinely person-centred care for LGBT* people with dementia remains, at the very least, profoundly challenging. In short, I wonder just how much, or indeed how little, in the past decade, things have really changed. As such, I decided to return to my earlier work (which focused specifically on the experiences of gay and lesbian carers who were supporting a person diagnosed with dementia) with a view to consolidating the issues it raised and to perhaps invite a new consideration of the experiences it reflects. This chapter represents, therefore, a range of chronologies – theoretical, practical and personal.

The L, the G, the B and the T: creating inclusive spaces in the study of dementia

One of the problems we have in exploring and understanding the experiences of LGBT* carers is the fact that sexual/gender identity are often invisible facets of the general caring project and experience. My own work purposefully focused only on the experiences of lesbian women and gay men – the work omitted to focus on the B and the T elements of the ubiquitous, and often uncritically employed, sexualities and gender identities abbreviation. Given the power of 'LGBT' as a shorthand, catch all, abbreviation, this approach perhaps requires some explanation (but not excuse), as it is undeniably out of vogue. My rationale for this was, as I note above, entirely purposeful, because the 'homogenising discourse' (Westwood, 2015: 2) that can be the result of research which makes claims of inclusivity can, ironically, marginalise and exclude, as Brotman *et al.* (2002) suggested:

> Research which claims to include bisexual and transgender populations alongside gay and lesbian populations, is actually focussed entirely on the latter groups. This reinforces the marginalized and invisible status of bisexual and transgender people.
>
> (p. 2)

There is, of course, a more generalised neglect of the lived experiences of bisexual and trans* people in the context of health and social care research and practice (it is not something peculiar to the experience of dementia). In studies of ageing, for example, sexuality itself has only relatively recently received any critical attention and, as I have outlined elsewhere, in the study of dementia in particular, the lack of attention afforded to issues of sexuality perhaps reflects a tendency 'to relegate certain issues, which are often difficult and challenging, to the margins of academic and professional discourses' (Innes *et al.*, 2004: 11). Jones (2010) reflects on these omissions in the context of bisexual people's access to, and use of, health and social care, whilst Westwood *et al.* (2015) focus on the same issue, but specifically from carers' perspectives (for a more comprehensive overview of these omissions and the ways in which various authors have addressed them, see Chapter 1, this volume).

At the inception of my work, I felt strongly that issues of bisexuality and trans* identities should deserve distinct and separate attention. Indeed, as Tarynn Witten's and Chryssy Hunter, Jenny-Anne Bishop and Sue Westwood's chapters (Chapters 8 and 9, respectively) in this volume suggest, we are, only now, beginning to try to understand the experiences of trans* people in the context of health and social care, and dementia in particular. Here again, there is still a very limited literature that focuses specifically on the experiences of trans* people who access health and social care services (see, for example, Fredriksen-Goldsen *et al.*, 2014; Hines, 2007). Nonetheless, the passage of time has thankfully begun to afford new insights into (and questions around) the thorny issue of inclusivity and, at last, bisexual and trans* people's experiences are assuming a more central and critically important aspect of health and social care research (as some of the chapters in this book amply illustrate). At the time of pursuing my own explorations, however, I felt that to artificially amalgamate the issues faced by gay, lesbian, bisexual and trans* people would be both conceptually and methodologically imprudent. It should be stressed that I remain to be convinced that a more contemporary methodological consideration would necessarily generate a different decision.

By way of further complication, of course, the grouping together of gay men and lesbian women, assuming that a gay or lesbian identity 'made these men and women more similar than gender made them unique' (Quam, 1993: 11) also requires some justification.

> Gay men and lesbians are more different from one another than they are similar, both in their orientation and their gender.... Thus any attempt to join them for the purpose of sociological research is both artificial and misleading. Joining them under one umbrella of research on 'homosexuals' has the effect of diluting our understanding of each and trivialising the experience of both.
>
> (Wahler and Gabbay, 1997: 2)

I would argue, however, that whilst I am conscious of the risk of producing simplistic or misleading conclusions, there are sufficient parallels, particularly with regard to the perception of gay men and lesbians in the public consciousness and, as I will demonstrate here, the subsuming nature of a diagnosis of dementia, to permit a collective consideration of gay men and lesbians' experiences in the context of providing support for a person with dementia. For the respondents in my work, commonality was generated through the experience of caring for a person with dementia which, as I will outline in this chapter, became, for many, an all-consuming and enveloping experience which cut across, and was reflected through, a person's sense of self and their identity, becoming, in the process, a catalyst for critically reflexive opportunities and outcomes.

It should be said at the outset, of course, that providing support for a person with dementia generates its own, very particular, commonality (whilst always being mindful of the specificities of individual experience) that centres on the collateral impact of the condition. Respondents left work, lost friends and a social life and experienced increasing isolation. The physical and psychological impacts of providing care also took their toll, as they would for anyone in this situation. What I am keen to do here, however, is to focus, purposefully, on the specificities of providing care for a person with dementia as a gay or lesbian person. Thus, the commonality is assumed (fully explicated elsewhere) whilst the specificity requires, I would argue, more critical attention.

Ways and means

Recruitment for my original project was initially obtained through a contact within the Alzheimer's Society and, subsequently, snowballing techniques accounted for the majority of other respondents via leaflet distribution, journal articles, conference presentations and personal recommendation. All participants were provided with project information outlining the aims and objectives of the study and each person completed consent forms. Semi-structured interviews were undertaken with participants in the style of a 'guided conversation' (Kvale, 1996), exploring a range of key themes focusing, specifically, on their experiences of providing care for a person diagnosed with dementia.

Respondents ranged in age from 23 to 67. The majority were caring (or had cared for) a parent who had a diagnosis of dementia. Only two people cared for a partner with dementia, whilst two people cared for friends. Over half the respondents were in partner relationships, some of these (8) were long term (more than 20 years). Only two of the older (post 50) respondents lived without a partner, a finding which is largely at odds with other research in this area, which suggests that older gay and lesbian people are more likely than their heterosexual counterparts to enter older age alone (see e.g. Cahill *et al.*, 2000). All interviews were recorded and transcribed verbatim and data analysis developed common and contrary themes using a constant thematic comparative method.

Families, friends and constructions of care

It is, of course, to the 'family', a uniquely privileged construct (McAlister *et al.*, 2014), that we customarily turn when seeking to understand the experience of caring for a person with dementia. There is an implicit expectation that 'family' will be available to 'care' when a family member requires support. 'Family' is, of course, a notion understood, for the most part, in the context of biology, not choice, though it is often a spouse who will be the person to provide support for a person with dementia, in whose absence adult children will take on the primary caring role (Collins and Jones, 1998; Hirst, 2004). The nature of this care is profoundly gendered, of course, the adult daughter being posited as the archetypal care giver (Price, 2011a), a role referred to by Manthorpe (2003) as the 'spinster model', and, by Hash (2001) as the 'woman in the middle' phenomenon. Care provided in and through the family is also filtered through a heteronormative lens, the provision of care embodying 'a whole conglomerate of linked institutions', including love, gender, and reciprocity (Plummer, 1992) and, those caring relationships which sit outside a normative heterosexual family model – those carers who transgress normative expectations of who should provide care and the nature of the care provided –

can be seen to simultaneously transgress expectations of who *should* care and *how* the role of 'carer' is most properly invoked and performed.

The interpersonal dynamics and relationships which constitute family practice are often poorly scrutinised or explored in the context of the provision of care for people with dementia. Rather, the 'family' simply has a presumed status and role to play. The minutiae of family relationships and family practices can, thus, become inadvertently marginalised, the result being the fact that individuals in the family are unproblematically re-cast as 'carers' or 'family carers' (Price and Walker, 2015) losing, in the process, critical facets of relationships that generate, constitute and maintain inter-family dynamics. Through various incarnations of community care policy in particular, family relationships have been formalised through the dual processes of policy guidance and legislative initiative which have obscured the particularities of family relationships in favour of the amorphous, and, legislatively useful, notion of 'family' which, by default, generates, operates and perpetuates heteronorms (the heterosexual ideas and values which guide and inform social, familial, cultural and political etc. beliefs and practices) – one of the reasons, I would argue, why LGBT* people are effectively invisible in the context of family 'care'.

The semantic shift, from 'family' member to 'carer' is, thus, particularly significant in the context of LGBT* people as, whilst it recognises the important role family members might play in supporting a person with dementia, it can also obscure the ways in which this semantic recasting might impact upon, and reflect, people's relationships and experiences. The family, as noted earlier, is, for many, a presumed generative institution where close and loving relationships are customarily enacted. For some LGBT* people, however, the family cannot be an uncritically assumed generative space, due, in no small part, to the ways in which issues around sexuality and gender identity might have impacted on family dynamics. This was certainly the case for many of the people who shared their stories with me. For Dawn and Lyn, who both found themselves caring for a mother with dementia, it was their relationship with sisters (similarly expected to 'care') which they reflected upon:

> DAWN: There's a long history, I've had a huge long relationship with my sister about my sexuality. I know she still feels it would be better if I was heterosexual. In her heart she still thinks it's a bit sad...
>
> (Price, 2011a: 1295)

> LYN: [my sister is an] Evangelical Christian, so has struggled massively with my sexuality ... has kind of campaigned ... thinks I should rot in hell really. She reads the Daily Mail and I did not need to hear anything she had to say to me. That was my point with it. You know, I'd explored it [sexuality] with the rest of my family and that felt very important to do, so normally I would do up front on the table, let's look at it. With my sister, I thought I just could not see anything useful in that. I knew what she thought.
>
> (Price, 2011a: 1295)

For these two women in particular, caring provided not only a contested relationship space, but also an ironically generative one. This generativity, for many of the respondents in my work, often centred upon the form and quality of people's relationships both pre- and post caregiving. For Dawn, the renegotiation and re-evaluation of her relationship with her sister was an unexpected benefit of her caregiving experience and, despite her complex pre-caregiving relationship she noted,

> DAWN: …the only thing positive was that we [sister and brother-in-law] formed such friendships over it and we had such a brilliant time together, surviving it.
>
> (Price, 2011a: 1295)

Dawn also reflected upon her relationship with her mother and focused on the ways in which the experience of dementia had shifted her understanding of her mother's reluctance to come to terms with the fact that Dawn was a lesbian.

> DAWN: I didn't love her, I never loved her … but I became very compassionate and fond of her as a dementing woman because she changed so much and became really sweet. This is bizarre isn't it, and me and my sister would arrive and we'd gird our loins, you know, and we'd be going to do this and do this and she'd say 'Oh, darlings, oh lovie' and we'd be like 'Who's she talking to?' And it took us ages to realise that this was the changed woman…. And for me, my experience of mum and her dementia was actually a lovely time to … not resolve issues because I could never say, 'Mum, why are you such a bitch?'… But I sorted it out with myself.
>
> (Price, 2011a: 1296)

For Lyn too, the nature of relationships began to shift as the realities of her mother's dementia became increasingly apparent. Despite their apparent differences, Lyn suggested that her mother's illness, and the necessity to work alongside her sister to help provide care, provided a range of possibilities for rethinking the relationship she and her sister shared:

> LYN: So interestingly, the point at which mum went into hospital … was the point at which we [she and her sister] started doing much better together…. 'Cos I was doing the sleep deprivation and falling apart thing and she was, she was very supportive actually, and I remember coming away thinking how strange, that something as awful as that should bring us to a place where, you know, it, I mean, it felt like it kind of cut through.
>
> (Price, 2011a: 1299)

Family relationships, then, and their inherent challenges and opportunities as a lesbian or gay person, are the starting point for this analysis of the journey through care. Long before dementia became an issue, relationships were sometimes strained and, occasionally, fractured by and around issues of sexuality and, whilst sexuality was not the prime mediator in caring relationships at this point, as dementia began to assume a more central position in daily life, people's lives began the subtle shift into the realities of supporting a person with cognitive loss.

The journey to diagnosis

The journey through dementia starts, for many people, with the act, or at least the process, of diagnosis – the starting point for a journey into 'the kingdom of the sick' (Sontag, 2001). For a person with dementia, in particular, diagnosis can be a critical point, which constitutes 'a salient juncture between illness and disease, patient and doctor, complaint and explanation' (Jutel, 2009: 278). Of course, the diagnostic journey can be long, as the onset of cognitive difficulty can be insidious, yet fraught with a developing sense that there is, most certainly, 'something wrong'. For many of the respondents who shared their stories of care with me, it was at the point of diagnosis where issues of sexuality began to shape the nature of the illness journey. These issues overlaid people's, largely, negative, experiences of diagnosis, the 'diagnostic moment' (Jutel, 2009) constituting an uncomfortable and unpredictable shift in time, but always marking a critical point in the illness journey. Quotations without reference are from my original data and have not been previously published elsewhere.

Anna, whose partner was diagnosed with dementia, related her experience of diagnosis:

> I think the whole thing wasn't handled well at that point. Not especially because we were a gay couple ... but it was like, [consultant] didn't just say, well, you know, are you ok? Do you want to come back next week and talk about this? This must be a shock, are you ok? How are you getting home? Nothing like that, it was 'Well, that's [dementia] what I think it is' and half an hour later, we were outside and I was thinking ... 'oh!'

For all respondents, it was in the assimilation and response to the diagnosis of dementia that sexuality began to emerge as a resonant theme. For many, it came to constitute a critical component of their understandings and experiences of dementia, as they negotiated both the condition and others' responses to their lifestyles.

For many people, the diagnosis of dementia (for a parent, in particular) added a further layer of complexity to the ways in which previously difficult relationships were married with the challenges of managing cognitive loss. The person with dementia, for example, might forget the fact that their son or daughter was gay or lesbian. People then were required to decide whether or not to engage in a ceaseless revelation of their sexuality.

TOM: It's [being gay] not in the forefront of experience, so I don't think he [dad] knows. So, if I went over today and mentioned Carl, my partner, I'd … it would be news to him…. And it would be news again tomorrow and the day after … so, it was one of those situations where, erm, I think we also decided, an unspoken decision, that it would cause, to keep bringing this into the situation would cause more strife than it was worth really.

In response, Tom decided it was better to effectively go back into a closet he had come out of many years earlier in his relationship with his father, negating and, arguably, invalidating his original coming out experiences.

Stereotypes and sensibilities

As the implications of diagnosis began to assert themselves, the specific dynamics of sexuality within family structures began to emerge as a critical theme in people's narratives. The trio of interpersonal dynamics, referred to by Plummer (1992) above, began to impact in very specific ways. For the women, gendered expectations were married with a lesbian specific pressure to care which was generated from stereotypical notions of lesbian women's lives. As women, they were mindful of gendered expectations, but these were exacerbated by biological families' heteronormative perceptions. They were, thus, simply available (without the heteronormative trappings of 'families' of their own) to care. As such, lesbian women were simply expected to 'get on with it'. One woman said that, as a single, lesbian woman with no children, she was presumed to have no other more pressing responsibilities. She was, therefore, simply 'available' and expected to provide care – an example, perhaps, of the ways in which a lack of heteronormative signifiers allows for a blanket negation of lesbian women's lifestyles and commitments.

DAWN: Oh yes, oh yes, we should be there. We should give up our lives and move into the village [to care for mother], you know, oh it was awful.
(Price 2011a: 1294)

CATH: I think we lesbian women pick up the pieces and clear up the crap – to put not too fine a point on it!
(Price 2011a: 1294)

It was, ironically, one of the male respondents who, perhaps best, summed up this perspective. Joe, and his partner, Ewan, cared for a friend, Violet. Violet had been a neighbour whom Joe had become firm friends with and, when Violet's difficulties meant she could no longer manage in her own home, Joe and Ewan had welcomed her into theirs.

JOE: I think maybe for lesbians, there's like stereotypes of, like, being a spinster and, you know, like all those kind of horrible stereotypes. And so, it might be like, if you're not 'the marrying kind' if you're a spinster type, then maybe you will look after your parents because you've got nothing better to do. You're not going to marry ... you know.

Stereotype was a resonant theme for Joe; one which had a great bearing on his own experience. He reflected on the ways in which service providers used stereotypes to underpin their attitudes and approaches:

> JOE: I think just generally their attitude would be that they would, the stereotype of, of gay men being quite kind of erm ... passive and accepting and nice.... You know, I think. And being accommodating and being like.... Err... a bit funny and not rocking the boat, not causing trouble. I think that social workers would tend to think that we'd be more flexible 'cos we've not got kids, we'd be more flexible 'cos we can be. We'd be more flexible because, err, because we don't have to kind of ... it's like we haven't got anything better to do, you know. And because we're, like, fun, we're fun, gay guys, we're like, all that kind of fun side of it and sometimes it would work for you, because you'd be chatting to the social worker who would take your call because they'd know you'd be like nice and everything. But then, other times, if you were expecting a visit from somebody or whatever, they'd quite happily phone you up and say 'Oh, we can't come today' because they'd know, as a kind of gay man who's a little bit camp, a little bit daft, a little bit accommodating, a little bit fun and all those kind of stereotypes, they'd see that in me and think, right, he'll be alright about it. Joe's always alright about everything. Whereas, if it was like a heterosexual bloke, like the stereotypes for that would be like not flex-ible, not this, not that. They would phone me and cancel, rather than phone them and cancel. They'd let me down before they'd let them down, because they know that I would, I wouldn't be complaining as quick as somebody else, I would take more on and I think they just took advantage of that...

Joe's understanding of the ways in which stereotypes operated on multiple levels was evident in his experiences of 'mundane heterosexism' (Peel, 2001) which he encountered on a regular basis when caring for Violet. He reported, for example, that service providers would refer to Ewan as Joe's 'special friend' and made erroneous assumptions about their lives together:

> JOE: We were talking [with a care provider]about getting Violet dressed and everything ... and I was saying Yeah, 'cos we bought all Violet's clothes, so we kind of erm, and, in a way, we made sure she was fantas-tic, you know what I mean, she wasn't just like, you know a lot of people who are like cared for, they just wear easy to wear clothes with elasticated things and t-shirts and stuff, but we liked, because Violet

always did look fantastic, so we tried to keep that up as much as we could. And so, when we'd be talking to people about what we'd do with her clothes and we'd kind of, you know, we'd go to certain shops to buy them and try and keep the standards as high as possible. And somebody said to us 'So, when you're getting her dressed then, do you love it? So, do you sometimes think, hey, I could wear that and I could put that on?' And I'm just like, 'No, no we don't think like that actually!'

Expectations of, and to, care were a common theme for men as well as women; perhaps less explicitly gendered, but clearly filtered through the lens of sexuality. Indeed, it was the men's experiences, in particular, which brought me to explore the notion of a gay sensibility (wherein gay and lesbian sexuality brings a particular understanding and articulation of care to the caring encounter). Of course, this is not to suggest that the experience of providing care (especially in the middle years of life) is a specially gay/lesbian specific experience, rather that, for gay men, in particular, there is, at least in the public consciousness, a critical, presumed, link between sexuality and the caring role.

> ANDREW: I've nursed friends who have died in my arms of AIDS and that's not been easy. I've had to care for them, wipe their arses, put them to bed, fit intravenous drips into their arms. I've had to do that and that's impacted on my life. I cared for my mother who had dementia, who, for years, supported me as a gay man and I had to nurse her as a child until she died ... I could only do those things *because* I am a gay man and being gay has informed the care I give. I would be arrogant enough to say it's ensured that the quality of care that I give is the best. I don't know whether people who haven't had that experience of oppression, of having to fight ... know, really, how to fight for someone else ... and when you've got vulnerable people who rely upon you to look after them, it makes you strong too and it makes you feel you can take on the world. Because you have to, because, if you don't, nobody else will.

As dementia becomes a critical mediator of everyday life, the fight to which Andrew refers often moves into the public arena. Previously private matters are inadvertently (and often very reluctantly) cast into the public gaze, as support and care provision in the home becomes a feature of daily life.

Private issues and public responses

It was often at the point at which formal service providers came into the picture that issues of sexuality were most explicitly framed in the experience of caring for a person with dementia. As private worlds were thrust into the public spotlight, it became necessary to carefully manage the flow of information into and out of people's houses. This shift in the visibility of the caring relationship also entailed the necessity to make critical choices about information sharing. The principle issue here was the decision as to whether or not to come out to service providers. Many people demonstrated profound anxieties in this context, being uncertain as to how sexuality might shape relationships with professional care providers.

People's coming out strategies were, thus, shaped and mediated by three interlinked factors: first, their concrete experiences of heterosexist and homophobic reactions, second, their *perceived* feelings of discrimination and lastly, their *anticipation of* that discrimination. These three factors tempered their willingness to make explicit their sexuality to service providers which, in turn, generated a variety of implications for their caring experiences.

> JOE: When the services started to get involved, their expectations of me and my partner, Ewan, as two gay men was kind of strange.... They kind of, their expectations of what we, what we would be like and what we would do ... and it's like, do they understand? Will they understand? Like, will these people who are coming, will they really understand, erm, about mine and Ewan's situation? Because a lot of them, well, all of them really, I mean, they only have like a kind of heterosexual model to follow.
>
> (Price, 2010: 163)

The management of service providers' knowledge of, and responses to, respondents' sexuality was managed in a variety of ways. Some people felt it necessary to come out in order to make their sexuality and/or relationship status explicit in order to avoid misunderstanding and misinterpretation, whilst others felt coming out unnecessary, as they perceived their sexuality as obvious, requiring no need for revelation or explanation. Other people decided not to come out to service providers for fear of possible negative responses (Price, 2010), whilst some were 'outed' by the person they were caring for, 'outed', in effect, by dementia. Cath's aunt, who lived in a residential home, for example, would often ask about Cath and her partner's relationship:

> CATH: 'Oh, that's right, how long have you two been together?' I'd have to answer in a very loud voice, because she was deaf.... And I'm like oh, God, shut up, you know.... And I could see out of the corner of my eye the whole staff turns round...
>
> (Price, 2010: 166)

A model developed by Hitchcock and Wilson (1992), in their own study of the disclosure behaviour of lesbian women to health service providers, proved to be a useful framework for understanding disclosure in the context of providing care for a person with dementia. Disclosures were very much 'situation-contingent' (Fish, 2006: 129) and people employed a range of strategies and control mechanisms that cut across the parameters of the model outlined here as circumstances dictated. *Active disclosure* (a purposeful act of telling) was often employed as a purposeful strategy to offset potential misunderstanding in service provider relationships, where it was important for people coming into a person's home to understand the nature of the relationships within it. *Passive disclosure*, by contrast, involved no explicit revelation, but a person's sexual identity was implicitly suggested by way of clues provided that related to their sexuality. The third strategy was that of *active non-disclosure* – passing as heterosexual and choosing not to challenge incorrect assumptions that were made about sexuality and, finally, *passive non-disclosure*, wherein the service user purposefully concealed aspects of their sexuality or actively avoided questions related to sexuality. Each strategy came with associated risks, as responses to disclosure (or non-disclosure) were not predictable and had the potential to add additional difficulty to already trying circumstances.

Keith's strategy, though, was uncompromising.

> KEITH: I'm a bit stroppy about it now, so, when people come in, I make a point of ... I do quite often just say, 'I'm gay and I live with my partner'. I tell everyone now. The person that I have who comes in on a Monday afternoon ... and when the manager came, I made a point of telling her that I was gay and that I lived with my partner, because people were going to be coming into the house, so stupid not to.
>
> (Price, 2010: 163)

Overtly negative responses to people's disclosures were rare, though the possibility of receiving a negative response was, of necessity, actively managed, again adding an element of additional difficulty to already strained circumstances. Luke's experience of accessing support from the Alzheimer's Society is, perhaps, indicative of this. For Luke, silence provided perceived safety, but at a considerable cost.

> LUKE: It's very ... I was very much appreciative of the support that I got at the time.... The things you see and sort of go through with different people on these things, and I met such wonderful people on this Alzheimer's group thing.
>
> LIZ: Did you come out to them [others in the support group] at all?
>
> LUKE: No, no and there was no gay people there, but it didn't need to be that really, because everyone was in the same boat...
>
> LIZ: Did you think that the whole kind of caring aspect kind of negated any sexuality issues? Was it, you know, that everyone was there because they were caring for somebody and really it didn't matter whether you're gay ... straight...
>
> LUKE: Well, except that as things went on, I think there was a feeling amongst the older, straight people, that being gay wasn't a good thing to be. The general feeling when we went to the meetings later, very much later on, in the proceedings, that you know, to be gay wasn't a good thing to be and that everyone should be straight. So it wasn't a

very good thing and that put me off … I just let it slide … I just fell in with everybody else and what they were talking about, I didn't, I gave nothing away about myself at all. I just said I was looking after my mother and it was very hard. They said, they asked me how she was and all, they had no idea I was gay at all…

LIZ: I guess in those groups you could never talk about [partner] and your relationship with him…

LUKE: No, no I couldn't.

(Price, 2010: 164)

Home from home?

As dementia gradually became the dominant feature in people's lives, choices about long-term care sometimes had to be made. For many people this involved moving the person they cared for into residential or nursing facilities where, again, choices about disclosure and the fear of homophobia became pressing issues for many people. It was Roger Newman who was, perhaps, the first to illuminate the nature of this experience as a gay man. His story of navigating dementia care services pre civil partnership, equal marriage and the anti-oppressive legislation we can now rely on for at least some degree of public protection, is, perhaps, the most telling and poignant explication of the fact that the experience of caring for a person with dementia *is* very particular for gay and lesbian people (Newman, 2010; Newman and Price, 2012; see also Roger Newman's chapter in this volume, Chapter 13). In addition to the already difficult decisions associated with finding, accessing and affording good residential care, gay and lesbian carers had to assess the LGBT* 'friendliness' of care providers and then, once the person they were caring for had moved into care, they were required to purposefully navigate increased visibility and, sometimes daily, disclosure (voluntary and otherwise), all issues which became additional stress factors for many people.

Even at the end of life, the specificities of caring as a lesbian or gay person were highlighted in the experiences of the people who shared their stories with me. As ever, each new encounter required a renegotiation and presentation of identity and relationship. Here again, Joe's experience was typical:

JOE: We'd built up relationships with, you know, all different people, because, over time, they'd got to know who we were in Violet's life and so we didn't have the same name or whatever, but they knew that we were like, you know, whatever, 'Legitimate Carers'. All that changed after she died 'cos we were meeting new people and they were saying 'Why are you doing this? What are you doing this for?' And, in that world, people don't, there's no understanding of like gay relationships at all, none, none at all. You know, people didn't, people, whereas the social workers over time would know that Ewan was my partner and they'd call him my partner and they'd have an understanding of what that was, if it was like somebody like the coroner or the coroner's office, or something, if I rang about Violet one day and then Ewan might phone the next day, 'cos of what, she had to have an autopsy on her body and I might have rang up one day to see how things were going and then Ewan would phone the next day, and they'd say 'Well, who are you then?' and 'What's?' you know, 'What's your relationship to Violet and what's your relationship to Joe, 'cos we've got him down as Joe Grant?' and you're like, you know, and they just didn't know, they just don't know and you just think God, why don't you just know!

An ending

For Joe, and the other people involved in my original study, the journey through dementia did not (and does not) end when one's active caring role is completed – the journey has no definitive ending and the impact and implications of caring, or having cared for, a person with dementia can be life changing and ongoing. The journey starts with the first rumblings of cognitive unease, through the maelstrom of diagnosis and accessing support and on into the shifts and changes, the negotiations and implications, associated with a condition such as dementia. For the people involved in my small study, this is a journey suffused with and overlaid by issues of sexuality in ways in which, at the outset, I could not have anticipated.

The initial absences I noted are, I would conclude and reiterate, related to heterosexuality's hegemonic control of everyday life, which continues to be 'an invisible package of unearned assets that can be cashed in daily' (Fish, 2006: 12). As such, the absence of gay and lesbian sexualities in the context of dementia is, perhaps, simply a reflection of its omission and invalidation in many other facets of daily life. Gay and lesbian people have, thus, historically been impelled to live opaque lives in politically legislated and personally safety conscious 'privacy' and, for them, the onset of dementia in later life may be a minefield of 'outings', particularly for carers who advocate for partners or friends who may lack the capacity to do so for themselves. Even for those people who are confidently 'out' in a range of contexts, the various crises that accompany dementia and the ensuing need for outside support mean that previously private living arrangements and relationships can be suddenly forced into the public domain and opened to, sometimes harsh and unwelcome, public scrutiny.

It is, however, in the more intimate space of the 'family' that the journey into care is most firmly situated. It is the 'family', despite the difficulties associated with its conceptualisation and operationalisation that critically shapes the experience of providing care in complex and sometimes contradictory ways. Thus, an effective understanding and appreciation of the context within which care is given to family members, particularly parents, who may have had a difficult relationship with their gay or lesbian child because of their inability or unwillingness to accept their sexuality, is central to the provision of care in this context. Paradoxically, perhaps, dementia, and the nature of care people required, also presented opportunities to re-visit and re-evaluate previously difficult and damaging relationships with family members and, for some, the caring process provided a catalyst for healing relationships and perceiving other family members anew.

In short, the issue of sexuality has proved to be a resonant thread that may be seen to weave in varying breadths and depths by and through gay and lesbian people's caring experiences. It has suffused, permeated and, in some cases, saturated the dementia journey in ways which are both predictable and genuinely surprising – from diagnosis to death. So, it is with some regret and a fond backward glance that I now leave the final words of my exploration into gay and lesbian carers' experiences with Andrew, a gay man who so lovingly cared for his partner. In response to my question, *why is it different for them?*, he stated: 'We have a culture of our own, we have a language of our own, we have a history of our own and we share a struggle which other people may not understand.' In one sentence, Andrew succinctly addressed my central question, effectively ending my original study, but allowing me to commence a much longer intellectual journey of my own. As such, I remain very grateful to those people who were brave enough to share their experiences with me. For the many other LGBT* people who make the similar (but never the same) journey through their own experiences of dementia, I sincerely hope the small body of work which has been the outcome of my original question might be of some value.

References

Brotman, S., Ryan, B. and Cormier, R. (2002) 'Mental Health Issues of Particular Groups: Gay and Lesbian Seniors'. *Writings in Gerontology: Mental Health and Aging.* **2**, 55–67. Ottawa, ON: National Advisory Council on Aging.

Cahill, S., South, K. and Spade, J. (2000) *Outing Age: Public Policy Issues Affecting Gay, Lesbian, Bisexual and Transgendered Elders.* Washington DC: The Policy Institute of the National Gay and Lesbian Task Force Foundation.

Collins, C. and Jones, R. (1998) 'Emotional Distress and Morbidity in Dementia Carers: A Matched Comparison of Husbands and Wives'. *International Journal of Geriatric Psychiatry.* **12**(12) 1168–1173.

Fish, J. (2006) *Heterosexism in Health and Social Care.* Hampshire: Palgrave Macmillan.

Fredriksen-Goldsen, K. I., Cook-Daniels, L., Kim, H.-J., Erosheva, E. A., Emlet, C. A., Hoy-Ellis, C. P., Goldsen, J. and Muraco, A. (2014) 'Physical and Mental Health of Transgender Older Adults: An At-risk and Underserved Population'. *The Gerontologist.* **54**(3) 488–500.

Hash, K. M. (2001) *Caregiving and Post-caregiving Experiences of Midlife and Older Gay Men and Lesbians.* Virginia Commonwealth University: Unpublished Doctoral Thesis.

Hines, S. (2007) 'Transgendering Care: Practices of Care within Transgender Communities'. *Critical Social Policy.* **27**(4) 462–486.

Hirst, M. (2004) *Health Inequalities and Informal Care: End of Project Report.* York: Social Policy Research Unit (SPRU), University of York. [Available] www.york.ac.uk/inst/spru/pubs/pdf/healthinequalities.pdf.

Hitchcock, J. M. and Wilson, H. S. (1992) 'Personal Risk Taking: Lesbian Self-Disclosure of Sexual Orientation to Professional Health Care Providers'. *Nursing Research.* **41**(3) 178–83.

Innes, A., Archibald, C. and Murphy, C. (2004) 'Introduction'. In A. Innes, C. Archibald and C. Murphy (eds), *Dementia and Social Inclusion*, pp. 11–21. London: Jessica Kingsley Publishers.

Jones, R. (2010) 'Troubles with Bisexuality in Health and Social Care'. In R. L. Jones and R. Ward (eds), *LGBT Issues: Looking Beyond Categories: Policy and Practice in Health and Social Care*, pp. 42–55. Edinburgh: Dunedin Academic Press.

Jutel, A. (2009) 'Sociology of Diagnosis: A Preliminary Review'. *Sociology of Health & Illness.* **31**(2) 278–299.

Kvale, S. (1996) *Interviews: An Introduction to Qualitative Research Interviewing.* Thousand Oaks, California: Sage.

Newman, R. (2010) 'Surely the World has Changed'. In L. Whitman (ed.), *Telling Tales about Dementia*, pp. 145–152. London: Jessica Kingsley Publishers.

Newman, R. and Price, E. (2012) 'Meeting the Needs of LGBT People Affected by Dementia'. In R. Ward, I. Rivers and M. Sutherland (eds), *Lesbian, Gay, Bisexual and Transgender Ageing: Biographical Approaches for Inclusive Care and Support*, pp. 183–195. London: Jessica Kingsley.

Manthorpe, J. (2003) 'Nearest and Dearest: The Neglect of Lesbians in Caring Relationships'. *British Journal of Social Work.* **33**, 753–768.

Manthorpe, J. and Price, E. (2003) 'Out of the Shadows'. *Community Care*, 3–9 April, 40–41.

Manthorpe, J. and Price, E. (2006) 'Lesbian Carers: Personal Issues and Policy Responses'. *Social Policy and Society.* **5**(1) 15–26.

McAlister, S., Carr, N. and Neill, G. (2014) *Queering the Family: Attitudes towards Lesbian and Gay Relationships and Families in Northern Ireland.* ACCESS RESEARCH KNOWLEDGE (ARK) Research Update 89, N. Ireland: Queen's University Belfast and University of Ulster www.ark.ac.uk/publications/updates/Update89.pdf [accessed 10 March 2015].

Plummer, K. (1992) 'Speaking its Name: Inventing A Lesbian and Gay Studies'. In K. Plummer (ed.), *Modern Homosexualities: Fragments of Lesbian and Gay Experience*, pp. 3–29. London: Routledge.

Price, E. (2005) 'Older Gay Men and Lesbians: All But Invisible'. *Nursing Older People.* **17**(4) 16–18.

Price, E. (2006) 'Ageing Against the Grain: Gay Men and Lesbians'. In P. Burke and J. Parker (eds), *Social Work and Disadvantage: Addressing the Roots of Stigma by Association*, pp. 97–111. London: Jessica Kingsley Publishers.

Price, E. (2008) 'Pride or Prejudice? Gay Men, Lesbians and Dementia'. *British Journal of Social Work.* **38**, 1337–1352.

Price, E. (2010) 'Coming Out to Care: Gay and Lesbian Carers' Experiences of Dementia'. *Health and Social Care in the Community.* **18**(2) 160–168.

Price, E. (2011a) 'Caring for Mum and Dad: Lesbian Women: Negotiating Family and Navigating Care'. *British Journal of Social Work.* **41**(7) 1288–1303.

Price, E. (2011b) 'Gay and Lesbian Carers: Ageing in the Shadow of Dementia'. *Ageing and Society.* **32**(3) 516–532.

Price, L. and Walker, L. (2015) *Chronic Illness, Vulnerability and Social Work: Autoimmunity and the Contemporary Disease Experience.* London: Routledge.

Quam, J. K. (1993) 'Gay and Lesbian Aging'. *Sex Information and Education Council of the United States Report.* **21**(5) 10–12.

Sontag, S. (2001) *Illness as Metaphor and AIDS and its Metaphors.* London: Picador.

Wahler, J. and Gabbay, S. G. (1997) 'Gay Male Aging: A Review of the Literature'. *Journal of Gay and Lesbian Social Services.* **6**(3) 1–20.

Westwood, S., King, A., Almack, K. and Suen, Y.-T. (2015) 'Good Practice in Health and Social Care Provision for Older LGBT People'. In J. Fish and K. Karban (eds), *Social Work and Lesbian, Gay, Bisexual and Trans Health Inequalities: International Perspectives*, pp. 145–159. Bristol: Policy Press.

11 One-day training courses on LGBT* awareness – are they the answer?

Sue Westwood and Sally Knocker

Introduction

There is a growing awareness of older lesbian, gay, bisexual and trans* (LGBT*) individuals' concerns about needing to use formal health and social care provision in later life (Cook-Daniels, 2006; Concannon, 2009; Ward *et al.*, 2011). For many individuals, loss of cognitive capacity associated with dementia, increased dependency upon others, and exposure to prejudice and discrimination are particular worries (Guasp, 2011; Bailey, 2012). Activists working with and/or on behalf of older LGBT* individuals (Adelman *et al.*, 2006; Knocker *et al.*, 2012; Meyer and Johnston, 2014) have recently begun to promote more 'LGBT* friendly' health and social care provision (including for individuals with dementia) via the delivery of one-off training sessions to public, private and voluntary sector organisations (Rogers *et al.*, 2013; Erdley *et al.*, 2013). At the heart of this training is the liberal hope (Harding and Peel, 2007) that raising awareness, and increasing LGBT* 'cultural competence' (Gendron *et al.*, 2013) among staff will lead to an improvement in the care experiences of older LGBT* individuals.

In this chapter, we explore both the possibilities and the potential limitations of training, particularly one-day training, as a tool to promote best practice among those providing services to LGBT* individuals living with dementia. We have both (Sue Westwood (SW) and Sally Knocker (SK)) delivered training on dementia and best practice in working with older LGBT* individuals, and will share our experiences of doing so in this chapter. We consider what can be achieved in a one-day training (sensitisation to, and awareness of, some of the basic issues affecting LGBT* individuals with dementia). We also consider what cannot be achieved in a day (wider organisational change, care cultures, entrenched attitudes, and the attitudes and behaviours of other service users, their families and friends). We suggest that there are real dangers that short training courses become tokenistic and ineffective, particularly when they address only knowledge and competencies rather than developing genuine empathy and emotional intelligence among staff. One-day training might even be counterproductive, in that it could enable an organisation to tick the 'LGBT* training' box and move on, rather than address more complex, systemic issues which might act as barriers to good practice. We discuss how deeper cultural changes within organisations, with a focus on inspired leadership and with training initiatives as only a part of the jigsaw of change, offer the real route to supporting LGBT* people to feel safe, respected, cared about, and able to be themselves in dementia care spaces. We propose that training supported by ongoing consultancy, located in a statutory requirement, embedded by commissioners of services, is the only way that real and lasting improvements can be achieved.

'Older LGBT*'/'LGBT* & dementia' training: content

There is at present very little LGBT*-specific training relating to dementia care. Instead, there is more often generic 'older LGBT*' training for health and social care staff working with older people, many of whom will be affected by a form of dementia, especially those living in residential care and nursing homes. In the UK, there is an under-prioritisation of equality and diversity training in general and (older) LGBT* training in particular (Monro, 2010; Monro and Richardson, 2011). A survey conducted by the CSCI (2008) found that, although 94 per cent of social care providers reported implementing equality and diversity initiatives, only 9 per cent of providers gave any examples of equality work relating to 'sexual orientation'. We are only aware of LGBT*-specific training being delivered in the UK, USA, Canada and Australia, by a small handful of agencies and/or independent trainers.[1] Apart from in the USA, where SAGE (the national organisation representing older LGBT* individuals)[2] has a training programme which it is rolling out nationally, the training content and style is determined by each agency or trainer. Training can include all, or some, of the following: regulatory context (e.g. equality and diversity, human rights, and care provision regulations relating to providing services to older LGBT* individuals); outline of LGBT* history; introduction to older LGBT* fears and concerns about health and social care provision; stories from older LGBT* individuals themselves, either as co-trainers, or via DVDs, audio recordings and/or written extracts; small and large group discussions and/or role play of scenarios trainees might encounter and how to deal with them; disclosure by trainer(s) of personal experiences. Some training is delivered to managers, some to non-managerial staff, some to both. Some training is delivered for free, but, more often, there is a charge. Training is usually delivered as a 'one-off', that is trainers come into an organisation once, deliver the training to staff, and then do not return again.

Some dementia-specific elements of the training might relate to the impact of disinhibition on an individual's ability to filter what they say or do (and so risk exposure for those who wish to conceal their sexuality/gender identity) or how early memories of prejudice and discrimination, and associated fears, might resurface. When looking at the work of Tom Kitwood (1997) on the importance of psychological needs being met in people living with dementia, there are particularly significant aspects to consider in relation to LGBT* individuals. It can be particularly important for marginalised individuals who have been socially excluded to experience *psychological* safety – and, arguably, this might become more important as our cognitive abilities are failing. Training should, therefore, focus on the emotional as well as physical aspects of safety and on mitigating the potential fear and isolation experienced by LGBT* individuals in dementia care contexts.

It is important to not only provide specialist training, but also to integrate LGBT* perspectives within *all* dementia training. Dementia Care Matters,[3] the organisation SK works for, for example, includes a one-day session on 'Sexuality, Intimacy and Relationships' as part of a one-year course on culture change in dementia care. LGBT* issues are integrated within this one day as well as within other training days, for example when referring to families and friends of people living with dementia ensuring that this might include same-gender partners and 'families of friends' (Roseneil, 2004). When looking at issues of privacy, confidentiality and dignity, there can also be important discussions about supporting trans individuals whose bodies may not conform to their gender identity and presentation which can have implications should they need personal care. One powerful story on a training course was of a man who was behaving in a very angry and distressed way to care workers when he moved into a care home. This, as is so often the case, was assumed to be a 'symptom' of his dementia, When his wife came in to talk to the manager, she explained that for many years her husband had dressed in women's clothes whilst he was at home, which was something that she had accepted and supported. The care home staff team were then able to support this man to continue to do this, and, unsurprisingly, his angry and distressed behaviour disappeared. In a training context, there might be facilitated discussions about how care workers feel about this example and how they might respond to the reactions of other people living in or visiting the care home.

What is achievable in a day?

One-off, standalone one-day (or even sometimes a half-day) training in this context can achieve a number of things: increase awareness; promote sensitisation to relevant issues; encourage reflective practice; open up a dialogue, and offer a language and framework for discussing older LGBT* issues and care practices and increase knowledge of local and national agencies with expertise in older LGBT* issues. However, empirical research on the outcome of such training is sparse and tends to report only on outcomes at the end of the training day, rather than over longer periods of time (Porter and Krinsky, 2014).

Increasing awareness is very important. One of the most common observations of trainers working with health and social care staff on older LGBT* issues is that staff will question the need for such training, often observing 'we treat everyone the same' (Knocker, 2006: 39). Exploring this during the training session can help staff to understand that achieving equal outcomes in care provision often means treating people differently, according to their individual lives, identities and care needs. We have often found telling the (imagined) 'coffee' story useful here:

On a training course, lunch is served, but there are no drinks. After lunch, when the group has reconvened, the trainer asks 'Would everyone like a drink?' Everyone responds enthusiastically. The trainer then says that there are mugs of hot coffee with milk available for everyone. Someone says she does not take milk in her coffee. Someone says he does not drink coffee. Another person says she does not drink hot drinks. Sorry, says the trainer, we treat everyone the same, and so, we serve the same drink to everyone.

(Unidentified source)

This very simple imagined scenario can help staff to understand how a 'sameness' approach to equality (i.e. treating everyone the same) does not always lead to equality of outcome (i.e. everyone getting an equally good outcome).

Another simple exercise which invites people to put themselves in the shoes of LGBT* individuals is to ask people to talk in pairs about a person who is very important to them without mentioning their gender at all. They cannot say 'he' or 'she' or use their name or anything which gives away their gender. Reflections after this exercise reveal how hard it is to talk about someone without alluding to their gender. The trainer is then able to make the point that the reality for many individuals in same-sex relationships is that they constantly have to censor their communications when talking about a partner, in particular, if they are not confident about the attitude of the person with whom they are in conversation.

One of the key aims of training is to encourage workers to think about things from a different perspective or put themselves in the shoes of other people. Staff who do not identify as LGBT* themselves may simply not appreciate that LGBT* individuals perceive and experience care differently, and that this is informed by historical and more recent experiences of marginalisation and discrimination, including in health and social care provision (McNeil *et al.*, 2012; River and Ward, 2012). Being given insights into (older) LGBT* individuals' lives can be extremely illuminating. In fact, we have both observed that this can be the time those staff members who have been sitting back in their chairs with their arms folded, lean forward, unfolding their arms. The story of Jo, whose girlfriend was knifed and murdered in a homophobic street attack in a film produced by Opening Doors London,[4] for example, always has a very powerful impact on people's realisation of the fear and hatred many LGBT* people experienced. Similarly the story of KrysAnn, (a trans woman dying without her biological family, who rejected her after she transitioned in later life) in the film GenSilent,[5] can also sensitise trainees to issues they had not previously considered. However, there can also be dangers of 'limiting classroom teaching to examples of outrageous and extreme forms of homophobic incidents' (Barnett, 2013: 51), as this can make it easier for workers to separate themselves from these and not acknowledge the many smaller ways in which society at large can exclude people who identify as LGBT*.

One-off training can also open up a dialogue, and offer a language and framework for, discussing LGBT* issues and care practices. Some trainees do not know what the 'LGBT*' abbreviation stands for, and some may have never used the words 'lesbian', 'gay', 'bisexual' and/or trans*, transgender and transsexual. Some do not even know what they mean. One training manual actually encourages people to say the words together in class.[6] But more than just giving people the words, it also gives people permission to use those words in professional contexts.

There have been some interesting occurrences of personal sharing within these training days which have had some very positive outcomes for the whole group's learning. There are nearly always staff members in the group who identify as LGBT* themselves or have relatives or friends who do. For example, on one course, run by SK, a mother talked about her own experience of struggling with her son coming out to her and then realising how much she loved him and how they subsequently became much closer. Some trainers invite older LGBT* individuals to share during a training event. However, it is important that the trainer creates a sufficiently safe environment for people to be able to feel open to share, which is not always possible when some very negative opinions are being voiced. It can also put a certain pressure on that individual to 'represent' the voice of all LGBT* people when, inevitably, all that they are sharing is their own unique story.

One-off training can also encourage reflective practice and provide workers with information about specialist providers who can offer advice and support, and this can lead to post-training advantages, as is highlighted by this UK trainer:

> We had a social worker who called us after an awareness-raising training who said 'I'm working with an older man and I believe he's gay. I've no idea how to approach it with him, I think he's so isolated and lonely, he would almost certainly benefit from your project, how do I raise it with him? I don't just want to say "excuse me, sir, are you gay?" and scare the hell out of him.' So we said if you get six or seven leaflets for different services you know, put in like one for the women's Bengali group. He's not a Bengali woman. So if there's six or seven leaflets, 'that's not for me', 'that's not for me', this is the toenail cutting service, this is the befriending scheme, this is for older lesbian and gay people, this is for Bengali … and just leave it with him. And, do you know what? She called back a few days later. It worked. He's going to give [us] a call. He was really excited. He was excited that he was presented with such an option and that such an option existed.
>
> (UK trainer, unpublished data from SW's PhD thesis, Westwood, 2015)

We can see here how training can help professionals recognise older LGBT* individuals' needs and identify the most appropriate strategy for offering support to address those needs, with external support if required. However, not all training, and trainers, offer this follow-up service.

So, to summarise, one-off training can increase awareness, promote greater sensitivity and encourage more informed, reflective and responsive practice. We shall now address what it is not possible to achieve in a day.

What is not achievable in a day?

One-off training can be problematic in a number of ways. At the most basic level, with the frequent and high turnover of staff in older age health and social care provision, and the reliance upon bank staff and agency workers, one-off training will only reach a fraction of all the staff working with older LGBT* people. As has been observed among older LGBT* trainers, 'changing attitudes may be an iterative process' (Porter and Krinsky, 2014: 213) and 'due to relatively high turnover among agency staff, a clear need to develop a strategy for ongoing training emerged' (Landers *et al.*, 2010: 326). Without an ongoing training programme, then, one-off training will have only limited effect.

Most traditional training programmes focus on 'skills' and 'behaviours' more than attitudes. However, increasing numbers of trainers are realising that to really implement meaningful change, courses need to involve more content that invites participants to share more of *themselves*. At Dementia Care Matters, for example, dementia training always starts with a memory box exercise where care workers are asked to bring along objects which relate to their own identity and life story and to talk about these. The aim of this is to reinforce the point that in order to work well with 'others', we need to be aware of what is important in our own lives – it is not about 'them', that is the older people living with dementia, it is about all of 'us' as human beings. The danger of doing a one-day course is it inevitably focuses on 'them', that is LGBT* people as different, when actually what we are trying to connect with is the humanity in all of us. Training which focuses on identity and beliefs is obviously much more difficult to achieve than just focusing on what you need to 'do'; we are actually trying to focus people on how they need to '*be*' when working alongside LGBT* people, which is a much more fundamental shift in thinking. This requires exercises that encourage participants to think about their own experiences in life of feeling different or 'on the outside'; what helps them feel safe, loved and relaxed, and what are things in life that help them feel they matter to others.

Training stems from the belief: 'that negative attitudes and behaviours towards lesbians and gay men can be challenged through education' (Peel, 2002: 255). However, attitudinal change is unlikely to be achieved in a one-off intervention without being located within the context of wider, ongoing, organisational development (Landers *et al.*, 2010). This is both at individual and collective levels. At an individual level, one-off training cannot address deeply entrenched attitudes, particularly among those staff members who hold strong negative views and beliefs about LGBT* individuals. These are the attitudes which most worry older LGB individuals who perceive older age care provision to be a source of 'ignorance at least, homophobia at worst' (Guasp, 2011: 22) and trans* individuals who have previously experienced prejudice and discrimination especially among mental health service providers (McNeil *et al.*, 2012). Some of these fears and concerns relate to religious organisations and/or individuals (staff and/or fellow service users) with strictly held religious beliefs (Knocker, 2013). There is virtually no literature on religion in the context of older age care provision, although there is growing anecdotal evidence of tensions between medical, nursing and social care staff with strict religious beliefs and LGBT* care users (CSCI, 2008; Carr, 2008), particularly among migrant staff who may come from cultures and/or faiths which are less favourably inclined towards LGBT* individuals (Walsh and Shutes, 2012). For example, this incident was reported in a recent small-scale study conducted by SK: 'One older disabled lesbian woman describes being given leaflets by religious care workers suggesting that she could be 'saved'; an experience that has made her feel unsafe and alienated in her own home' (Knocker, 2012: 10).

Other trainers have also reported resistance among staff attending training who hold particularly strong, negative, religious opinions. For example, SW has worked with staff informed by a strong faith who have remained silent and passive throughout an entire day's training. Other trainers have reported overt prejudice:

> One woman said that if her daughter was lesbian she'd have to 'exorcize the demon out of her' and another man just starting from the point of 'where does this perversion come from?'
> (UK trainer, unpublished data from SW's PhD thesis, Westwood, 2015)

> I suspect that, at the back of the room there was somebody who was praying all the time … he had his head bent forward and he was muttering all the time … and I've heard that from other trainers as well, people praying throughout the training, some even having to be removed because of it.
> (UK trainer, unpublished data from SW's PhD thesis, Westwood, 2015)

The impact of this on the trainers themselves should also not be under-estimated. Whilst the aim of the training might be to encourage people to talk openly about any fears, stereotypes or prejudices they may have, this can be a very stressful experience for even the most robust LGBT* trainer to try and respond to.

At a collective level, older LGBT* trainers are generally agreed that training is most effective if it is embedded at a wider organisational level as 'part of a bigger plan of action addressing the systems, the structures, and the culture of the organization' (Lai and Kleiner, 2001: 16). As these three trainers, in a study SW recently conducted, observed,

> So I tell them 'I can come in once and I can turn the light bulb on, but I can also come back and do some consulting with you over time to help really set some roots in'.
> (USA trainer quoted in Westwood, 2015)

> Changing cultures is not about skills and competencies and training days. It's about leadership, it's about working alongside workers, being alongside them for a specific period, about having specific areas to target.
> (UK trainer, unpublished data from SW's PhD thesis, Westwood, 2015)

> I think you've got to train right from the top, because you've got to get them, the senior management team, involved, because then it filters down, and then you can embed it in your policies, and you can ensure that your staff do what your policies set out you should do.... It's not enough to have it sat in the policy book, is it? You have to use it.
>
> (UK trainer, unpublished data from SW's PhD thesis, Westwood, 2015)

These three trainers are each articulating the importance of working with an organisation, at multiple levels, across an extended period of time, in order to effect real and substantive collective changes. Developing strategies to challenge homophobic and/or transphobic service users, their families and friends, and being sure of managerial support in doing so, needs to be included in training (Willis *et al.*, 2013). But, it also must be embedded within a broader managerial and/or organisational context. It is important to pay attention to 'how diversity is managed by policies, work design, structural integration, corporate culture, and top management commitment to the cause and communication of its importance' (Jonsen *et al.*, 2011: 46). In particular, whether the organisation provides a safe working environment for its LGBT* staff needs to be addressed (Manthorpe and Price, 2005; Buddel, 2011). Some of this under-attention to a whole system approach can be based in pragmatism, with limited, and diminishing, financial resources in difficult economic times, necessitating that trainers 'get in' where and how they can (King, 2013), but this situation is far from ideal. There is even a risk that it may be counter-productive, encouraging a 'tick-box' approach to training, with managers feeling they have 'covered' LGBT* issues by facilitating a one-off training event.

A lot of older LGBT* training involves the notion of 'cultural competence' (Gendron *et al.*, 2013, Hardacker *et al.*, 2013; Portz *et al.*, 2014; Fredriksen-Goldsen *et al.*, 2014), which is understood as:

> When the staff, using the systems within the organization, are able to identify and address the needs of a particular group within the larger pool of all constituents. In this case, the cultural group is LGBT* older adults.
>
> (Meyer, 2012: 25)

The problem with notions of cultural competence is that they imply older LGBT* individuals comprise a single cultural group, which, clearly, they are not. This blanket collectivism (Johnson and Munch, 2009), tends to under-represent diversity among older LGBT* individuals. This diversity does not just involve differences between lesbians, gay men, bisexual women and men, and trans* individuals, it also involves more nuanced differences among them as well, particularly in relation to dementia. These subtleties and variations are very difficult to convey in a one-off training, particularly when it is being delivered to staff who may not have addressed these issues before.

People living with dementia are facing many significant losses and changes as cognitive decline impacts on their abilities, their memories, and potentially also their sense of self. In the context of these losses, there are various aspects of a person's identity that will contribute to a preserved sense of well-being and security. Wendy Hulko (2009) and other authors have highlighted the significance of social location and 'how social location shapes the subjective experiences and responses of persons with dementia' (O'Connor *et al.*, 2010: 30). Other authors have emphasised the significance of 'the continuing personhood of the individual with dementia' (Twigg and Buse, 2013: 326) and the need to understand that personhood at an embodied level (Kontos and Naglie, 2007). This embodiment is nuanced at the intersection of not only ageing, gender and sexuality (Calasanti and Slevin, 2007), and gender identity (Cook-Daniels, 2006) but also their intersection with other social divisions (ethnicity, class, religion, disability, etc.). Again, trying to convey the complexities of intersectionality and the implications for practice with LGBT* individuals with dementia, and to emphasise the importance of taking a person-centred approach to care, is nigh on impossible across a single day. What happens instead is that we resort to generalisations to convey an approximate picture. In those generalisations, diversity is lost.

Training exercises which encourage participants to reflect on the various identities that are important to them can help emphasise that many of us fall into different groups in which we have a sense of belonging, for example as sons and daughters, parents, our work identity, our political or religious affiliations, our hobbies and interests. But this can also mean that we find it hard when some of these 'worlds' we inhabit do not always sit comfortably together. Gill Valentine's case study with a deaf lesbian, for example, showed how she felt marginalised by disablism when among hearing lesbians and gay men, and by heteronormativity and homophobia when among heterosexual deaf people (Valentine, 2007). In this way, both her deafness and her sexuality/sexual identity intersected to shape how she was positioned in different groups. The deeper issues to explore here are what it is that helps us feel that others understand and appreciate who we are, and how might it feel when we *don't* experience this? How easy is it for us to challenge attitudes that do not match our own when we are in a group of people who we do not know well and where we want to 'fit in'? Just as it should not be the sole responsibility of people from Black, Asian and minority ethnic (BAME) communities to challenge racism, so it should not be the responsibility of LGBT* individuals to tackle prejudice and discrimination towards them. These kinds of broader questions can help workers make connections with LGBT* issues even if they do not identify as LGBT* themselves.

So, in summary, whilst one-off LGBT* training for staff working with individuals with dementia has a number of advantages, it also has a number of limitations as well. These include: that wider organisational issues are not addressed; that diversity among and between older LGBT* individuals is not fully explored and understood; that individual staff attitudes towards LGBT* individuals are not dealt with; and that systematic disadvantage goes unchallenged.

Conclusion

In this chapter we have explored the advantages and disadvantages of one-off training for those providing services to LGBT* individuals with dementia. We propose that standalone training, whilst arguably 'better than nothing', is insufficient in order to ensure that LGBT* individuals with dementia experience safe, respectful, responsive and attuned services. Training can be only one part of a wider change strategy, and that training itself must be frequent, ongoing, and not just a one-off. It also has to be located within a change process which addresses organisational systems, management processes, policies, and procedures. It also has to address how an organisation deals with equality and diversity more broadly, and whether LGBT* staff themselves feel comfortable being open about themselves at work. If they do not, service users certainly will not (Hubbard and Rossington, 1995). Deeper cultural changes within organisations, with a focus on inspired leadership, as well as training initiatives, offer the real route to supporting LGBT* people to feel safe, valued and able to be themselves, if and when they develop dementia. More also needs to be done to encourage trainers in dementia care to integrate LGBT* issues within a wide range of courses including in relation to person-centred care, life story work, safeguarding, dignity and confidentiality and other general care topics.

Working with mainstream providers to ensure more responsive and effective services for older LGBT* individuals is to be lauded. However, this should also not be at the expense of those individuals who want specialist provision (e.g. lesbian-only; women-only; gay-men only; LGBT*-only) (Carr and Ross, 2013). Whilst improving mainstream provision via training and consultancy is essential, activists should not lose sight of also representing those individuals who want something beyond the mainstream.

Notes

1 E.g. in the USA – SAGE (Services and Advocacy for LGBT* Elders) (www.sageusa. org/) and The LGBT* Aging Project of Massachusetts (www.LGBT*agingproject.org/); in Australia – Val's Café (http://valscafe.org.au/index.php/our-story/history), The GLBTI Retirement Association Inc (GRAI) (http://grai.org.au/) and Queensland LGBT* Ageing Action Group (www.qahc.org.au/seniors#LGBT*); in Canada – Rainbow Health Ontario (www.rainbowhealthontario.ca/home.cfm): in the UK – Age UK London, 'Opening Doors' project (www.openingdoorslondon.org.uk/), Age Concern Central Lancashire, 'Older and Out' (www.fiftyfiveplus.org.uk/index.php?news=3417) and Stonewall Housing Older People's Project (www.stonewallhousing.org/insights/category/older-LGBT*-housing.html).
2 SAGE (Services and Advocacy for LGBT* Elders): www.sageusa.org/.
3 Dementia Care Matters: www.dementiacarematters.com/.
4 Opening Doors London DVD: www.youtube.com/watch?v=JpKSRU900y0.
5 'GenSilent Training Kit': http://stumaddux.com/gen_silent_TRAINING_ORDER_PAGE.html.
6 www.healthdirect.gov.au/news/better-aged-care-for-sexual-minority-groups-LGBT*i.

References

Adelman, M., Gurevich, L., de Vries, B. and Blando, J. (2006) 'Openhouse: Community Building and Research in the LGBT* Aging Population'. In D. Kimmel, T. Rose and S. David, (eds) *Lesbian, Gay, Bisexual and Transgender Aging*, pp. 247–264. New York: Columbia University Press.

Bailey, L. (2012) 'Trans Ageing'. In R. Ward, I. Rivers and M. Sutherland (eds) *Lesbian, Gay, Bisexual and Transgender Ageing: Biographical Approaches for Inclusive Care and Support*, pp. 51–66. London and Philadelphia: Jessica Kingsley Publishers.

Barnett, C. (2013) *An investigation into heterosexism in social care policies for older people in the lesbian, gay, bisexual, transgender (LGBT*) community and its implications for social work practice*. Dissertation for MSc in Social Work, London Metropolitan University.

Buddel, N. (2011) 'Queering the workplace'. *Journal of Gay & Lesbian Social Services*, **23**(1): 131–146.

Calasanti, T. and Slevin, K. (2007) 'Introduction'. In T. Calasanti and K. Slevin (eds) *Age Matters: Realigning Feminist Thinking*, pp. 247–268. New York: Routledge.

Carr, S. (2008) 'Sexuality and religion: A challenge for diversity strategies in UK social care service development and delivery'. *Diversity in Health and Social Care*, **5**: 113–122.

Carr, S. and Ross, P. (2013) *Assessing Current and Future Housing and Support Options for Older LGB People*. York: Joseph Rowntree Foundation.

Commission for Social Care Inspection (CSCI) (2008) *Putting People First: Equality and Diversity Matters 1: Providing Appropriate Services for Lesbian, Gay and Bisexual and Transgender People*. London: CSCI.

Concannon, L. (2009) 'Developing inclusive health and social care policies for older LGB citizens'. *British Journal of Social Work*, **39**: 403–417.

Cook-Daniels, L. (2006) 'Trans Ageing'. In D. Kimmel, T. Rose and S. David (eds) *Lesbian, Gay, Bisexual and Transgender Ageing*, pp. 20–35. New York: Columbia University Press.

Erdley, S. D., Anklam, D. D. and Reardon, C. C. (2013) 'Breaking barriers and building bridges: Understanding the pervasive needs of older LGBT* adults and the value of social work in health care'. *Journal of Gerontological Social Work*, **57**(2–4): 362–385.

Fredriksen-Goldsen, K. I., Hoy-Ellis, C. P., Goldsen, J., Emlet, C. A. and Hooyman, N. R. (2014) 'Creating a vision for the future: Key competencies and strategies for culturally competent practice with lesbian, gay, bisexual, and transgender (LGBT) older adults in the health and human services'. *Journal of Gerontological Social Work*. Advanced online access. DOI: 10.1080/01634372.2014.890690.

Gendron, T., Maddux, S., Krinsky, L., White, J., Lockeman, K., Metcalfe, Y. and Aggarwal, S. (2013) 'Cultural competence training for healthcare professionals working with LGBT* older adults'. *Educational Gerontology*, **39**(6): 454–463.

Guasp, A. (2011) *Lesbian, Gay and Bisexual People in Later Life*. London: Stonewall.

Hardacker, C. T., Rubinstein, B., Hotton, A. and Houlberg, M. (2013) 'Adding silver to the rainbow: The development of the nurses' health education about LGBT* elders (HEALE) cultural competency curriculum'. *Journal of Nursing Management*, **22**(2): 257–266.

Harding, R. and Peel, E. (2007) 'Heterosexism at work: Diversity training, discrimination law and the limits of liberal individualism'. In V. Clarke and E. Peel (eds) *Out in Psychology: Lesbian, Gay, Bisexual, Trans and Queer Perspectives*, pp. 247–271. Chichester: John Wiley & Sons.

Hubbard, R. and Rossington, J. (1995) *As We Grow Older: A Study of the Housing and Support Needs of Older Lesbians and Gay Men.* London: Polari.

Hulko, W. (2009) 'From "not a big deal" to "hellish": Experiences of older people with dementia'. *Journal of Aging Studies*, 23(3): 131–144.

Johnson, Y. M. and Munch, S. (2009) 'Fundamental contradictions in cultural competence'. *Social Work*, **54**(3): 220–231.

Jonsen, K., Maznevski, M. L. and Schneider, S. C. (2011) 'Special Review Article: Diversity and its not so diverse literature: An international perspective'. *International Journal of Cross Cultural Management*, **11**(11): 35–62.

King, A. (2013) 'Prepare for impact? Reflecting on knowledge exchange work to improve services for older LGBT* people in times of austerity'. *Social Policy and Society/FirstView Article/November 2013*, pp. 1–13. DOI: 10.1017/S1474746413000523, Published online: 19 November 2013.

Kitwood, T. (1997) *Dementia Reconsidered – The Person Comes First.* Buckingham: Open University Press.

Knocker, S. (2006) *The Whole of Me: Meeting the Needs of Older Lesbians, Gay Men and Bisexuals Living in Care Homes and Extra Care Housing.* London: Age Concern England.

Knocker, S. (2013) *Perspectives on Ageing Lesbians, Gay Men and Bisexuals.* London: Joseph Rowntree Foundation.

Knocker, S., Maxwell, N., Phillips, M. and Halls, S. (2012) 'Opening Doors and Opening Minds: Sharing One Project's Experience of Successful Community Engagement'. In R. Ward, I. Rivers and M. Sutherland (eds) *Lesbian, Gay, Bisexual and Transgender Ageing: Biographical Approaches for Inclusive Care and Support*, pp. 150–164. London and Philadelphia: Jessica Kingsley Publishers.

Kontos, P. C. and Naglie, G. (2007). 'Bridging theory and practice: Imagination, the body, and person-centred dementia care'. *Dementia*, **6**(4): 549–569.

Lai, Y. and Kleiner, B. H. (2001) 'How to conduct diversity training effectively'. *Equal Opportunities International*, **20**(5–7): 14–18.

Landers, S. Mimiaga, M. J. and Krinsky, L. (2010) 'The Open Door Project Task Force: A qualitative study on LGBT* aging.' *Journal of Gay & Lesbian Social Services*, **22**(3): 316–336.

Manthorpe, J. and Price, E. (2005) 'Lesbian carers: Personal issues and policy responses'. *Social Policy & Society*, **5**(1): 15–26.

McNeil, J., Bailey, L., Ellis, S., Morton, J. and Regan, M. (2012) *Trans Mental Health and Emotional Wellbeing Study 2012*. Edinburgh: The Scottish Transgender Alliance.

Meyer, H. (2012) 'Aging in the US: The next Civil Rights Movement? Federal policy, activism, and LGBT* older adults'. *Temple Political & Civil Rights Law Review*, **21**(2): 511–520.

Meyer, H. and Johnston, T. R. (2014) 'The National Resource Center on LGBT* Aging provides critical training to aging service providers'. *Journal of Gerontological Social Work*, **57**(2–4): 407–412.

Monro, S. (2010) 'Sexuality, space and intersectionality: The case of lesbian, gay and bisexual equalities initiatives in UK local government'. *Sociology*, **44**(5): 996–1010.

Monro, S. and Richardson, D. (2011) 'Intersectionality and Sexuality: The Case of Sexuality and Transgender Equalities Work in UK Local Government'. In Y. Taylor, S. Hines and M. E. Casey (eds) *Theorizing Intersectionality and Sexuality*, pp. 99–118. Basingstoke: Palgrave Macmillian.

O'Connor, D., Phinney, A., and Hulko, W. (2010) 'Dementia at the intersections: A unique case study exploring social location'. *Journal of Aging Studies*, **24**(1): 30–39.

Peel, E. (2002) 'Lesbian and Gay Awareness Training: Homophobia, Liberalism, and Managing Stereotypes.' In A. Coyle and C. Kitzinger (eds) *Lesbian and Gay Psychology: New Perspectives*, pp. 255–270. Chichester: Wiley-Blackwell.

Porter, K. E. and Krinsky, L. (2014) 'Do LGBT* aging trainings effectuate positive change in mainstream elder service providers?' *Journal of Homosexuality*, **61**(1): 197–216.

Portz, J. Dickman, Retrum, J. H., Wright, L. A., Boggs, J. A., Wilkins, S., Grimm, C., Gilchrist, K. and Gozansky, W. S. (2014) 'Assessing capacity for providing culturally competent services to LGBT* older adults'. *Journal of Gerontological Social Work*, **57**(2–4): 305–321.

River, L. and Ward, R. (2012) 'Polari's Life Story: Learning from Work with Older LGBT* People'. In R. Ward, I. Rivers and M. Sutherland (eds) *Lesbian, Gay, Bisexual and Transgender Ageing: Biographical Approaches for Inclusive Care and Support*, pp. 135–149. London and Philadelphia: Jessica Kingsley Publishers.

Rogers, A., Rebbe, R., Gardella, C., Worlein, M. and Chamberlin, M. (2013) 'Older LGBT* adult training panels: An opportunity to educate about issues faced by the older LGBT* community'. *Journal of Gerontological Social Work*, **56**(7): 580–595.

Roseneil, S. (2004) 'Why we should care about friends: An argument for queering the care imaginary in social policy'. *Social Policy & Society*, **3**(4): 409–419.

Twigg, J. and Buse, C. E. (2013) 'Dress, dementia and the embodiment of identity'. *Dementia*, **12**(3): 326–336.

Valentine, G. (2007) 'Theorizing and researching intersectionality: A challenge for feminist geography'. *The Professional Geographer*, **59**(1): 10–21.

Walsh, K. and Shutes, I. (2012) 'Care relationships, quality of care and migrant workers caring for older people'. *Ageing and Society*, **1**(1): 1–28.

Ward, R., Pugh, S. and Price, E. (2011) *Don't Look Back? Improving Health and Social Care Service Delivery for Older LGB Users*. London: Equality and Human Rights Commission.

Westwood, S. (2015). *Ageing, gender and sexuality: Equality in later life*. PhD Thesis. Keele University, UK.

Willis, P., Maegusuku-Hewett, T., Raithby, M. and Miles, P. (2014) 'Swimming upstream: The provision of inclusive care to older lesbian, gay and bisexual (LGB) adults in residential and nursing environments in Wales'. *Ageing & Society*, **1**(25): 282–306. DOI: 10.1017/S0144686X14001147.

Part III
Rights

Introduction to Part III

Sue Westwood and Elizabeth Price

This section addresses a range of rights-based issues relating to LGBT* people living with dementia. In Chapter 12, Nancy Knauer considers the variable legal recognitions afforded to LGBT* people and to people with dementia in the USA. She explores their implications for choice, or lack of it, and issues of (dis)empowerment for LGBT* people living with dementia, particularly within the conservative, religious, sociocultural contexts of the USA. In Chapter 13, we go from national issues to the experience of a single individual. Roger Newman, from England, cared for his partner who had dementia. This prompted both a personal journey, discovering what it means to be a gay carer of a partner with dementia, and a public journey, as Roger became more involved in championing the rights of LGBT* carers of people with dementia. Roger reflects on the progress made, and the challenges still ahead, in terms of LGBT* people living with dementia carers' rights.

In Chapter 14, Paul Willis, Michele Raithby and Tracey Maegusuku-Hewett report on the findings from a recent research project with care staff working in residential care homes for older people in Wales. They reflect on how lesbian, gay and bisexual (LGB) sexualities in care spaces can be obscured and ignored, which, in turn, impedes a rights-based approach to the expression of sexuality in care contexts: without recognition of LGB sexual identities/sexualities, associated rights issues are not triggered. In the final chapter, Chapter 15, Richard Ward considers issues of rights and recognition for people with dementia in a Scottish socio-legal context. Ward interrogates the categories mobilised to assert the rights of people with dementia, considering their exclusionary processes, including with regard to LGBT* people with dementia. He advocates a deconstruction of these categories.

All four chapters highlight the importance of recognition for rights, both in terms of being recognised as being entitled to any rights at all, and then which rights, and how. Access to rights also informs access to resources, both the provision of health and social care provision, but also the quality of that provision, and the extent to which it is, or is not, responsive to LGBT* individuals' needs and wishes. Issues of mental capacity, and loss of capacity associated with dementia, prompt questions about who speaks up on behalf of the LGBT* person with dementia, and how, and the extent to which the views and preferences of the person concerned are accurately reflected by those purporting to be representing them. This is of particular concern among biological families who may hold enduring homophobic and/or transphobic attitudes which may inform the decisions they make on behalf of the LGBT* individual who has lost capacity. As Sue Westwood has considered in Chapter 2, Nancy Fraser (1997) has argued that recognition, resources and representation form three interlocking arms of equality. As these chapters demonstrate, rights, issues and concerns relating to LGBT* people living with dementia, are reflected in each of these arms, highlighting how dementia is a critical and pressing (in)equality issue for LGBT* people.

Reference

Fraser, N. (1997) *Justice Interruptus*. New York: Routledge.

12 LGBT* individuals living with dementia

Rights and capacity issues in the United States

Nancy J. Knauer

Introduction

In the United States, the unique challenges facing lesbian, gay, bisexual and trans* (LGBT*) individuals living with dementia have been largely overlooked by both national policy initiatives and the LGBT* rights movement. Although the LGBT* rights movement has begun to embrace issues related to LGBT* ageing, it has often remained silent on the more problematic aspects of ageing, including issues related to dementia. The federal government has recently identified the prevention and treatment of Alzheimer's disease and related dementias as a top national priority, but its policy proposals have not addressed issues of sexual orientation or gender identity. As a result, LGBT* individuals living with dementia and their carers have been underserved by their community, the legal system, and the health care system.

The distinct needs and concerns of LGBT* individuals living with dementia are the result of a complex set of interrelated factors, including the demographic patterns of older LGBT* adults, the evolving nature of LGBT* rights, the stubborn persistence of anti-LGBT* bias and prejudice, and heteronormative caregiving and health policies. After discussing the barriers facing LGBT* individuals living with dementia, this chapter focuses on guardianship reform, culturally competent practices, and advance care planning as ways to address these concerns. It also explores how anti-LGBT* bias can complicate questions of capacity and erase LGBT* identities. Recognizing that legal reform may take years to institute, this chapter urges all LGBT* individuals to develop an expanded advance care plan to safeguard and memorialize their values and preferences. An expanded advance care plan can address important issues that may not be covered by the traditional estate planning documents, including gender identity, housing, caregiving, visitation, and funeral instructions.

The intersection of LGBT* ageing and dementia policy

Over the last several years, there has been increased interest in issues related to LGBT* older adults and LGBT* ageing, but very little has been done to identify LGBT*-specific concerns within dementia policy. National LGBT* advocacy organizations have begun to address LGBT* ageing issues, as have mainstream ageing and senior organizations. The federal government has recognized LGBT* older adults as an especially vulnerable population in administrative guidance interpreting the Older Americans Act, which is the primary funding mechanism for programmes directed at those aged 65 and older (WIG, 2012). State governments have also addressed LGBT* ageing issues. California passed anti-discrimination protections specifically aimed at LGBT* older adults and has mandated cultural competency training for certain professionals (Schevker, 2013). Massachusetts has convened a state-wide Commission on LGBT Ageing to study the issues and make policy recommendations (Wu, 2014). Much of this new focus on LGBT* ageing has understandably concentrated on models of 'successful ageing' and often overlooks some of the more problematic issues related to LGBT* ageing, such as financial insecurity, re-closeting, the lack of informal caregivers, social isolation, and dementia.

At the same time, there has also been a sharp increase in research and spending in areas related to the treatment and care of dementia. An estimated 3.8 million Americans were living with dementia in 2014, including nearly 40 per cent of the population aged 85 and older (Shih *et al.*, 2014). A conservative estimate of the number of LGBT* older adults living with dementia is 350,000 (McGovern, 2014). The total number of individuals living with dementia is expected to more than triple by 2050, which will create an unprecedented need for long-term support and services and place significant strain on health and family resources (Shih *et al.*, 2014). To address this looming crisis, Congress enacted the National Alzheimer's Project Act (NAPA) in 2011 (Belluck, 2010: A26; Library of Congress, 2011). The NAPA mandated the creation of an inter-agency advisory council and the development of a national strategic plan. The following year, the U.S. Department of Health and Human Services (HHS) released the National Plan to Address Alzheimer's Disease (the 'National Plan') (U.S. Department of Health and Human Services, 2014a). Updated annually, the National Plan provides a detailed policy blueprint for the prevention and treatment of Alzheimer's Disease and related dementias. The National Plan specifically targets certain populations who face barriers to diagnosis, treatment, and care, such as racial and ethnic minorities. However, the 87-page document does not address the unique challenges experienced by LGBT* individuals and their carers.

LGBT* older adults in the United States

In the United States, LGBT* older adults came of age at a time when homosexuality was widely criminalized and gender conformity was strictly policed. As a cohort, older LGBT* individuals have experienced high levels of anti-LGBT* violence, harassment, and discrimination, and studies suggest that these life experiences continue to inform their behaviour, specifically their relationship to the medical profession, willingness to use the closet as an adaptive strategy, and fear of encountering anti-LGBT* bias (METLIFE, 2006). In the case of dementia, these characteristics present numerous barriers to effective diagnosis, treatment and care.

Homosexuality was classified as a severe sociopathic personality disorder until 1973, and states were permitted to criminalize homosexual behaviour until 2003. To provide some historical perspective, this means that LGBT* individuals who turned 65 in 2014 were 24 years old before homosexuality was declassified as a mental illness. As they were growing up and well into young adulthood, today's older LGBT* adults were subject to involuntary commitment and a wide range of 'therapeutic' interventions, such as electro-shock therapy, psychoanalysis, aversion therapy, and even lobotomy. Beyond the medical field, the classification of homosexuality as a mental illness and its continued criminalization was used to justify a wide range of legal and social disabilities. LGBT* people were disqualified from most employment and considered per se unfit parents.

Estimates of the current number of LGB elders in the United States range from between 1.6 million and 2.4 million (Knauer, 2012). The wide variation is the result of differing estimates on the number of LGB individuals more generally and the absence of reliable statistics on the number of trans* elders (Grant, 2010). Regardless of the estimate used, however, it is clear that the number of LGBT* elders will increase remarkably as the Baby Boom generation transitions to senior status, and the total population of individuals 65 years of age and older in the United States doubles by 2030 (U.S. Administration on Aging, 2014).

In terms of demographics, older LGBT* individuals are more likely than their non-LGBT* peers to be single and to live alone (De Vries and Blando, 2004). It is also common for LGBT* older adults to be estranged from their family of origin, and they are much less likely to have children (De Vries and Blano, 2004). Older same-sex couples are geographically diverse and broadly distributed across the United States. Same-sex partnered households where at least one partner is 65 years of age or older reside in 97 per cent of the counties in the United States, with 15 per cent of these couples residing in areas that are classified as rural (Gates, 2003). The largest concentrations of older same-sex partnered households are not located in traditionally LGBT*-friendly jurisdictions, but rather in states with high concentrations of older adults generally, such as Florida and Arizona (Grant, 2010: 39).

Same-sex couples where at least one partner is aged 65 or older struggle disproportionately with financial insecurity and report greater levels of disability (Fredriksen-Goldsen *et al.*, 2013a, 2013b). As long-time survivors of homophobia and transphobia, it is not surprising that older same-sex households lag well behind their non-LGBT* peers on all economic indicators. Female same-sex partnered households where one partner is 65 years of age or older are nearly twice as likely to live below the poverty level than different-sex married households in the same age cohort (Shih *et al.*, 2014: xii). Widespread financial insecurity means that older same-sex couples will have fewer financial resources to pay for long-term support and services. In the United States, the cost of care for individuals living with dementia is estimated to be between \$159 billion and \$215 billion annually (Shih *et al.*, 2014: xi). Medicare is the primary government-provided health insurance for older Americans, but it does not cover the cost of long-term support and services that can easily exceed $80,000 annually for a skilled nursing facility (U.S. Department of Health and Human Services, 2014b). Long-term care is covered by Medicaid, which is a government-provided health insurance programme for low income and low wealth individuals. In order to qualify for Medicaid, individuals must have total assets worth less than $2000 (Shih *et al.*, 2014: xiv note 4). Middle and upper income individuals often purchase long-term care insurance, but the high cost of the insurance is out of reach for many middle income Americans and prohibitive for those struggling with financial insecurity (Waggoner, 2014).

Chosen family and caregiving

Financial insecurity will limit an individual's access to care and treatment for dementia. In the United States, ageing policy assumes that the primary responsibility for caregiving will be shouldered by family members. Estimates indicate that over 80 per cent of all caregiving is provided on an 'informal' or unpaid basis, with the vast majority of that care being performed by younger relatives (Kling and Kimmel, 2006). This caregiving pattern obviously places LGBT* individuals living with dementia at a severe disadvantage because they are more likely to be estranged from their families of origin and much less likely to have children than their non-LGBT* peers. Instead, they rely on what anthropologists refer to as 'chosen family' for support (Weston, 1991). Although chosen family structures represent a creative way to form relationships and community in the face of a hostile society and disapproving family, they also have two major drawbacks. They are legally very fragile, and they are often single-generational. The single-generational nature of chosen family means that a friendship group will age in unison, thereby creating reciprocal and overlapping caregiving responsibilities that can tax the resources of a friendship group.

Without the typical informal caregivers, LGBT* individuals living with dementia will be more likely to require assisted living arrangements or home health care support sooner than their non-LGBT* peers. However, LGBT* older adults are often determined to 'age in place' because they fear encountering anti-LGBT* bias in long-term care facilities at the hands of service providers and other residents. This fear also causes them to underutilize supportive services that are designed to help elders live independently in the community. As a result, LGBT* older adults are at an enhanced risk of self-neglect and social isolation, both of which will delay diagnosis and treatment for dementia.

Re-closeting as a public health concern

Advancements in LGBT* rights and recognition in the United States has decreased the number of LGBT* individuals who feel compelled to remain 'closeted' and hide their identity and basic facts about their lives from family, friends, and service providers. However, not all members of the older generation have fully embraced the new levels of openness. Many older LGBT* adults remain closeted and estranged from relatives and friends and are only 'out' with members of their close knit chosen family. Some members of this generation are only 'out' to their partners. Even those older LGBT* individuals who are 'out' report pressure to 're-closet' as they age because they fear encountering medical professionals, home health aides, and other service providers who harbour anti-LGBT* bias. LGBT* older adults report a widespread distrust of the medical profession and a lack of confidence that they will receive treatment that is not tainted by anti-LGBT* bias. Some LGBT* residents of long-term care facilities report that they create an alternate set of memories to share with the other residents by changing the facts of their life, such as describing a partner as a cousin or a best friend. With respect to re-closeting, one older gay man explained, 'as strong as I am today … when I am in front of the gate of the nursing home, the closet door is going to slam shut behind me' (Gross 2007: A1).

In addition to the dignitary harm of concealing an essential part of oneself, it is clear that re-closeting has adverse health consequences and should be treated as an important public health issue. In the words of a prominent geriatric psychiatrist, closeted LGBT* older adults face 'a faster pathway to depression, failure to thrive and even premature death' because 'there is something special about having to hide this part of your identity at a time when your entire identity is threatened' (Gross 2007: A1). The re-closeting of LGBT* individuals living with dementia also has direct consequences for certain cognitive psychosocial dementia therapies, including reminiscence programmes and validation therapy. These treatment options will not only fail to reach closeted LGBT* individuals living with dementia, but they may create further distress by introducing false and incongruent memories.

For trans* elders, the closet is not a viable option because many older trans* individuals transitioned without medical intervention and, even those who did transition with medical assistance, often have not had surgical genital reconstruction (Cook-Daniels, 2006). As a result, a trans* resident's physical characteristics may not conform to his or her gender identity and performance, making the resident vulnerable to the prejudice and hostility of personal health aides and other service providers. Sex-segregated living facilities also present particular challenges. Anecdotal accounts suggest that trans* residents in long-term care facilities have been forced to wear gender inappropriate clothes and to room with members of the opposite sex because the facility refused to honour the resident's gender identity. There have also been reports of service providers refusing to wash or provide personal care assistance for trans* residents. For these older trans* adults, entering long-term living facilities can mean a forced re-transition to the sex they were assigned at birth.

Fear of anti-LGBT bias and access to services*

The fear expressed by LGBT* older adults that they will experience anti-LGBT* bias as they age is not misplaced. This bias can range from simple ignorance to outright hostility on the part of service providers and their non-LGBT* peers

(National Senior Citizens Law Center, 2011). In long-term care facilities, service providers have failed to respect long-term partners or other chosen family by deferring to the wishes of next of kin and separating partners. As noted above, they also have forced trans* residents to wear inappropriate clothing and addressed residents by the wrong name and incorrect pronoun. Non-LGBT* peers may engage in shunning and bullying behaviours. There are reports of LGBT* older adults receiving inadequate care and abusive treatment from health care workers on account of their sexual orientation or gender identity. Some workers have openly expressed distaste over having to touch an LGBT* person. Religiously motivated workers have been known to harangue LGBT* elders who are in their care and urge them to repent before it is too late.

In 2007, the *New York Times* reported that long-term care facilities have sometimes moved residents who are perceived to be LGBT* to secure 'memory' or dementia wards without cause in order to placate the complaints of other residents or their family members (Gross, 2007: 13). The dementia wards are considered optimal places to put an offending LGBT* resident because the other residents of the dementia ward will not complain. The same *New York Times* article reported that this practice led to tragic results when an older gay man was confined to a dementia ward without cause and eventually hanged himself (Gross, 2007).

Older LGBT* persons and social isolation: the case of Clay Green and Harold Scull

The case of Clay Greene and Harold Scull provides an example of what can happen when isolated older LGBT* individuals attempt to age in place without supportive services. In 2008, Sonoma County, California used secure 'memory' wards to separate long-time partners, Harold Scull and Clay Greene (Bajko, 2010). Sonoma County is part of the generally progressive San Francisco Bay area. At the time, Clay was 76 years of age and Harold was 88. They had been committed partners for over 25 years and had lived together for 20 years. They shared a small house with their cats, Sassy and Tiger. When Harold fell on the front porch steps of their home, Clay called 911, over Harold's objections (*Green v. Cnty. of Sonoma*). Suspecting violence, the County immediately took both men into care and separated them. According to Clay, Harold was taking medication that made him unsteady on his feet, and he was still bruised from an earlier fall. Without the necessary medical screening and against his will, Clay was placed in a secure dementia facility. Four months later, Harold died alone in a board and care facility, and Clay was not told until several days after the fact (James 2010: A18). By the time Harold died, the County had removed their cats, sold all of the couple's possessions, and assumed control of their finances. Clay continued to be held in the secure facility until early 2009 when his court-appointed attorney was finally able to secure his release. Even after his release, his lawyer reported that Clay remains fearful that county workers will come to his home and harm him (James 2010: A19).

In 2010, Clay, along with Harold's estate, sued Sonoma County and related defendants alleging that the defendants' actions were motivated by anti-gay bias and the desire for financial gain (*Green* v. *Cnty. of Sonoma* at 1, 9, 14, and 17). Clay further alleged that he was verbally harassed and demeaned by the defendants who 'expressed displeasure at having to deal with expressions of grief by a gay man who had lost his partner' (*Green* v. *Cnty. of Sonoma* at 9). Shortly before the trial began, the defendants settled the claims for an amount in excess of $600,000 (Egelko 2010). Sonoma County denied any wrongdoing, but agreed to modify its conservatorship procedures to prevent similar incidents in the future.

Avenues for advocacy and reform

The last several decades have seen tremendous progress in the area of LGBT* rights in the United States. LGBT* individuals now enjoy unprecedented social and political acceptance. Although nationwide marriage equality was achieved in 2015, there are no comprehensive anti-discrimination protections for LGBT* individuals on the federal level and fewer than one-half of the states extend non-discrimination protections on the basis of sexual orientation and gender identity (Human Rights Campaign (HRC), 2014). As a result, in the majority of states, same-sex couples can be married on Saturday and fired from their jobs or evicted from their homes on Monday. Comprehensive non-discrimination protections would clearly improve the lives of LGBT* adults, but the attainment of these goals will not be sufficient to safeguard the interests of LGBT* older adults. The advent of marriage equality will resolve many of the disadvantages imposed on same-sex partners, but it will not address the larger issues raised by the reliance of LGBT* individuals on chosen family. Marriage allows an individual to make his partner part of his family, but there is no comparable mechanism to make his best friend part of his family. This limitation has obvious consequences in areas where the law gives priority to next of kin for decision-making and vests them with other types of authority. Existing state-level non-discrimination protections are also generally under-inclusive because they tend to focus on the employment context, whereas LGBT* older adults are more likely to encounter LGBT* bias in more private venues, such as housing and health care settings. Accordingly, non-discrimination measures must be universal and far-reaching to protect LGBT* older adults in all aspects of their lives.

This section outlines areas of reform in addition to the general goal of comprehensive non-discrimination protections that will improve outcomes for older LGBT* individuals, specifically those living with dementia. The starting point for all of these reforms is a recognition that LGBT* individuals face unique barriers with respect to the diagnosis, treatment, and care of dementia due to their demographic patterns, financial insecurity, reliance on chosen family, and justified fear of encountering anti-LGBT* bias. As such, LGBT* older adults represent a special population who should be expressly targeted in the National Plan, along with racial and ethnic minorities. Beyond this national acknowledgement, there are numerous opportunities to improve outcomes for LGBT* individuals living with dementia in the areas of guardianship laws and cultural competency training. Moreover, as discussed in the final section, all LGBT* individuals should be strongly encouraged to use advance care planning to memorialize their preferences and safeguard their dignity in the event of cognitive impairment.

Guardianship laws

An estimated 1.5 million adults in the United States are living under a plenary guardianship, which removes all legal decision-making capacity from the ward (as distinct from a limited guardianship where only certain spheres or types of decision-making ability are vested in the guardian) (Uekert and Van Duizend, 2011). Guardianship is governed by state law and varies considerably from state to state. Over the last 20 years, there has been considerable reform in the area of guardianship law designed to enhance respect for the core concepts of dignity and self-determination. These reforms have included revising the capacity standards, rejecting plenary guardianships, increasing procedural safeguards, and imposing certification and monitoring requirements on guardians. However, they have not addressed issues related to sexual orientation and gender identity. This silence leaves guardianship law open to the influences of anti-LGBT* bias that can range from cultural insensitivity to outright hostility. When this occurs, capacity standards, choice of guardian rules, and decision-making standards can operate to erase LGBT* identity and ignore LGBT* families. Accordingly, guardianship law should mandate that respect for an individual's sexual orientation and gender identity is integral to the concepts of dignity and self-determination.

Tests evaluating capacity or measuring undue influence may disadvantage LGBT* individuals, especially where the individual in question is closeted and estranged from his legally recognized next of kin. Capacity doctrines typically take into account an individual's ability to engage in deliberative decision-making and, in some instances, the perceived reasonableness of an individual's actions. When an individual experiences dementia, it is common for family members to be expected to arrange care. If the individual living with dementia was closeted and estranged from his family, the family members may be alarmed to find their 'bachelor' uncle living with another man and immediately assume that he is being taken advantage of by the 'roommate'. In these situations, the confused relatives may also be able to use criminal undue influence laws to stop the 'roommate' from having further contact with their uncle. In the state of Wisconsin, for example, it is possible to get a restraining order against the 'roommate' regardless of whether the uncle has capacity and consents to the contact (Kohn, 2012: 7).

In order avoid these misunderstandings, capacity doctrine should acknowledge the right of an individual to self-identify her sexual orientation and gender identity. It should also take steps to ensure that the determination of capacity is done in a culturally competent manner that takes into account the unique socio-legal status and background of LGBT* individuals. *A Handbook for Psychologists* prepared by the American Bar Association's Commission on Law and Aging notes that 'a person's race, ethnicity, culture, gender, sexual orientation, and religion may impact his or her values and preferences', but provides no further guidance (American Bar Association and American Psychological Association, 2008: 27) The only other time it mentions sexual orientation is in connection with the capacity to engage in sexual activity, ignoring more expansive issues related to identity.

Guardianship law also establishes an order of priority to determine who serves as guardian, and these provisions invariably privilege legally recognized next of kin. Preferences for traditional family disadvantage same-sex partners who are not married, and they uniformly exclude chosen family. As a result, the individuals most familiar with the person in need of assistance can be foreclosed from consideration in the absence of a durable power of attorney that nominates a guardian.

The 2008 case of *In re Guardianship of Atkins* from Indiana demonstrates the potential fragility of LGBT* families under guardianship law and how a 'best interest' standard can operate to give voice to anti-LGBT* bias and disapproval (*In re Guardianship of Atkins*). At the time, the state of Indiana did not have marriage equality, but Patrick Atkins and Brett Conrad had lived together as a committed couple for 25 years. When Patrick suffered a debilitating stroke, his family immediately restricted Brett's ability to visit, eventually forbidding it completely. Patrick's family disapproved of his same-sex relationship and his mother later testified that if her son were going to return to his life with Brett, then she would prefer that he not recover.

Brett petitioned the court to be appointed Patrick's guardian, but Patrick's parents had clear priority under the Indiana guardianship statute, and Patrick had not executed a durable power of attorney. The trial court appointed Patrick's parents co-guardians of his estate and person. The court further ruled that, as guardians, Patrick's parents had 'the ultimate and sole responsibility ... to determine and control visitation with and access of visitors to Patrick Atkins in his best interest' (*In re Guardianship of Atkins* at 882). The intermediate appellate court unanimously upheld the appointment of Patrick's parents as co-guardians, citing the clear mandate of the statute. The majority opinion granted Brett's request for visitation and described the animosity that Patrick's mother expressed toward her son's relationship as 'astonishing' (at 882). The opinion also stated that 'we are extraordinarily skeptical that [Patrick's parents] are able to take care of [his] emotional needs' (at 884). The Indiana Supreme Court ultimately refused to review the case (*Conrad* v. *Atkins*). After three years of litigation, Patrick was left in the care of his disapproving parents, despite strong judicial misgivings regarding his emotional well-being.

The case of Patrick involved estranged relatives working at odds with the interests of the LGBT* person in need of assistance, but for LGBT* older adults struggling with social isolation there may be no relatives interested in assuming responsibility. When this occurs, as it did with Harold and Clay, public guardians will be appointed, and these parties may be even less inclined to familiarize themselves with the individual's values and preferences. Consequently, it is imperative to provide public guardians with training designed to equip them with culturally competent practices to represent LGBT* individuals.

Culturally competent practices

Cultural competency training can be an effective way to educate service providers about the needs and concerns of LGBT* older adults. It can be mandated by statute as part of a licensing or accreditation requirement or adopted voluntarily. For example, California requires licensed health professionals who have regular contact with seniors and residential care administrators to have LGBT* cultural competency training (Schevker, 2013). HHS, in conjunction with LGBT* advocacy organizations, has developed an online training module, *Building Respect for LGBT Older Adults*, to raise awareness of the needs of LGBT* residents in long-term care facilities (U.S. Administration on Aging and U.S. Administration for Community Living, 2014). LGBT* Advocacy organizations have also produced a range of training materials (National Resource Center on LGBT Aging, 2014).

In addition to cultural competency training, it is important to adopt culturally competent policies and programmes that are inclusive and take into account the particular needs of LGBT* older adults. For example, facilities serving older adults should adopt well-publicized non-discrimination policies and policies that guarantee respect for an individual's LGBT* identity. These policies can include anti-bullying provisions to prevent residents and staff from bullying LGBT* older adults, as well as inclusive programming. Parallel efforts to institute culturally competent practices have been very successful in the workplace. Today, the overwhelming majority of Fortune 500 companies have anti-discrimination policies that include sexual orientation and gender identity.[1] The Human Rights Campaign (HRC, 2013) rates companies based on a Corporate Equality Index that measures how welcoming the company is toward its LGBT* employees. HRC has recently started an analogous rating index in the health care context; both are designed to provide useful information to consumers and employers, creating new industry norms (HRC, 2014b).

Advanced care planning

For LGBT* older adults, the traditional estate planning documents – wills, durable powers of attorney, and advance directives – are not sufficient to preserve their preferences and protect their chosen families. As typically drafted, health care powers of attorney and advance directives do not address a number of important decisions that are customarily left to family, such as funeral or burial instructions, and they do not address issues specific to trans* individuals. To supplement the traditional estate planning documents, LGBT* older adults should develop an integrated advance care plan that may require the assistance of financial advisers and medical service providers, as well as the coordination of both formal and informal caregivers. The comprehensive advance care plan should incorporate the traditional estate planning documents while also providing clear written instructions with respect to gender identity, housing, caregiving, visitation, funeral and burial arrangements, and anything else an individual feels strongly about, such as the care of their pets or organ donation.

In many instances, the actual legal force of these instructions may be unclear, but, at the very least, they will provide some indicication of what the individual would have wanted had she been able to express her wishes. They should be designed to speak beyond incapacity and provide protection for both the individual and her chosen family from the potentially conflicting values of next of kin or public guardians. In each case, the individual's wishes and preferences can be reflected in a separate document or incorporated in a more comprehensive document, such as an advance directive. Whenever possible, the document should be executed with the same legal formalities applicable to wills: signed, dated, witnessed by two disinterested witnesses, and notarized. Given the potential for a will challenge, it is also important to document that the individual had the requisite capacity to execute the documents. The following briefly outlines five areas of common concern for LGBT* older adults: gender identity, housing, caregiving preferences, visitation issues, and funeral and burial arrangements.

Gender identity

With respect to gender identity, ageing and the onset of dementia can pose a specific set of challenges for trans* individuals, who often express deep concern that they will encounter transphobic service providers, especially in assisted or long-term care facilities. As discussed above, long-term care facilities sometimes refuse to respect an individual's gender identity by forcing a resident to wear gender inappropriate clothing or calling the resident by the wrong name and using the wrong pronouns. These actions can produce extreme dignitary and psychological harm while undermining psychosocial dementia treatment that stresses reminiscence and validation therapy. For these reasons, it is extremely important for LGBT* older adults to leave express and detailed directions regarding gender identity issues, including preferred pronouns and clothing, as well as desired supportive medical therapy. These directions can be easily incorporated into a durable medical power of attorney or advance directive to the extent they are directed at service providers and involve medical care. However, it is also important to make sure that any substituted decision-makers are aware of the individual's wishes, especially if estranged next of kin might be hostile to these wishes or a public guardian might be involved.

Housing

In terms of housing options, LGBT* individuals overwhelmingly report that they would prefer to 'age in place' and express extreme trepidation about entering any form of congregate living facility, such as a nursing home or assisted living facility. If an individual intends to age in place, the goal of her advance care plan should be to maximize autonomy and the ability to live independently for as long as possible. The plan should identify and organize supportive services and informal caregivers, but it should also identify acceptable housing options for when the individual can no longer live independently. Although the market has recently begun to respond to the concerns of LGBT* older adults by creating LGBT*-centred senior housing developments, there are very few expressly LGBT*-centred facilities, and these facilities generally do not provide dementia care. In the absence of an LGBT*-centred facility, the advance care plan should identify acceptable LGBT*-friendly facilities that, at a minimum, have an anti-discrimination policy covering sexual orientation and gender identity. Ideally, the facility should also have adopted the types of culturally competent practices discussed above.

Caregiving

LGBT* older adults who rely on chosen family should take special care to spell out their wishes with respect to their preferred caregivers and appoint substitute decision-makers through health care proxies and durable medical powers of attorney. All states currently recognize durable powers of attorney that survive the incapacity of the grantor of the power. They also allow individuals to appoint the persons whom they wish to serve as guardian should one be needed. In the absence of a durable power of attorney, the law will privilege next of kin over chosen family, regardless of the closeness of the relationship. When no next of kin is available or willing to serve, the state will assume the responsibility for the adult in need of assistance through the office of the public guardian or, if the adult has private funds, through a private fiduciary. Generally, the state will be considered to have a greater interest than chosen family, who are considered strangers under the law.

Visitation

Another area of concern is visitation. Older LGBT* individuals should execute a document that lists the individuals whom they would like to have visiting privileges at either a hospital or long-term care facility. Hospital visitation authorization forms have been a common feature of LGBT* estate planning since the first wave of the HIV/AIDS epidemic in the 1980s when partners and friends were barred from visiting sick and dying patients due to hospital policies that restricted visitors to 'family members'. Although it had long been unclear whether these documents carried any legal force, HHS recently issued regulations requiring all hospitals and long-term care facilities that accept Medicaid and Medicare payments to extend visitation privileges without regard to sexual orientation or gender identity (Centers for MEDICARE & MEDICAID Services, U.S. Dep't Health & Hum. Services, 2014). For long-term care facilities, the regulations expressly provide that visitors must be given 'full and equal visitation privileges, consistent with resident preference.' (Director, Survey & Certification Group, Centers for MEDICARE & MEDICAID Services, U.S. Dep't Health & Hum. Services, 2013). The regulations were issued in response to a Presidential Memorandum affirming a patient's right to visitation that President Obama issued after a heart-wrenching case in Florida where hospital workers refused to allow a same-sex partner access to her dying partner despite the fact that she was her partner's attorney-in-fact (Parker-Pope, 2009; Obama, 2010).

Funeral and burial arrangements

The lack of recognition for chosen family and family estrangement has sometimes produced conflict over funeral arrangements and burial instructions. For example, one family of origin pursued a lawsuit for three years attempting to stop a surviving partner from including the term 'life partner' in an epitaph (Ginanni, 1997). Given the importance of this issue and the strong emotions it can trigger, LGBT* older adults should execute a separate document that sets forth their directions and preferences for their funeral and burial arrangements. The states vary as to whether individuals have the authority to direct the terms of their funeral and burial, but the document will serve as indication of the individual's wishes.

When individuals do not leave instructions, the law will typically look to legally recognized next of kin for direction. For individuals who do not have any legally recognized next of kin or are totally estranged from their families of origin, the state will assume control. In a 2009 case from Rhode Island, it took a surviving long-time partner 32 days to convince the medical examiner to release his partner's remains, even though they were legally married in a neighbouring state and the surviving partner was the executor of his partner's estate (Edgar, 2009). In the absence of any legally recognized next of kin, his partner's remains were considered the property of the state, illustrating the lack of legal standing afforded chosen family.

Conclusion

Currently, national dementia policy fails to address the unique challenges facing LGBT* older adults. The first step to improving outcomes for LGBT* individuals living with dementia is to expand the National Plan to acknowledge LGBT* older adults as a population with special needs, as it does for racial and ethnic minorities. Recognition on the national level will signal the importance of providing culturally competent care for the estimated 350,000 LGBT* Americans living with dementia. As LGBT* rights in the United States continue to evolve, the adoption of marriage equality and expanding non-discrimination protections will improve outcomes for LGBT* individuals, but more targeted reform is necessary to safeguard their interests, including changes in the guardianship laws and the implementation of cultural competent and inclusive policies and programmes. In the meantime, all LGBT* individuals should augment their estate planning documents with an expanded advance care plan that addresses issues and values important to them, such as gender identity, housing, care-giving, visitation, and funeral and burial arrangements.

As a final note, it bears mentioning that some of the challenges facing the current cohort of LGBT* older adults may be generational. Younger generations of LGBT* individuals have benefitted more directly from greater freedom, recognition, and legal protections. They are less likely to be estranged from their families and more likely to parent by creating intentional LGBT* families. Despite these changing demographics, the experiences of LGBT* older adults may provide a cautionary tale about the effect of the ageing process on the ability to withstand and navigate bias. Surveys show that older LGBT* individuals are more fearful of ageing than their non-LGBT* peers (METLIFE, 2006: 4). The practice of re-closeting in later life suggests that the ageing process may amplify feelings of difference and vulnerability. Incidents that one may have successfully weathered at 35 may be much more menacing when experienced at 85 years old. Accordingly, reform is imperative to protect the future of all LGBT* individuals who one day will encounter the special challenges presented by LGBT* ageing.

Note

1 Ninety-one per cent of all Fortune 500 companies have non-discrimination policies for sexual orientation and 61 per cent extend protection based on gender identity (Human Rights Campaign, 2013).

Case law

Conrad v. *Atkins*, 891 N.E.2d 34 (Ind. 2008).
Green v. *Cnty. of Sonoma*, First Amended Complaint, p. 2 (Cal. App. Dep't Super. Ct. Mar. 22, 2010) (No. SPR-81815) [Online] Available from: www.nclrights.org/wp-content/uploads/2013/04/cases_GreenevSonomaCounty_Complaint.pdf.
In re Guardianship of Atkins, 868 N.E.2d 878, 880 (Ind. App. 2007).

Statute

Centers for MEDICARE & MEDICAID Services, U.S. Dep't Health & Hum. Services (2014) Final Rule: Changes to the Hospital and Critical Hospital Conditions of Participation to Ensure Visitation Rights for all Patients, 42 C.F.R. §482.13(h); 42 C.F.R. §485.635(f).

References

American Bar Association and American Psychological Association (2008) *Assessment of Older Adults with Diminished Capacity: A Psychologist's Handbook*. [Online] available from: www.apa.org/pi/aging/programs/assessment/capacity-psychologist-handbook.pdf. [accessed: 31 December 2014].

Belluck, P. (2010) With Alzheimer's patients growing in number, Congress endorses a national plan. *New York Times.* 16th December. p. A26.

De Vries, B. and Blando, J. (2004) The Study of Gay and Lesbian Aging: Lessons for Social Gerontology. In G. Herdt and B. De Vries, *Gay and Lesbian Aging: Research and Future Directions*, pp. 3–28. New York: Springer Publishing Company.

Director, Survey & Certification Group, Centers for MEDICARE & MEDICAID Services, U.S. Dep't Health & Hum. Services (2013) Memorandum to State Survey Agency Directors, Reminder: Access and Visitation Rights in Long Term Care. 28th June. [Online] available from: www.cms.gov/medicare/provider-enrollment-and-certification/surveycertificationgeninfo/downloads/survey-and-cert-letter-13-42.pdf. [accessed 31 December 2014].

Edgar, R. (2009) Lack of funeral rights turns mourner into gay activist. *Providence Journal.* 15th November. [Online] available from: http://connectingdirectors.com/articles/905-lack-of-funeral-rights-turns-mourner-into-gay-activist. [accessed: 31 December 2014].

Fredriksen-Goldsen, K. I., Cook-Daniels, L., Kim, H.-J., Erosheva, E. A., Emlet, C. A., Hoy-Ellis, C. P., Goldsen, J. and Muraco, A. (2013a) Physical and mental health of transgender older adults: an at-risk and underserved population, *The Gerontologist*, first published online 27 March 2013, DOI: 10.1093/geront/gnt021.

Fredriksen-Goldsen, K. I., Emlet, C. A., Kim, H.-J. Muraco, A., Erosheva, E. A., Goldsen, J. and Hoy-Ellis, C. P. (2013b) The physical and mental health of lesbian, gay male, and bisexual (LGB) older adults: the role of key health indicators and risk and protective factors, *The Gerontologist* **53**(4), 664–675.

Gates, G. (2003) Gay and Lesbian Families in the Census: Gay and Lesbian Seniors. *The Urban Inst.* [Online]. 30 May. Available from: www.urban.org/url.cfm?ID=900627 [accessed: 31 December 2014].

Ginanni, C. N. (1997) Cemetery to inscribe headstone, pay $15,000. *Legal Intelligencer.* 8th September. p. 5.

Grant, J. (2010) Outing age 2010: public policy issues affecting lesbian, gay, bisexual and transgender elders. Nat'l Gay And Lesbian Task Force Policy Inst. [Online] www.thetaskforce.org/downloads/reports/reports/outingage_final.pdf [accessed: 31 December 2014].

Human Rights Campaign (2013) Corporate America Champions LGBT Equality in Record Numbers. [Online] 9 December. Available from www.hrc.org/press-releases/entry/corporate-america-champions-LGBT-equality-in-record-numbers [accessed: 31 December 2014].

Human Rights Campaign (2014) Statewide Employment Law and Policies. 9 October. [Online] available from: http://hrc-assets.s3-website-us-east-1.amazonaws.com//files/assets/resources/statewide_employment_10-2014.pdf [accessed: 31 December 2014].

James, S. (2010) An unlikely plaintiff. At issue? He dares not speak its name. *New York Times.* 7 May.

Kling, E. and Kimmel, D. (2006) SAGE: New York City's Pioneer Organization for LGBT Elders. In D. Kimmel, T. Rose, and S. David, (eds) *Lesbian, Gay, Bisexual, and Transgender Aging: Research and Clinical Perspectives*, pp. 265–276. New York: Columbia University Press.

Knauer, N. J. (2012) Gen silent: advocating for LGBT elders, *Elder Law Journal* **19**(2), 289–349, fn 55.

Kohn, N. (2012) Elder (in)justice: a critique of the criminalization of elder abuse, *American Criminal Law Review* **49**(1), 1–29.

Library of Congress (2011) National Alzheimer's Project Act. Bill Summary & Status 111th Congress (2009–2010) S.3036 [Online] 11 January. Available from: http://thomas.loc.gov/cgi-bin/bdquery/z?d111:s3036 [accessed: 31 December 2014].

McGovern, J. (2014) The forgotten: dementia and the aging LGBT community, *Journal of Gerontological Social Work* **57**(8), 845–857.

METLIFE, (2006) Out and aging: the MetLife study of lesbian and gay baby boomers. [Online] November 2006. Available from: https://www.metlife.com/assets/cao/mmi/publications/studies/mmi-out-aging-lesbian-gay-retirement.pdf [accessed: 31 December 2014].

National Resource Center on LGBT Aging (2014) Culturally Competent Care and Training. [Online] Available from: www.LGBTagingcenter.org/resources/index.cfm?s=4 [accessed: 31 December 2014].

National Senior Citizens Law Center (2011) LGBT Older Adults in Long-Term Care Facilities: Stories from the Field. [Online] available from: www.LGBTlongtermcare.org/wp-content/uploads/NSCLC_LGBT_report.pdf accessed: 31 December 2014].

Obama, B. (2010) Memorandum to Kathleen Sebelius, Sec'y Health & Hum. Services, Respecting the Rights of Hospital Patients to Receive Visitors and to Designate Surrogate Decision Makers for Medical Emergencies. 15 April. [Online] available from: www.whitehouse.gov/the-press-office/presidential-memorandum-hospital-visitation [accessed: 31 December 2014].

Parker-Pope, T. (2009) Kept from a dying partner's bedside. *New York Times*. 19 May. p. D5.

Schevker, M. (2013) Governor signs bill to ensure LGBT seniors receive respectful, competent elder care. West Hollywood Patch. [Online] available from: http://patch.com/california/westhollywood/governor-signs-bill-to-ensure-LGBT-seniors-receive-respectful-competent-elder-care-westhollywood [accessed: 31 December 2014].

Shih, R. A., Concannon, T. W., Liu, J. L. and Friedman, E. M. (2014) Improving dementia long-term care: a policy blueprint. [Online] available from: www.rand.org/content/dam/rand/pubs/research_reports/RR500/RR597/RAND_RR597.pdf [accessed: 31 December 2014].

Uekert, B. K. and Van Duizend, R. (2011) Nat'l Ctr. for State Courts, Adult Guardianships: A 'Best Guess' National Estimate and the Momentum for Reform. p. 107 [Online] available from: www.guardianship.org/reports/Uekert_Van_Duizend_Adult_Guardianships.pdf [accessed: 31 December 2014].

U.S. Administration on Aging (2014) Aging statistics, [Online] available from: www.aoa.gov/Aging_Statistics/ [accessed: 31 December 2014].

U.S. Administration on Aging and U.S. Administration for Community Living (2014) Building Respect for LGBT Older Adults [Online] available from: http://LGBTagingcenter.org/training/buildingRespect.cfm [accessed: 31 December 2014].

U.S. Department of Health and Human Services (2014a) National plan to address Alzheimer's Disease: 2014 update [Online] available from: http://aspe.hhs.gov/daltcp/napa/NatlPlan2014.shtm [accessed: 31 December 2014].

U.S. Department of Health and Human Services (2014b) Costs of Care. [Online]. Available from: http://longtermcare.gov/costs-how-to-pay/costs-of-care/ [accessed: 31 December 2014].

Waggoner, J. (2014) Long-term care insurance: peace of mind at a price. USA Today. [Online] 31 March. Available from: www.usatoday.com/story/money/columnist/waggoner/2013/12/02/long-term-care-insurance/3807147/ [accessed: 31 December 2014].

Weston, K. (1991) *Families We Choose*. New York: Columbia University Press.

Wisconsin Gazette (WIG) (2012) U.S. agency: older LGBTs a population of 'greatest social need'. Wisconsin Gazette.com. [Online]. Available from: www.wisconsingazette.com/breaking-news/us-agency-older-LGBTs-a-population-of-greatest-social-need.html [accessed: 31 December 2014].

Wu, J. (2014) Equal dignity at every stage of our lives: the MA commission on LGBT aging, Gay & Lesbian Advocates & Defenders [Online] Available from: www.glad.org/current/post/equal-dignity-at-every-stage-of-our-lives-the-ma-commission-on-LGBT-aging [accessed: 31 December 2014].

13 The needs and rights of LGBT* carers of individuals with dementia

A personal journey

Roger Newman

Beginnings

'So how long has he been like this?' The consultant looked at me, clearly seeking an answer to help her but also perhaps, in my guilty mind, trying to shift some of the blame onto me. My answer was a definitive 'I just don't know'. Now, years afterwards, I regularly meet carers of newly diagnosed loved ones with dementia, for whom dementia seemed to have crept up on them. It was a condition which was not like flu, where one day you were fine and then the next day laid low. This was something which involved behaviour, progressively out of the ordinary, but which you could, for a while, simply incorporate into your relationship as an explanation of ageing, stress, or just not feeling especially up to the mark.

My partner, David, was a case like that. Having been together for 18 years, I had got used to his quirks, in the same way that he had got used to mine, but, at the same time, when there were perceptible changes, I just assumed they were blips and would put themselves right, like most of the physical and mental issues which hit you when you are older. It was, however, other people who seemed to see things more clearly than me. David's job had always been demanding but his talent, as a display manager for a large retail furniture company, had not failed him during his 18 years of service. He had been regularly congratulated on, and financially rewarded for, the quality of his displays in the ten or so shops he was responsible for. It was a shock, therefore, when he told me that he had been summoned to his head office for an interview, where he had been told that his managers felt his heart was no longer in his work. Not long after, I discovered that his proposals for new displays were being rejected, and that he had been taking time off work for no apparent reason. It was then only a matter of months before he came home with the news that he was to be made redundant, with almost immediate effect.

David's communication skills also started to change. There were long periods of silence and few extended conversations. A holiday in California became difficult to cope with, especially at meal times. Was it depression over the redundancy, I wondered? But I also remembered that on a previous holiday he had taken to talking to anyone sitting close by and mentioning his sister in a way in which he assumed the person knew her. When I saw people backing off, it was clear to me that this wasn't normal.

Our relationship also began to suffer. The warmth, love and camaraderie, which had been so admired by others, started to go and a gulf began to appear between us. At dinner parties, I felt that I needed to explain to others what he meant and even to apologise if his behaviour appeared to be strange. Again, I and others put this down to stress or the depression following his redundancy, but there were also deeper things happening to our relationship and I was beginning to suspect that actually he didn't want or love me anymore.

Having put up with this for long enough, I decided that we needed to separate and I left him. I was quite shocked by the lack of concern he showed about this, but soon the separation started to betray signs which indicated that there was something else happening. He crashed his car and phoned to tell me, but the information he gave was confused. His conversations now always included a curious laughter. We continued to visit each other, but the conversation was becoming even more difficult, almost as if he couldn't go further than using repeated stock phrases. Friends, also in touch with him, told me about his behaviour such as walking into other people's gardens and phoning them with bizarre information, and there were worrying signs of strangers visiting him and taking objects away.

I decided to intervene. A letter to his doctor yielded no more than the advice that David should go to see him if he was worried. Numerous phone calls to social services also failed to get the attention he clearly needed and, in spite of the fact that we had taken out power of attorney for each other, there was a wary approach from all which indicated that I had no real role other than being a concerned friend. This was, after all, 1992, and well before the more recent UK legislation providing greater legal rights and protections for LGBT* people.

A further phone call from David's neighbours convinced me that I had to intervene and do something. My visits to him were now enough to assure me that he had lost the power to look after himself. His power of speech was declining even further. When, on one of my visits, I suggested he get us some food, he served us frozen food on a plate, still frozen. He was smoking and discarding both ash and finished cigarettes on the floor. In short, he was no longer safe.

It took some time to establish my role with his medical centre, but eventually they agreed for a doctor to visit. David was given what I now know to be a mini mental state test. He couldn't answer most of the questions, but the doctor simply told me that he had seen worse. That was no help and I replied forcibly that David was unsafe and I feared that something serious was going to happen. I positioned myself between the front door and the doctor and told him quietly and firmly that he wasn't going until he did something. It didn't then take long for the arrangements to be complete and David was sectioned. I will never forget the look of fear and confusion on his face as they took him away in the ambulance. Neither will I forget the guilt I felt for making it happen.

Becoming a carer

From then on I knew that there was no alternative but to accept the role of David's primary carer. You couldn't just walk away from the experience of spending 21 years with someone as if it counted for nothing, and, in any case, I still loved him for who he was. The diagnosis of pre-senile dementia followed and then my painful induction into a new and totally unknown world of dementia care.

Very early on, I had decided that it was necessary to be as open about our sexuality as was possible. David and I had never discussed how we would react to the challenges which a serious illness might bring and what would be the implications for our relationship. Perhaps we were part of just a handful of gay men who had created powers of attorney for each other, but the onset of AIDS within our community had forced that need in front of our eyes. From now on, seemingly every new situation which related to David's care had to involve a coming out process. Later, David's frequent kissing of me, wherever we were, made the acknowledgement unnecessary, but phone calls and form-filling were a different matter.

We never experienced downright discrimination, but, instead, there was a more regular response of people accepting my explanation about the nature of our relationship and then conveniently seeming to ignore it. There were a few enlightened people who engaged with me, following my disclosure, but generally it didn't happen. I have to say that, decades later, there remain service providers and health professionals who choose to do the same following their client's admission about something as profound as their sexuality.

For me, as carer, there were hugely important decisions to make about meeting David's care needs, especially since I was still working. He was already showing signs of incontinence; his behaviour in public was liable to create attention and even possibly aggression; his now almost total loss of speech made conversation impossible. I was not helped when, in the hospital following his sectioning, he was tested for HIV without my permission, and a few weeks later moved to a residential home without consulting me. Both incidents galvanised me to make clear to service providers exactly what the limits of their responsibilities might be and what I required from them, namely, 'no decision about him, without me!' I decided that residential care was the only option for us in our situation and that I would seek a residential home close to where I lived, where I could visit David and bring him back to my home virtually every day. Thus began almost eight years of caring and many more years of learning just what this condition, generically called 'Alzheimer's Disease', was all about.

More than anything, I wanted to get things right and ensure that my care for David was not just good but had real quality to it. The consultant had told me that David wasn't my problem, and that I should leave them to look after him. But how could I do that? Yet, having accepted responsibility, and told his family that I would look after him, I wasn't sure what this care might involve. What was made quickly clear to me was that a second house, registered in his name, but paid for by both of us, would now have to be sold to pay for his care. Like so many carers, I had to juggle my time between sorting out the sale, holding down a job and seeing David daily. Whatever decisions and actions had to be undertaken it was me, and largely me alone, who had to deal with them. I felt that there was just no one to tell me what my rights were, what services might be available to help me and what good care in a residential setting looked like. If anyone had offered me advocacy I would have cried in gratitude.

Navigating long-term care

Gradually I gained a picture of what ideal residential care needed to be like. It would not be where a new member of staff appeared almost every week. It would be where activities were organised and photographed, and celebrated. It would not be where the minibus, bought for outings, never seemed to move from its parking spot. It would be a place where the residents would be taken out individually and regularly. The current place David was in did not fulfil any of these criteria.

The time had come to look around for something better than his current home and I found such a place just a mile from my house. Staff turnover was low. There was a good atmosphere. The walls were festooned with courses which staff had attended and they had had some experience of caring for residents as young as David, who was only 56. To be sure, the place was no more qualified to look after someone with profound dementia than I was, but I felt that their hearts were in the right place. Thus began, for David, seven years of residence where they struggled to stop him from regularly 'escaping', where they coped unbelievably with his double incontinence, and where they showed in so many ways that they really did care for him.

Now began my life as a carer in earnest. The word 'carer' is such a sanitised and offhand one, and conjures up delightful images of people in need, surrounded by devoted husbands/wives/families. I didn't have that. David's family lived long distances away and none of them could take on the central task of caring, so there was nothing else for it but for me to do it. But I had no idea where to start, what my goals might be, and what the demands would be like. I knew nothing about dementia, indeed I'm not sure that I even knew the word 'Alzheimer's'. It didn't take long to find out the truth!

David took a long time to settle and so there were numerous phone calls from the home asking me to go and help them with such basic tasks as dressing and feeding. They arranged appointments with podiatrists, nurses, and social services but it soon appeared that very little could be achieved without me being there to facilitate David's cooperation. If he needed his flu jab, I was the only person who could ensure that it happened successfully, and achieving a successful dental appointment at the hospital was nothing short of a nightmare. The confusion from health service providers about how to deal with me continued, as did the endless round of 'coming out' situations. Questions about 'next of kin' surfaced regularly, as did some about why I had power of attorney over David's affairs. Visitors at the residential home weren't quite sure what to say to me either. On one occasion, a kindly man asked me how my father was and then, like so often, I had to explain that he was my partner. David was variously regarded as a friend, a brother, and my father, but not my partner and never my lover.

These challenges would have been impossible to cope with had I not had the support of friends, most of whom were gay. They visited David and did their best to cope with being in the presence of someone who could no longer speak and who was clearly trying to work out who they were. Their concern was invaluable, but their willingness to visit was an added strain on my time because they clearly felt far less anxious if I was there with them, which I was, because I wanted them to continue to come. But it meant their visits did not give me the break I so badly needed.

Increasingly, every hour of my day, and often at night, David and his needs became central to my own life. Gay friends recognised that I was doing it because our relationship had significance to me, but it took others longer to understand. Sometimes I did need others to speak up for me, but fairly early on I acquired the skill of eye-to-eye contact and firmly spoken words, whenever a situation cropped up where I was at risk of being rejected as David's significant other. Having done the explaining, there was rarely a warm feeling of acceptance and engagement with our situation, which only added to its stress

It didn't take long to learn that those with dementia desperately need the assurance that close affectionate physical contact can bring. David's kissing of me, wherever we were, was sufficient to tell me that he craved such contact and it didn't take me long to choose his needs over the reactions of other people watching. It helped David if I brought him down to the house, almost every day, so that he could be hugged and I soon learned how powerful the smile, the holding of hands, the singing of songs, which he mouthed with me, actually were.

Carer support

If that was what David needed, then so did I, and after five years of caring alone, I found my lovely partner Michael, who never saw his role as supplanting David, but proactively did what he could to shoulder the burden, and that was never more so than when David died.

There were other issues, related to my caring role, which were a source of concern. Although I had power of attorney over David's affairs, there was, at the time, no legal civil partnership available to reinforce this. I felt deeply that I needed to be accountable especially where the management of David's finances were concerned. The details of every item purchased and every bill paid were recorded and I regularly made it clear that these accounts were available to be seen, especially by David's relatives. A solicitor had given me the saying 'where there's a Will, there's a relative!' and although I never felt that there was ever any suspicion about my conduct of David's affairs, later, when the Lesbian and Gay Carers Network was in operation, there were a number of members who described instances where conflict over finances had taken place, underpinned by homophobia among family members.

I needed to feel that I was being supported and recognised for my caring. Carers need to feel good about what they are doing; they need support for when things get on top of them; generally they don't want the responsibility taken from them even though they might be exhausted and burned out. It helps to be celebrated for one's devotion. For me, there seemed also a strange, but I hope understandable, need for this caring to be seen and recognised that this was a gay man who was similarly getting it right for his gay partner. One of the ways of achieving this was by joining the Alzheimer's Society, both locally and nationally.

At the local level, the branch welcomed me with open arms. I was phoned almost immediately on joining and they seemed genuinely glad to have me. I joined a carers' support group and attended other meetings organised by the group. It wasn't long either before I became a member of the committee, but it was then that I was aware of a barrier still to be overcome. My involvement with the support group was active and vocal – after all, my status as a gay carer was as equal as any other and meant that I spoke about David and his needs freely. However, at one session, another carer was clearly unhappy about my involvement and said both loudly and forcibly, 'but I am talking about my husband' and therefore by implication was saying 'you are only talking about a friend'. In a similar way, I became very much aware from some in the group (though I hasten to add, by no means all) that they were glad to have me there, were friendly, and did want to know how I was, but also rarely asked me how David was. On one occasion when I shared the experience of being openly and publically kissed by him, one said 'oh my god!'. Out of all this was a realisation that there was some way to go before full recognition and understanding that dementia does not discriminate.

At national level I perceived a further issue. It was always a pleasure to receive the Alzheimer's Society's regular newsletter and, in those days, the 1990s, it was a lifeline, because so little literature was available locally about dementia. For most LGBT* people, visible signs of acceptance and welcome have always been a powerful tool, and I looked for such signs in the Society's publications, and found none. The photos and the articles in their literature all seemed to suggest that dementia was a White person's illness and that those with the condition were usually surrounded by devoted husbands, wives and families. That rankled, and I wrote a letter to the editor expressing my sadness at the approach and wondered if there were any others out there who were carers for someone they were not married to or were even of the same sex. I was not inundated by replies, but those that arrived were significant enough to start considering how the needs of minorities, and particularly lesbian and gay carers, might be met.

The emotional toll on a carer of someone with dementia cannot easily be quantified and only those who have been in their shoes can truly know the reality. Having people around you cannot take the burden from you, but can ease the journey in unbelievably helpful ways. Yet to say to someone 'my husband has Alzheimer's' is comparatively 'straightforward' but to have to face a double admission of dementia and being gay is much more demanding.

Lesbian and Gay Dementia Carers' Network

As our plans for the creation of a lesbian and gay carers group started to take shape, the acknowledgement by non-gay, but caring, people that there might be an issue here started to take shape and it was ground breaking. The logic was clear, people with dementia are multifarious, and some are gay. If they are fortunate enough to have carers, they are likely to be gay too. The person with dementia and their carer are likely to be of an age where they bring with them heavy baggage about having concealed their sexuality. Service provision, therefore, has to enable them to feel that they and their situation are safe in their hands and free from any judgement or discrimination.

With superb support from the Alzheimer's Society, a carers' group gradually came into being. There was to be no fudging about the issue and an understanding that public commitment 'from the top' could be the only way that we could succeed as a lesbian and gay carers' organisation. An article about us appeared in the newsletter and an editorial word of support from the Chairman nailed the Society's rainbow colours to the mast.

It was not all plain sailing from then on. We were told that a number of members had resigned from the Society and the directors did receive some very nasty letters opposing our existence. Some doubted whether there should be a separate group for such a small minority of people (one lady wouldn't even accept that there could possibly be as many as 5 per cent of the adult population as homosexual). The main comment was, however, that support for carers and those with dementia, at its best, should never differ whatever the situation because it was a principle that everyone with the condition should be treated the same. Our reply, seemingly mouthed endlessly, was that it was not a matter of treating everyone the same, but it was a matter of recognising the distinctive needs of people like lesbian and gay individuals, and ensuring that those needs were met. It was our task within the now established Lesbian and Gay Carers Network to show what those needs were.

So, strangely, my two worlds informed each other. My experience of caring for David and being co-founder and co-organiser of the Lesbian and Gay Carers Network informed my desire to bring together and support others in similar situations. That experience was powerful. When people pointedly asked why we needed a separate organisation, those of us caring simply were able to say, 'there are things we need to say to each other and provide for each other because we are gay. If we feel the need to have a separate group then simply accept that this is what we want and need'. For me it all stemmed from the baggage we bring from the past in terms of society's attitudes and treatment of lesbian and gay people. In short, the way we have been treated has created in us a feeling of alienation and a desire to create families of our own choosing. It was not surprising that one of our contacts whose partner was showing signs of dementia said that they were both anxious about how service providers might deal with them and their needs, once they admitted their sexuality.

David's legacy

In the most extreme circumstances, David died on 16 March 2000. He went missing from the residential home, which had cared for him so well, and was found dead on a beach. The trauma was overwhelming and, for years afterwards, my dreams, whatever their content, regularly seemed to include him going missing. Incredibly, the support which followed was almost overwhelming too. What David had achieved through his dementia was that so many people working in the field had started to recognise that the condition was just as much a gay one as it was a straight one. Huge awareness-raising had started to take place and our work on the Network started to bear fruit as, little by little, calls came in to the dedicated telephone helpline from lesbian and gay people, caring for partners, relative and friends. Many had inspiring tales to tell and some were full of outrage at the lack of understanding of their situation by those around them. A prime example was of a gay man caring for a parent who was told by a doctor that he could not possibly care for his parent properly considering the fact that like most gay men he had multiple partners! There were other similar examples but, thankfully, there were also examples of service providers who were asking for some insights about sexuality which might enable them to provide the best possible support.

My experience of caring and those of the other extremely dedicated people in the team ensured that our work went from strength to strength. Numerous opportunities arose, both at home and abroad, to talk about our work and the tentative start to our service; of when, at first, we had feared we would have no clients, and how it had eventually resulted in a steady stream of lesbian and gay people who valued what we were offering. It had become, in fact, the only organisation of its kind in the world.

Lessons learned

Gradually, and with surprise, we realised that, in fact, we had become activists. David's photo appeared in articles and eventually even in a film and I was proud that such a lovely, handsome and sensitive man had achieved so much because of his illness. But, in our Network, we were acutely aware that in reality our work had only just begun. We knew that HIV dementia (Brew and Chan, 2014) existed and that a sizeable proportion of gay men, over the age of 60 had the virus, but little had been planned to support them should they develop dementia. We were also aware that, statistically, more women than men would have the condition and there were clear implications for the lesbian community in terms of preparing to offer support (Westwood, 2014). Just as, if not more significantly, we knew that the vast majority of lesbian and gay people did not have partners (Guasp, 2011) and the needs of those living alone with the condition had not even begun to be considered (Cook, 2013).

A further issue also needed confronting, and forcefully too, namely that the LGBT* community's attitude and concern for its elders was virtually non-existent. Older LGBT* people were often grouped together in an 'over 50s slot' but our experiences and needs are far more complicated than that (Ward *et al.*, 2012). Coupled with that is the unsurprising, but largely ignored, fact that, like the general population, one in three lesbians and gay men aged over 65 will also develop dementia (Knapp *et al.*, 2007).

Sadly, the Network closed in 2010 (Newman and Price, 2012). It was in the closing days of the life of the Network that we had started to look at how best to meet the needs of trans carers and trans individuals with dementia. In the space of one week, we had received calls from three trans carers, but we had to acknowledge that the scope of our expertise was extremely narrow. Even since then, in terms of the support needs of carers of trans individuals with dementia, very little is known at present (see Witten, Chapter 8, this volume). Similarly, there is very little knowledge or research about the needs of trans carers more broadly and/or trans individuals', especially older trans individuals', health issues (Bailey, 2012). Activists in Australia (Chad, 2009) and the USA (McFadden *et al.*, 2012) have suggested that trans individuals are concerned that dementia may expose them to prejudice, discrimination and a lack of respect from care providers, and this issue probably extends to all carers of trans people with dementia and/or trans carers of LGBT* people with dementia. It is highly likely that carers of trans individuals with dementia will need to take on a strong advocacy role, making sure that an individual's gender identity is validated and supported in care contexts, at end-of-life and after death. Much more research is needed to understand these important issues and how they affect carers.

Looking back at the group

As I have already indicated, in spite of clear support from the LGBT* community and overwhelming evidence of its use and value, the Network, ultimately named 'LGBT* Alzheimer's Support Group' of the Alzheimer's Society, was abolished in 2010. This was in the middle of turbulent days for the Society and the Network was a victim of those changes.

What did we achieve and, more importantly, what did we learn about the needs of LGBT* individuals and those with dementia? For starters, we took heart from one of our supporters, who at the beginning of our work, and with initially silent phone calls, eventually told us 'never underestimate the psychological and social significance of your mere existence'. From my experience of caring for David, and from comments we had received from delegates at conferences, it was clear that few had even imagined that there might be LGBT* carers of people with dementia and, more importantly, that there might also be some LGBT* people with dementia, all bringing with them needs which were distinctive and even unique.

From the moment of the Network's first client, it was clear that we had to rethink our assumptions about the sort of LGBT* person who might be contacting us. My situation and experience of caring turned out to be extremely limited compared with some of those who contacted us. Those in the media and those who supported us seemed sometimes to want to slot us into a gay alternative of the straight carer/family pattern. It soon became clear that LGBT* caring relied far more on the principle of 'families of choice' than we had first realised. Over the years, we had contacts who were not partners of those with the condition, might not even be living with them, might be part of alternative patterns of relationship and might be in international partnerships which brought complicated issues of nationality status and caring. We dealt with partnerships which had existed for decades, with friendships which were equally as strong, and both of which were now under severe strain because of the nature of the condition they were dealing with. As with my experience with David, there were things to be said to service providers about caring for LGBT* people which had never been considered. We sometimes needed to say, quite forcibly, that effective caring for LGBT* people with dementia cannot be squeezed into your own narrow world view and your own limited view of relationships.

It did not take long, therefore, before a picture emerged of the rainbow of issues which callers to the Network were presenting. Naively, we had assumed from the start that the issues which David and I had to deal with would largely be the same for those contacting us. We hadn't even got close to it and our learning curve was a steep one. We did have callers who wanted to offload their guilt about needing sexual contact with others now that their partner's dementia was profound. There were women who had become the carer for a parent as a result of other family members assuming that, being single, they were a natural choice for caring. There were couples who now had to face a coming out process, when dealing with service provision, some of whom had never acknowledged the fact, to anyone, that they were gay. There were some who were facing the death of a partner, whose family simply assumed that their relationship was nothing more than friendship. And there was the person living alone who asked us if we could find a gay careworker to give a feeling of security when care visits took place. There were some wanting legal advice once diagnosis had taken place; and there were two significant situations where families had resorted to law in order to deprive a caring partner of their power of attorney. And, finally, there were those who were coping with the demands of caring but just wanted to talk with another gay person – someone who was family. Of the 20 new contacts a year, many of them were not simple one-off calls, and, with a few, the contact lasted for years, and even beyond the time when their caring responsibilities had ceased.

It was true that we had underestimated the psychological and social significance of our existence as an organisation, and the awareness-raising achieved was huge. Others working in the field, and not a part of our Network, began to present us with their own case histories and examples where LGBT* people with dementia, or their carers, had faced some form of discrimination or a lack of empathy when dealing with health professionals or service providers. There was occasional evidence also of care workers having their own personal agendas when dealing with LGBT* people or of objecting to performing care tasks required to meet the healthcare needs of known lesbian and gay people. There was also the fear expressed of not being in control of one's life should dementia take hold and of having to deal with less-than-sympathetic care workers and service providers who might be covertly or overtly homophobic.

Conclusion

The experience of caring for David, and our experience in the Network, identified a need from others for literature for use by practitioners and for research too. Very little has been written so far about the needs of carers of LGBT* people, especially those with dementia. I have shared my lived experience in various ways: as a representative on special interest groups; in publications (Newman, 2005, 2009; Newman and Price, 2012); and in a training video for the Social Care Institute for Excellence (SCIE, 2010). A few authors have written about the challenges face by older LGBT* individuals in terms of 'coming out to care' when their LGBT* loved ones have care needs (Brotman *et al.*, 2007) and of the under-recognition and lack of support for LGBT* carers in general (Willis *et al.*, 2011). An even smaller number have addressed the issues of LGBT* carers of individuals with dementia (e.g. Price, 2010, 2012). Elizabeth Price has highlighted how the experience of 'coming out' to dementia service providers, particularly when it may not always be in a time or manner of their choosing (they may be outed by a loved one's loss of inhibitions), can shape how carers understood their entire engagement with those services (Price, 2010). Price has highlighted how the experiences of caring for a loved one with dementia can also inform lesbian, gay and bisexual carers' anxieties about their own care futures, and concerns that their own needs will not be met, especially if they themselves develop dementia (Price, 2012). This intensifies the need for far more research in this area.

For all people, whatever their sexual orientation, the prospect of a dementia diagnosis is one that understandably they are most anxious about. My outline, in this chapter, of what dementia meant for David's well-being and quality of life, and the stresses involved in caring for him has, I hope, been set out truthfully. I also hope it might stir others into action.

Were I to be confronted by a similar diagnosis, today, bearing in mind the beneficial changes in the law in the UK (e.g. same-sex civil partnerships and marriage, the Equality Act 2010, etc.), I would not expect discrimination to take place, and, if it did, then I would also expect those caring for me to scream and shout their outrage. Homophobia is, however, something less tangible and more difficult to confront but, assuming that my care is both good, enlightened and empathic then I would expect the following:

1   I would hope that I would recognise that a key to me being treated holistically would be found in my willingness and in my carers' willingness to

'come out' to service providers, and I would hope that, in their turn, they would honour that acknowledgement and engage with it.

2   I would hope that my sexuality (and/or gender identity) might be a constituent feature of memory work and social activity provided by service professionals and I would especially hope that any of those professionals who are LGBT* themselves might ensure that these needs are recognised and met by their colleagues.

3   I would hope that as my condition declines, and should my behaviour become more extreme, that if my sexuality is expressed more blatantly than usual, then service providers would treat that in a professional and informed way as a result of specific training they have received on the issue.

4   Should my dementia result in me needing to live in a residential care home, then I would hope that my home would state quite clearly and with proactive training that the place is dedicated to ensuring that diversity and inclusion are the bedrock of its existence. I would also hope that informal carers ensure this is the residential home's approach before agreeing to the person with dementia taking up occupancy there.

5   I would hope that the activities organised by the home reflect its dedication to diversity and inclusion.

6   Finally, I would hope that the LGBT* community, which I am so proud to be a part of, will recognise its duty of care towards all of its members, whatever their age and/or disability. This would include having in place strategies, projects and programmes which ensure that all of its members are respected, supported and served, including those who have dementia, and those who care for them. Were this not to happen, then I believe that all the struggles of the past to achieve our rights and status would have been for nothing.

In this chapter I have looked back at my own experiences, and the support in the past for carers of LGBT* individuals living with dementia, and then considered the current situation. I have highlighted that there is much that is not yet known, in terms of the support needed by LGBT* carers of people with dementia, and, sadly, much that we do know is needed that is not yet being met.

References

Bailey, L. (2012) 'Trans Ageing'. In R. Ward, I. Rivers and M. Sutherland (eds) *Lesbian, Gay, Bisexual and Transgender Ageing: Biographical Approaches for Inclusive Care and Support*, pp. 51–66. London and Philadelphia: Jessica Kingsley Publishers.

Brew, B. J. and Chan, P. (2014) 'Update on HIV dementia and HIV-associated neurocognitive disorders'. *Current Neurology and Neuroscience Reports*, **14**(8), 1–7.

Brotman, S., Ryan, B., Collins, S., Chamberland, L., Cormier, R., Julien, D., Meyer, E., Peterkin, A. and Richard, B. (2007) 'Coming out to care: caregivers of gay and lesbian seniors in Canada'. *The Gerontologist*, **47**(4), 490–503.

Chad, R. (2009) *Bisexual, transgender, intersex & dementia: What about us?* Alzheimer's Australia. Downloadable from: https://fightdementia.org.au/sites/default/files/1530-Alford.pdf.

Cook, L. (2013) *People with dementia living alone*. London: Alzheimer's Society. Available from: www.alzheimers.org.uk/site/scripts/documents_info.php?documentID=550.

Guasp, A. (2011) *Lesbian, gay and bisexual people in later life*. London: Stonewall.

Knapp, M., Prince, M., Albanese, E., Banerjee, S., Dhanasiri, S., Fernández, J.-L., Ferri, C., McCrone, P., Snell, T. and Stewart, R. (2007). *Dementia UK: A report to the Alzheimer's Society*. London: Alzheimer's Society.

McFadden, S. H., Frankowski, S. and Witten, T. (2012) *Anticipating the possibility of developing dementia: Perspectives of older transgender/intersex persons*. Downloadable from: www.alzheimer-europe.org/EN/content/download/24282/173003/file/P18.5%20Mcfadden.pdf.

Newman, R. (2005) 'Partners in care'. *BJPsych Psychiatric Bulletin*, **29**(7), 266–267.

Newman, R. (2009) 'Surely the World has Changed?'. In L. Whitman (ed.) *Telling Tales about Dementia: Experiences of Caring*, pp. 134–151. London: Jessica Kingsley Publishers.

Newman, R. and Price, E. (2012) 'Meeting the Needs of LGBT* People Affected by Dementia'. In R. Ward, I. Rivers and M. Sutherland (eds) *Lesbian, Gay, Bisexual and Transgender Ageing: Biographical Approaches for Inclusive Care and Support*, pp. 183–195. London: Jessica Kingsley Publishers. [Accessible via: http://bit.ly/1dGiQCbb].

Price, E. (2010) 'Coming out to care: Gay and lesbian carers' experiences of dementia services'. *Health and Social Care in the Community*, **18**(6), 160–168.

Price, E. (2012) 'Gay and lesbian carers: Ageing in the shadow of dementia'. *Ageing & Society*, **32**, 516–532.

Social Care Institute for Excellence. (SCIE) (2010) *Working with LGBT* people – older people and residential care: Roger's story*. [Accessible via www.scie.org.uk/social-caretv/video-player.asp?guid=CACAAE12-7375-429A-9D9A-1D28E29E65BD].

Ward, R., Rivers, I. and Sutherland, M. (eds) (2012) *Lesbian, Gay, Bisexual and Transgender Ageing: Biographical Approaches for Inclusive Care and Support*. London: Jessica Kingsley Publishers.

Westwood, S. (2014) 'Dementia, women and sexuality: How the intersection of ageing, gender and sexuality magnify dementia concerns among older lesbian and bisexual women'. *Dementia: The International Journal of Social Research and Practice*, DOI: 1471301214564446.

Willis, P., Ward, N. and Fish, J. (2011) 'Searching for LGBT* carers: Mapping a research agenda in social work and social care'. *British Journal of Social Work*, **41**, 1304–1320.

14 Navigating stormy waters

Consent, sexuality and dementia in care environments in Wales

Paul Willis, Michele Raithby and Tracey Maegusuku-Hewett

Introduction

Within the United Kingdom (UK), it is currently estimated that one in every 14 older adults over the age of 65 has a diagnosis of dementia, with an expectation that the total population living with dementia will exceed one million by 2025, in parallel with an ageing population (Alzheimer's Society, 2014). Supporting significant others with dementia places strain on the lives of unpaid carers and on the financed provision of health and social care in residential and nursing environments (Alzheimer's Society, 2014). This strain may be simultaneously felt by carers and service providers contributing to the care of older individuals with increasing cognitive impairments. Arguably, the intersection of sexuality and dementia represents the 'last taboo' in providing care to older people with dementia, particularly when seeking to uphold the safety, quality of life and wellbeing of older adults in receipt of care services (International Longevity Centre UK (ILC-UK), 2011).

Sexuality may be widely recognised as an integral aspect of health and wellbeing throughout the life course, however, older people are often assumed to be asexual and lacking sexual desires (Ward *et al.*, 2005; Doll, 2012). This is in spite of increasing evidence that older adults in Britain remain sexually active in later life (Mercer *et al.*, 2013). Small-scale research capturing the views of older Australians indicates that sex still matters to individuals living with early onset dementia, regardless of changes in cognition (Bauer *et al.*, 2013). Older adults are also frequently presumed to be heterosexual and this can obscure recognition of differences on the basis of sexual identity (Ward *et al.*, 2010). Sex and sexuality is recurrently associated with younger bodies and identities. Within gay men's communities, loss of sexual attractiveness can be acutely felt by men in later life because of the socio-cultural and commercial emphasis given to sex and desirability as belonging to younger generations (Lyons *et al.*, 2014). Older lesbian women report experiences of discrimination across three intersecting axes: homophobia, ageism and sexism (Averett *et al.*, 2013). The recognition of older lesbians in the UK may be clouded by the historical invisibility of lesbians in social and legal discourse (Oram and Turnbull, 2001). Taking sexuality into the context of dementia care, care staff, registered nurses and managers of care environments face complex demands in balancing the desires, rights and well-being of residents alongside overarching legal and ethical imperatives in place to protect older people with declining mental capacity from harm. Adjacent to this, the biographies, interests and identities of lesbian, gay and bisexual-identifying (LGB) residents are frequently absent from discussions about managing concerns for capacity and consent.

In this chapter, we explore how staff and managers employed in residential and nursing care environments across Wales respond to issues of consent and capacity in the context of providing long-term care to residents who are sexually active. In particular, we examine three dimensions to care provision and dementia: first, how staff and managers seek to be facilitative of intimate relationships between residents with declining mental capacity; second, how the primacy of risk underpins care work in this domain; and third, the absence of LGB-identifying residents and same-sex relationships in professional discussions of sexuality, care and consent. Here, we attend to the ways in which older people's sexualities are represented by care staff and managers in their discussions about care. We refer to these discussions as 'care talk' to communicate the ways in which residents' sexual lives are represented in dialogue about everyday care. To illustrate care talk, we draw on qualitative evidence from a mixed-methods study into the provision of inclusive care to older adults in care environments across Wales (Willis *et al.*, 2013). The research was guided by the question, 'How are the identities and relationships of older LGB residents perceived and supported in residential care environments in Wales?' The perspectives of care staff and managers were obtained through focus groups. All participating homes provided residential care to older people with dementia. First, we elaborate on the policy context of the research before outlining findings from focus group discussions. We conclude with recommendations for developing a more affirming approach to negotiating care, consent and dementia in care environments that encompass the lives of older LGB people.

Supporting older adults with dementia: the Welsh context

As a small nation with a rapidly ageing population, Wales has recently adopted a rights-based stance in its policies for older adults culminating in the creation of a Declaration of Rights for Older People (Welsh Government, 2014). Founded on the UN Principles for Older Persons (www.un.org/documents/ga/res/46/a46r091. htm), the six core statements all bear relevance to the wellbeing of older adults in receipt of health and social care. In relation to the protection of sexual freedoms and expression, the following three statements are highly pertinent:

- 'I have the right to be who I am',
- 'I have a right to be valued' and
- 'I have the right to decide where I live, how I live and with whom I live'.

(Welsh Government, 2014)

As an identity-based cohort, older LGB adults feature, albeit fleetingly, in Welsh policy targeted at improving services for older adults. Within its Strategy for Older People, the Welsh Government represents older LGB people as a 'minority' group with differing care needs from the mainstream older population (Welsh Government, 2013), but does not elaborate on how these needs may differ from other older cohorts.

Older LGB adults in Wales are legally protected from sexuality-based discrimination – under the Equality Act 2010 (England and Wales), public and private services are prohibited from direct and indirect discrimination in the provision of services. Both age and sexual orientation are protected characteristics (Section 29, 'Provision of services, etc.'). Within health and social care policy, the National Service Framework for Older People (Welsh Assembly Government (WAG), 2006) stipulates a requirement to 'root out' discrimination from service providers, including on the grounds of sexual orientation. However, these requirements remain limited in application, as care and nursing staff are currently not mandated to undertake equality and social inclusion training, potentially leaving a gap in their professional development.

Building on the rights-based approach, citizenship, community and commitment to public services have been distinctive themes running through recent Welsh policy (WAG, 2011a), culminating in the Social Services and Well-being (Wales) Act 2014. Due for implementation in 2016, the Act notably changes the deficit-based terminology in which adult community care has traditionally been couched. Instead, it refers to 'people who need care and support', so that 'need' is no longer defined in medical terms. In consolidating and replacing previous 'community care' and carer legislation, it includes a duty to promote preventative services and to promote wellbeing; to safeguard people 'at risk' (replacing the previous disempowering term of 'vulnerable'), and an innovative requirement to promote service user-led design and provision of services.

The drivers for such root and branch reform in Wales are the wider need in the UK to reform adult care legislation (Law Commission, 2011), but also the rising levels of complex and long-term health conditions (including dementia) in Wales, coupled with shrinking resources. The Alzheimer's Society (2014) estimates that there are 43,477 people living with dementia in Wales. The numbers are projected to rise by 31 per cent across Wales by 2021 and by as much as 44 per cent in some rural areas (WAG, 2011b). As part of its integrated response, the Welsh Government seeks to establish 'dementia-supportive communities' (WAG, 2011b), building on local grass-roots improvements for the involvement of people living with dementia. At the time of writing, it remains to be seen whether these improvements will enhance recognition and participation of older LGB adults living with dementia and their carers.

Methodology

Care staff and managers participating in focus groups were employed in private residential and nursing homes in North, South and mid-Wales, encompassing rural and urban areas. In 2012–2013, three focus groups were facilitated with staff (*n*=14) providing direct care to older residents and two focus groups with service managers (*n*=27) (private and local authority) or people involved in the management of residential and nursing environments. Focus groups were co-facilitated by two members of the research team and ran between 45 to 90 minutes. Topics explored included: knowledge and awareness of LGB residents in their care; good practice for making residents feel included; barriers to inclusion; and staff training and policy on sexual relationships and sexual identity. Focus group discussions were audio recorded, transcribed and coded thematically line-by-line using the NVivo qualitative data analysis software to develop primary and subsidiary codes.

Nursing and residential homes were randomly selected for invitation from a sampling frame utilising the Care and Social Services Inspectorate for Wales' 2011 directory online. In the managers' groups (*n*=27), the majority were women (23) and over half the group (17) were between the ages of 26 and 50 years. The majority of participants (25) were White British with two people identifying as 'non-White' descent. All identified as heterosexual. In focus groups with care staff, the majority (9) were between 30 and 50 years of age. Again, nearly all participants (12) were female, with two men. Ten staff members were White and four indicated 'Asian/Chinese/mixed ethnic' background. The majority of staff indicated they were 'heterosexual'; one employee identified as 'lesbian'.

Findings: representations of sexuality and dementia in care talk

1 Supporting normative intimate relationships between residents with declining mental capacity

Throughout participants' conversations of care talk, there was a continual thread of discussion about the ways in which care and nursing staff negotiated the (hetero)-sexual expressions and intimacies of residents in their care on a daily basis. In this context, care homes were depicted as sexually charged environments; elsewhere we have discussed the recognition of care homes as sexualised environments (Willis *et al.*, 2014). On one level this is important because the recognition of sexual expressions, desires and relationships within care environments counteracts the desexualisation of older adults and strengthens the argument that, as a social dimension in residents' lives, sexuality is a critical aspect of care. Conversely, the discussion of supporting residents in long-term heterosexual relationships reinforces the absence of discussion about relationships outside this normative circle, for example same-sex and polyamorous relationships or casual sexual relationships. Within sociological circles, there have been attempts to 'denaturalise' heterosexuality as a social structure that generates taken-for-granted assumptions about socio-sexual relationships (Jackson and Scott, 2010). Concerted efforts have been made to bring attention to the ways in which heterosexual norms are privileged in everyday life and across institutions, inclusive of social care and welfare settings. The acute absence of discussions about non-normative sexual relationships and practice can implicitly reiterate heteronormative arrangements within care settings. Sexual relationships and activities outside of heterosexual norms are neglected or silenced.

Care staff and managers spoke with positive regard about providing care to residents in existing, long-term, heterosexual relationships. Relationships between different-sex residents who had been in a relationship prior to entering the home did not present immediate concerns, in spite of identified declines in mental capacity of one or more of the residents. One staff member discussed the measures in place to ensure two residents could sleep in the same bed without risk of injury:

> Well, there is a couple and the only thing that we've had to do is we had to stop them sleeping in a bed because of the dangers of one of them falling out … and we have spoken about getting a bigger bed for them and things like this…'
>
> (Care staff, Focus Group [FG] 1)

Other care staff explained, at length, the ways in which residents entering the home in heterosexual relationships were supported, for example the use of 'do not disturb' signs on bedroom doors. This included the protection of couples' privacy and shared space:

> When we have married couples in we ask them do they want to share a bedroom or don't they want to share a bedroom 'cos not everybody does. And if they do we make one room as a lounge and one room as the bedroom, put double beds, single beds, whatever they want in it.
>
> (Manager, FG2)

While acts of public affection between couples, such as kissing and cuddling, were not discouraged, sometimes care work involved diplomatically managing the emotive responses of other residents. One staff member described herself as a politician:

> It's trying to be a politician basically … one of the older gentlemen down the bottom was getting very upset, he said 'there are people kissing and canoodling in here in front of the children', there were no children around but he's got dementia so he might think there are children around. So I said [to the staff] 'you know, you have to speak to the other two and suggest they find somewhere a bit more quiet' 'cos in some places it's not suitable. That's it.
>
> (Care staff, FG3)

Existing heterosexual relationships between residents with dementia were permissible, supported and, to a certain degree, shielded from interference by staff and other residents, albeit within boundaries and in recognition of other residents' wellbeing.

2 Problematic intimacies: the primacy of risk with residents who are sexually active

Sexuality is often located as a problematic dimension in discussions of care pro-vision, more so in the delivery of care to older people as 'sex-less' individuals (Ward *et al.*, 2005). Alongside the recognition and support of long-term partner-ships, some heterosexual relationships were framed as problematic and risk-laden in discussions of dementia care. This was acutely so in the context of new relationships forming where one partner was living with dementia and there were questions raised about the capacity of individuals involved to consent to sexual relations. This form of care was framed as complex and ethically challenging work in which there were no obvious solutions beyond the prescribed legal response.

Within England and Wales, sexual activity with a person lacking capacity to give informed consent is an unlawful and criminal activity under the Sexual Offences Act 2003 (Laird, 2014). In Wales, current policy and procedures on safeguarding 'vulnerable adults' (SSIA, 2013) are based on principles of the European Convention on Human Rights 1950 and the Human Rights Act 1998; that everyone has the right to live their lives free from coercion, intim-idation, oppression and physical, sexual, emotional or mental harm. Critical to the protection of individual autonomy and decision-making is Article 8, 'the right to privacy and family life' (Royal College of Nursing, 2011). The Social Services & Well-being (Wales) Act 2014 introduces a duty for any partner of a local authority (such as a commissioned service) to inform that local author-ity if it has reasonable cause to suspect that an adult residing in its area is at risk of neglect or abuse, including sexual harm. Accordingly, care and nursing staff may seek to operate in the 'best interests' of older adults with dementia, which encompasses protecting residents from potential abuse or harm and reporting concerns to local authorities and police. However, the law does not provide a clear definition of what constitutes the 'best interests' of adults in what is fundamentally complex interpersonal work (Laird, 2014). Assessing capacity requires balancing the wishes and rights of residents, including rights to sexual expression and autonomy in decision-making, with an overarching duty of care to older adults who may be mentally incapacitated in some areas of decision-making. Mahieu *et al.* (2014) argue that this leads to an overriding pre-occupation with decision-making and residents' ability to give verbal consent to sexual relations; other means of indicating assent to sex are not discussed.

Under the shadow of this legal framework, care staff and managers discussed at length the imperative to ensure residents could give consent. Two managers discussed the steps followed to prevent sexual activity between two adults living with varying degrees of dementia. A referral to the local POVA team (Protection of Vulnerable Adults team, led by local authorities) ensued and led to police involvement. However, uncertainties remained about the best course of action to pursue:

F1: 'Yeah and he's a difficult one to assess really because he wouldn't come out of his bedroom for the psychiatrist to assess him but the lady that he was getting friendly with and she was getting friendly with him was severely demented too … I sort of felt that if they both were consenting anyway that it should be okay but because she didn't have the capacity we weren't prepared to allow it to happen and I mean obviously we turned to everybody and it was just thought that it shouldn't happen but it actually made her happy, didn't it?'

F2: 'Yeah, she was happy.'

F1: 'She was getting quite aggressive with us when we tried to lead her away and they were only little tête-a-têtes in the corridor really and things like that but she was quite…'

F2: 'She went back as well, didn't she?'

F1: 'Well she kept going back, didn't she?'

(Care staff, F1 and F2)

The inherent dangers of risk-averse practice have been discussed in social work and social care literature (Clarke, 2000; Laird, 2014; Stanford, 2009, 2011). A fundamental concern is the ways in which risk-averse practice more often serves professional interests than the interests and wishes of service users (Laird, 2014). Dementia care with older people represents another domain of risky practice in which different stakeholders (for example, care providers, medical staff, family members) can identify different levels of risk according to their relationship to the person in receipt of care (Clarke, 2000). Stanford (2009, 2011) has discussed the ways in which risk discourse materialises in social workers' representation of clients-within stories about professional practice, service users can embody risk identities and be depicted as 'at risk' or 'a risk'. Risk-averse practice may intensify when issues of sex and sexuality are situated alongside discussions of declining mental capacity. However, providing person-centred care instead requires recognition of residents' rights to take 'reasonable risks' (Mahieu *et al.*, 2014), including any risks associated with sexual relationships.

Previous research in England has flagged the dangers of framing older LGB residents' sexualised behaviours as problematic (the need for lesbian and gay residents to 'behave themselves'), which can pathologise the individual actions of LGB residents as inherently irresponsible and undesirable (Hubbard and Rossington, 1995). Here, we are interested in the gendered dimensions of risk-averse practice in which men's and women's sexualised behaviours are imbued with different meanings. Older women lacking capacity were frequently represented as vulnerable and requiring protection from potential harm. In contrast, older men were not always discussed as being 'at risk', more so presenting 'a risk' to others. One older man, who appeared to lack capacity due to learning disabilities, was framed as 'predatory' in his pursuit of intimate contact with female residents. This led to him being evicted from one home and re-housed in another:

> It started off as a friendship. He could be seen as a bit of a predator, maybe because he's got learning difficulties. It's difficult to say really but mentally he's an adolescent basically and he likes affection, he likes a bit of a friend and he formed a relationship and he does this, forms a relationship and then he gets obsessive and then when they back off he won't allow it to happen and the Police were involved in that one and both families were involved...
>
> (Manager, FG2)

A further challenge for care staff and managers involved mediating between family members as they adjusted to residents' new (heterosexual) relationships and attachments forming:

> And that, again, is a very difficult thing to deal with, and a very delicate subject, because.... We've had situations where we've had a husband and wife actually living in the home, and the husband's passed away and then a month later the wife is striking up a relationship with another male member. Now, how the hell do you try and discuss that with the family?... It's ... it's so difficult, and the pressure on staff to deal with these situations is.... It's a nightmare.
>
> (Manager, FG4)

There are limitations on how supportive family members may be towards the sexual expressions of loved ones, particularly when new affective ties are forged between residents (Bauer *et al.*, 2014). Individual family members may hold divergent expectations of care providers, placing additional demands on staff in managing family member's responses (Mahieu *et al.*, 2014). While some family members were accepting of their loved ones entering new relationships, other family members, such as adult children, required additional support. These changes are inevitably confronting for some family members as they require reconfiguring of long-held perceptions of loved ones' identities as 'partners/husbands/wives' or as parental figures:

> I've had a few problems within my home recently as I run a home with people with dementia, and two men completely separate had attached themselves to ladies in the home, very innocently, you know, holding hands, the occasional kiss and that sort of thing but both these men had wives, and it was awfully difficult then. One of the wives was absolutely wonderful, she just said, 'He's in a safe place, he's comfortable, he's obviously very happy, you know, I'm quite happy with this,' but his daughter was absolutely devastated, absolutely devastated...
>
> (Manager, FG2)

Sometimes, care staff had to contend with the ageist assumptions conveyed by family members: 'the gentleman's family that we've got at the moment, he's [adult son] not very keen on it and he is of the opinion that people of a certain age shouldn't be having sex' (care staff, FG1). While the latter accounts do not entail managing direct risks of harm to residents, there are inherent challenges to the reputation of the home through potential blame being attributed by family members; to the emotional wellbeing of family members as they experience the loss associated with partners and parents forging new relationships; and finally, to the residents as family members. As a consequence, staff may seek to prevent contact between new partners.

3 Restricted lens on sexuality: limited representations of older LGB adults in care environments

As discussed above, older LGB-identifying adults were missing from discussions about supporting the relationships of residents living with dementia – this is a glaring absence in which the needs, rights and wellbeing of older LBG residents, and their significant others, remain unacknowledged. Silence surrounding LGB identities was reinforced through a number of rhetorical means. First, through the active avoidance of asking questions about residents' sexual lives and histories: 'We don't pry, you know, we don't ask them to be too explicit' (care staff, FG2). Second, through locating sexual relationships between older adults of the same-sex away from public attention:

> I will say this though, but and I would say that on a normal couple. I shouldn't say 'normal', I shouldn't use that word, husband and wife, if two men are together or two women that's quite a thing like anybody in a marriage but don't flaunt it in front of people, I will say that...
>
> (Care staff, FG3)

Third, through avoiding speaking aloud words such as 'lesbian', 'gay' and 'bisexual', some staff members appeared uncomfortable with speaking about LGB identities and instead opted to refer to a collective 'it':

> It's not a problem is it? It's not a problem anyway but you just wouldn't say it when we were young would you? It was a, not a bad word, but you just didn't say it and I think that's because it was hidden, yeah.... I wouldn't pry or ask questions but if they're quite happy then you go along with the flow then.
>
> (Care staff, FG3)

Some staff members discussed their concerns about the ways in which other residents would respond with hostility towards other residents that openly identified as LGB; they were uncertain about how to respond to homophobic commentary. These concerns were amplified in the context of challenging residents with dementia in fear of causing distress to the offending party:

> It's quite difficult particularly if someone has dementia, and I don't have this example but I've heard racist comments or fascist comments, and

depending where they are on their dementia journey it can be quite difficult to challenge, you shouldn't challenge them 'cos it can cause a lot of upset. And sadly once they've got to that point you can't teach them new things, so it's a very difficult one.

(Manager, FG5)

Others expressed monolithic, highly limiting views of LGB people that frequently conveyed social stereotypes about lesbian and gay lives. In contrast, there was no discussion or mention of bisexual identities. One staff member explained to the group facilitator the 'jealous nature' of lesbian women:

I find lesbians are very protective of their partners more than the men … I've noticed a lot of the lesbians I know are very protective of their partners and very jealous, so can you imagine a lesbian, a young woman coming in here, her partner's coming and we're in there touching and seeing to her, can you imagine how … she could be saying, 'I don't want you doing it like that'.

(Care staff, FG3)

Another manager bundled gay men and sexual offenders under the same umbrella:

… but since doing the questionnaire I have thought of it, reflected on it and I think then why haven't I met any gay old men? I met one who was a paedophile. I've probably met loads that are [gay] but I don't know about it because they haven't told me they were. You know unless they've been in jail or on a register how am I to know what their … you know what they did in their past but it is strange, I just can't think, I can't think of any old men. Do they just come into a care home and not want to discuss it? I think it's the generation, they just cover it up. Things will change though and it will just be like everything else.

(Manager, FG2)

Implicit within this discussion is an assumption that change will happen regardless of the individual's actions – the social landscape will inevitably change and so automatically will older people's views and practices. It is important to recognise that these restricted, and in many ways oppressive, views were not voiced by all participants and indeed numerous participants identified significant issues about the prospect of providing care to LGB adults with dementia. Two managers across separate groups reflected on the ways in which dementia may trigger the emergence of LGB identities that residents had previously not discussed:

I would say, probably one of the hardest things to deal with, and that is if you have an admission into the home with somebody that is suffering with dementia, they could have basically been a gay or lesbian individual that's got a family, that's never demonstrated that sexuality at all. And yet when they have dementia, the inhibitors go down, and all of a sudden they revert back to type, that's how they are as an individual, and yet they may have brought up three children, they may have a complete family unit around them. So how do we, as a home, deal with that? Because there is nothing.

(Manager, FG4)

Several managers discussed the importance of establishing a culture of inclusion within the home, from initial contact with prospective residents onwards. One identified strategy was to explicitly state this in the home's statement of purpose:

...that's another way of promoting your nursing home to say, 'Look, we're quite open and we'll be looking to take anyone, treat them as an individual, but there could be someone in here that's gay and you know if you're not as happy with that then look elsewhere.

(Manager, FG2)

Others sought more information about the sexual history and life-stories of residents entering their care – no such information had been provided through accompanying paperwork such as social service care plans. In one instance, while sexuality was mentioned on a care plan form, it was listed as 'optional': 'we have Section 13, relationship and expressing sexuality, it is optional so for some residents we may have it, for some residents we will not have it' (care staff, FG1). It is reassuring to see sexuality listed as a domain requiring the attention of care staff. However, this is compromised by its listing as 'optional' as this gives employees permission to 'opt out' of this discussion. There was a demand from managers and care staff alike for training about working supportively with older LGB adults. Some staff had received dementia awareness training that included discussions about sexual activity. However, the focus of training appeared to be on managing problematic ('difficult' or 'challenging') behaviours associated with loss of social inhibitions rather than geared towards supporting sexual health and activity in later life.

Concluding comments

In this chapter, we set out to examine the ways in which sexual identity and LGB lives are represented in care talk about older people with dementia. While care providers and policy makers across the UK come to grips with an expanding population living with dementia, our findings indicate that staff and managers of care environments in Wales require (and indeed request) additional support and training in meeting the needs of LGB adults with dementia. In the context of providing care to heterosexual couples living with dementia, staff and managers convey sensitivity, respect for privacy and concern for significant others. This same level of care is not tangible when discussing support to LGB adults for a number of reasons. First, LGB identities are only partially visible in staff and managers' care talk and, when present, are frequently misrepresented in a negative, demoralising or restricted way. The use of depersonalised nouns such as 'it' can be highly dehumanising and is out of kilter with a person-centred approach and the recognition of individual personhood and dignity. Second, staff and managers express reluctance to initiate discussions with residents about sexual identity, same-sex relationships and homophobic commentary. In connection to dementia care, this reluctance is heightened out of concern for causing offence and distress to other residents with declining capacity. Elsewhere, we have argued that sexuality is frequently located as an extraneous dimension to everyday care in residential services (Willis *et al.*, 2014). For older adults located at the sexual margins, including LGB adults, this can result in their desires, relationships and histories being hidden from positive recognition. Separating sexuality from care inhibits a fully holistic approach to person-centred care.

From our discussions with care staff and managers, it is evident that care homes lack more positive, affirming approaches and protocols for addressing concerns about capacity, consent and sex. The primary response appears to be risk-averse in which residents can only be located as either 'at risk' or a risk to others – this is a restrictive binary that limits the ways in which staff can respond to and support the sexual wellbeing of residents while ensuring residents remain safe from harm and distress. Morgan and Williamson (2014) advocate a positive risk-taking approach to supporting older adults with dementia – this means decision-making about risk is shared and the positive benefits of risk-taking are carefully balanced against the potential harms.

The new Social Services and Well-being (Wales) Act 2014 prioritises the delivery of services to people in 'need of care and support' (for example, Section 5, 'Well-being duty'). With this language in mind, is it possible to think about sex, capacity and consent outside the rhetoric of risk and, alternatively, consider how to provide care that protects older adults from harm while supporting sexual wellbeing? Mahieu *et al.* (2014) advocate an 'anthropological-ethical' approach that poses alternative questions for care staff to ascertain assent to sexual relations beyond verbal consent, for example 'Does the resident in question willingly engage in sexual activity? Are there signs that indicate coercion?' (p. 9). There is no denying that this is a complex and emotionally demanding work for staff in which there are no easy solutions – care work that is often performed by staff on low wages with little professional development and support.

Finally, our discussion adds further weight to the demand for an enhanced training and education framework for care staff and their managers to ensure all the needs of older adults with dementia are being met, inclusive of sexuality. Based on our discussions of care talk, training needs to be three-fold in focus: breaking down barriers to viewing older people as sexual beings; enhancing recognition of differences in sexual expression, relationships and identity; and initiating and sustaining discussions about sexual lives and histories with residents living with dementia and their significant others. Within Wales, the policy and legal framework is in place to progress dementia care towards a person-centred approach that encompasses sexual personhood. The Social Services and Well-being (Wales) Act 2014 will require a cultural shift in service provision from a service-led model to a more active citizen-directed approach to assessment and provision of services. There is significant work ahead in ensuring that the Act's new promotion of 'wellbeing' encompasses 'sexual wellbeing' as an integral aspect of dementia care.

References

Alzheimer's Society (2014) *Dementia UK: overview* (2nd edition). London. Accessed 3 October 2014, ww.alzheimers.org.uk/site/scripts/download_info.php?fileID=2323.

Averett, P., Yoon, I. and Jenkins, C. L. (2013) Older lesbian experiences of homophobia and ageism. *Journal of Social Service Research*, **39**(1), pp. 3–15.

Bauer, M., Fetherstonhaugh, D., Tarzia, L., Nay, R., Wellman, D. and Beattie, E. (2013) 'I always look under the bed for a man'. Needs and barriers to the expression of sexuality in residential aged care: the views of residents with and without dementia. *Psychology and Sexuality*, **4**(3), pp. 296–309.

Bauer, M., Nay, R., Tarzia, L. and Fetherstonhaugh, D. (2014) 'We need to know what's going on': views of family members toward the sexual expression of people with dementia in residential aged care. *Dementia*, **13**(5), pp. 571–585.

Clarke, C. (2000) Risk: constructing care and care environments in dementia. *Health, Risk and Society*, **2**(1), pp. 83–93.

Doll, G. A. (2012) *Sexuality and Long-Term Care: understanding and supporting the needs of older adults*. Baltimore: Health Professions Press.

Hubbard, R. and Rossington, J. (1995) As we grow older: A study of the housing and support needs of older lesbians and gay men. London: Polari. Accessed online, www.openingdoorslondon.org.uk/resources/As_We_Grow_Older.pdf.

International Longevity Centre UK (ILC-UK) (2011) *The Last Taboo: a guide to dementia, sexuality, intimacy and sexual behaviour in care homes*. London: ILC-UK.

Jackson, S. and Scott, S. (2010) *Theorizing Sexuality*. Maidenhead: Open University Press.

Laird, S. (2014) The law, professional ethics and anti-oppressive social work. In Cocker, C. and Hafford-Letchfield, T. (eds) *Rethinking Anti-Discriminatory and Anti-Oppressive Theories for Social Work Practice*. Houndmills: Palgrave Macmillan, pp. 45–59.

Law Commission (2011) *Adult Social Care*. London: TSO.

Lyons, A., Croy, S., Barrett, C. and Whyte, C. (2014) Growing old as a gay man: how life has changed for the gay liberation generation. *Ageing & Society*, Advanced access 27 August 2014, DOI: 10.1017/S0144686X14000889.

Mahieu, L., Anckaert, L. and Gastmans, C. (2014) Intimacy and sexuality in institutionalized dementia care: clinical-ethical considerations. *Health Care Analysis*, Advanced access 1 October 2014, DOI: 10.1007/s10728-014-0287-2.

Mercer, C. H., Tanton, C., Prah, P., Erens, B., Sonnenberg, P., Clifton, S., Macdowall, W., Lewis, R., Field, N., Datta, J., Copas, A. J., Phelps, A., Wellings, K. and Johnson, A. M. (2013) Changes in sexual attitudes and lifestyles in Britain through the life course and over time: findings from the National Surveys of Sexual Attitudes and Lifestyles (NATSAL). *The Lancet*, **382**(9907), pp. 1781–1794.

216 P. *Willis* et al.

Morgan, S. and Williamson, T. (2014) *How Can 'Positive Risk-taking' Help Build Dementia-Friendly Communities?* York: Joseph Rowntree Foundation.

Oram, A. and Turnbull, A. (2001) *The Lesbian History Sourcebook: love and sex between women in Britain between 1780 and 1970.* London: Routledge.

Royal College of Nursing (RCN) (2011) *Older People in Care Homes: sex, sexuality and intimate relationships: an RCN discussion and guidance document for the nursing workforce.* London: RCN.

Social Services Improvement Agency (SSIA) (2013) *Wales Interim Policy and Procedures for the Protection of Vulnerable Adults from Abuse.* Cardiff: SSIA.

Stanford, S. (2009) 'Speaking back' to fear: responding to the moral dilemmas of risk in social work practice. *British Journal of Social Work*, **40**(4), pp. 1065–1080.

Stanford, S. N. (2011) Constructing moral responses to risk: a framework for hopeful social work practice. *British Journal of Social Work*, **41**(8), pp. 1514–1531.

UK Government (1998) Human Rights Act 1998. London: HMSO.

UK Government (2010) Equality Act 2010. London: HMSO.

Ward, R., Pugh, S. and Price, E. (2010) *Don't Look Back? Improving health and social care service delivery for older LGB users.* Manchester: Equality and Human Rights Commissioner.

Ward, R., Vass, A. A., Aggarwal, N., Garfield, C. and Cybyk, B. (2005) A kiss is still a kiss? The construction of sexuality in dementia care. *Dementia*, **4**(1), pp. 49–72.

Welsh Assembly Government (WAG) (2006) *National Service Framework for Older People.* Cardiff: WAG.

Welsh Assembly Government (WAG) (2011a) *Sustainable Social Services: a framework for action.* Cardiff: WAG.

Welsh Assembly Government (WAG) (2011b) *National Dementia Vision for Wales: dementia supportive communities.* Cardiff: WAG.

Welsh Government (2013) *The Strategy for Older People in Wales 2012–2023.* Cardiff: WG.

Welsh Government (2014) Social Services and Well-Being (Wales) Act 2014. Cardiff: WG.

Welsh Government (2014) *Declaration of Rights for Older People.* Cardiff: WG.

Willis, P., Maegusuku-Hewett, T., Raithby, M., Miles, P., Nash, P., Baker, C. and Evans, S. (2013) *Provision of Inclusive and Anti-Discriminatory Services to Older Lesbian, Gay, Bisexual-Identifying (LGB) People in Residential Care Environments in Wales: final research report.* Swansea: Centre for Innovative Ageing, Swansea University.

Willis, P., Maegusuku-Hewett, T., Raithby, M. and Miles, P. (2014) Swimming upstream: the provision of inclusive care to older lesbian, gay and bisexual (LGB) adults in residential and nursing environments in Wales. *Ageing & Society* advanced Access 14 October 2014, DOI: 10.1017/S0144686X14001147.

15 To equality – and beyond?

Queer reflections on an emerging rights-based approach to dementia in Scotland

Richard Ward

Introduction

With a population of approximately 5.4 million, Scotland is one of the smaller of a growing number of nations to have developed their own national dementia strategy (Scottish Government, 2010, 2013). The very existence of this strategy is an indicator of the degree of autonomy that currently exists at a national level over decisions on how best to meet the needs of Scots living with dementia. Recent developments in Scotland have also been shaped by the advent of 'user-led' groups and networks of people affected by dementia campaigning for change. As these networks have grown they have helped to foster an emergent collective awareness and identity while seeking to influence policy at regional and national levels.

In light of these changes, Scotland has begun to embrace a rights-based approach to dementia (Alzheimer Scotland, 2015), a shift in thinking reflected not only at the level of policy but increasingly with the aim of embedding this approach within service delivery and care practice (e.g. Alzheimer Scotland, 2011). Hence, the potential now exists for more explicit recognition of the differences amongst those affected by dementia; protection from unfair and discriminatory treatment across one or more protected characteristics; and even the prospect of a better understanding of the particular perspectives and experiences of LGBT* individuals as they seek care or support. However, the story of the development of (LGBT*) inclusive dementia services and provision via a rights-based framework is currently one of future potential rather than of existing hard evidence of change.

For instance, recent years have witnessed a move toward greater control over services by their users, marked by the growth of co-productive approaches to service delivery (e.g. East Dunbartonshire Council, 2014) and greater attention to user-defined outcomes (Joint Improvement Team, 2012). There is, however, little evidence to date that such developments have moved beyond a catch-all category of 'people with dementia' to specifically seek out and listen to the voices of LGBT* individuals affected by dementia. At the same time, the introduction of personalisation (i.e. a move toward greater control over services at the level of individual service users) has marked a shift away from pre-determined, group-based forms of provision which in the past drew people together purely on the basis of their diagnosis and residence within a specified geographical catchment area. While the personalisation agenda chimes with messages from research with older LGBT* individuals who have fervently rejected the prospect of such collective forms of care (Ward, 2012), we have yet to witness efforts to test or evaluate direct payments or personal budgets (intended to give service users spending power to exercise greater choice in how to meet their assessed needs) as a route to 'LGBT-friendly' support within care provision for older people let alone within dementia care services.

Arguably, one of the single most significant influences upon a rights-based agenda for dementia in Scotland has been the establishment and work of the Scottish Dementia Working Group.[1] One of the first and largest 'user-led' networks of people with dementia in the UK, the group campaigns for change across many different fields, raising awareness of dementia but also agitating for rights and recognition. The network has been closely studied, for instance in the work of Bartlett (2012, 2014a, 2014b) who has been keen to explore the way in which activism around dementia is beginning to emerge. Yet, it remains unclear whether LGBT* individuals have had a voice or played a role within this or other similar networks. Indeed, in regard to user involvement in general there remains very limited commentary on how individuals are recruited or engaged. Webb (2008) has observed that where service user groups are active they are usually self-selecting and their forms of accounting to a wider public are often uncertain. While Tait and Lester (2005) have found that many mental health user groups are small, poorly funded and non-representative of minority groups.

Another foundational development in the rights-based framework for Scotland was the creation of a Charter of Rights for People with Dementia by a cross-party group on Alzheimer's in the Scottish Parliament (Alzheimer Scotland, 2009). The Charter draws upon the UN Convention on the Rights of Persons with Disabilities and other related legal frameworks including the Human Rights Act 1998 and was prompted by the widespread reporting of experiences of inadequate and inappropriate services by people with dementia and carers often detailing the contravention of their rights. The Charter has also helped to frame a commitment to rights within the Scottish National Dementia Strategy (Scottish Government, 2013) and the policy agenda of Alzheimer Scotland. The Charter includes a commitment to non-discrimination and equality based on characteristics such as age, gender, race and sexual orientation. As such, there is much potential here to underpin work with LGBT* individuals affected by dementia but, thus far, no reported instances or exemplars that might inform practice.

This is similarly the case for another driver for a rights-based approach to dementia; the work of the Scottish Human Rights Commission, whose project 'Care about Rights' has sought to translate human rights legislation into an accessible framework for the care of older vulnerable people.[2] Kelly and Innes (2013) suggest human rights legislation can be used to drive improvements to the care of people with dementia through the creation of an 'everyday human-rights based culture of care' (p. 62) that includes upholding freedom of expression and the prohibition of discrimination.

Alzheimer Scotland (a national third sector organisation supporting people with dementia) has formulated an eight-pillar model of community support to people with dementia (Alzheimer Scotland, 2012). This model identifies eight key areas of commitment which include promotion of continued social participation and greater awareness of how environmental design can support access to local communities. In seeking to achieve these commitments, the charity has engaged with UK-wide initiatives such as 'dementia-friendly communities' and 'Dementia Friends',[3] in order to raise awareness of dementia at a community level.

There are, however, assumptions driving these developments, examined in more detail as this chapter progresses, that require rethinking in the context of working with LGBT* groups and individuals; not least the existing emphasis upon geographical communities over communities of identity. Yet, the notion of a dementia-friendly community does prompt some compelling questions regarding LGBT* communities and what forms dementia-friendliness might take in such contexts. There is an opportunity here for LGBT* campaign groups and activists working with LGBT* individuals affected by dementia to take a lead in answering such questions. One clear implication is that for practitioners to adequately support LGBT* people affected by dementia there is a need to both understand and engage with the communities to which they belong. This alone suggests the prospect of quite radical change to mainstream dementia care practice as it currently stands.

Having briefly considered some of the ingredients to an emerging rights-based framework within a Scottish context the discussion now turns to explore certain tensions in this field before seeking to learn from an existing critique of other more established rights-based campaigns.

Tensions within a rights-based approach to dementia

Consensus vs conflict

As the brief overview above makes clear, a rights-based agenda for dementia in Scotland holds out a number of opportunities for working with LGBT* people affected by dementia, although many of these are yet to be realised in practice. There has, to date, been a reluctance within dementia policy to engage with the particular experience of specific groups despite growing evidence of inequalities in terms of access to, and appropriateness of, existing provision. As a result, we are still a long way from understanding what 'living well with dementia' might mean for the diverse individuals who fall under the 'LGBT*' umbrella. One reason for this is the unstinting emphasis on consensus within much mainstream research and policy.

A consensus paradigm is one that both presumes and promotes a dictum of shared interests where commonality is emphasised and questions of difference are consequently underplayed. It runs throughout many current policies that assume, rather than question, lines of affiliation and social connection such as the 'dementia friends' and 'dementia-friendly community' initiatives mentioned earlier. These recent policy developments are part of a wider decentralisation of support arrangements for people with dementia and 're-spatialising' of care. Such changes point to the need for practitioners to work at creating a more welcoming and inclusive environment within community-based venues but largely ignore the possibility of other forms of exclusion that may operate for certain groups affected by dementia. This applies not least to the heteronormative and, at times, overtly heterosexist and hostile character of some public spaces and community resources.

As Power (2014) has argued in relation to similar initiatives in the field of intellectual disabilities, such policy developments reflect an intention to 're-sculpt the social ecology of disabled people' (p. 166). As attention turns to geographically defined communities as a resource in supporting people with dementia, emphasis has been given to the more 'natural' affiliations embedded within them, such as the informal assistance that exists within shops, cafes or leisure centres instead of the more formal support on offer in designated spaces such as day centres or other care facilities. Such policies assume a willingness and desire to help and care for one another both within networks of people affected by dementia and more widely in local communities. Yet, the lived experience of many LGBT* individuals suggests differently, be it hostility from neighbours and in public spaces (Council of Europe, 2011) or in other areas of health and social care where (past and present) discrimination from fellow services users and practitioners creates an overwhelming sense of being unsafe and ultimately a reluctance to be identified (Ward *et al.*, 2010).

In the debate that surrounds these initiatives, an emphasis on consensus can be understood as underplaying our understanding of difference and dementia, and the tensions that arise from it. For instance, the mantra of 'we're all in the same boat' used to characterise peer support pilot initiatives for the English national dementia strategy (see Keyes *et al.*, 2014) is illustrative of a much broader appeal to a consensus paradigm in the literature on peer support. Similarly, in the field of user involvement, commentators assume shared interests and goals not only within groups of people with dementia but also between service users and the practitioners who support them. Thus, in arguing for a more relationship-centred approach to user involvement in dementia care and research, Nolan *et al.* (2007) propose that it is 'productive to talk about creating a new shared world with a common set of concepts and values' (p. 196). Again, the (reported) experience of LGBT* individuals of user involvement and user-led networks in related fields of mental health and disability suggest a rather different reality (Ward *et al.*, 2011, Wintrip, 2009, see also King, Chapter 4 in this book). Hence, the situation of LGBT* individuals affected by dementia and the diversity and differences between and amongst them provides a standpoint both to critique these new arrangements and to question some of the underlying assumptions that drive policy in this area.

Questions of equivalence and stability

Another tension within a rights-based agenda concerns our conception of dementia itself. In calling for the rights of people 'with dementia' how should we now understand this 'condition'? In such a context, it would seem that dementia no longer refers simply to a diagnosis but has become a fixed and stable category of identity from which to lay claim to certain rights and status. But, how helpful is this for the interests of minoritised groups such as LGBT* people living with dementia?

In her efforts to document dementia activism, Bartlett (2014b) addresses people with dementia as a 'marginalised group' and traces the emergence of a collective identity which she found was conceptualised by many of the campaigners she interviewed as linked to a workplace identity. She concludes 'I would suggest that people with dementia have only just begun their "struggle for citizenship" and could learn a great deal from the insights of the disability movement' (p. 1301). The suggestion here is that dementia activism is embarking on a trajectory that is all too familiar to feminism and gay liberation as well as the disability movement. But, what are the implications of this and are there lessons to be learned from what has gone before?

It is helpful to recall that the emergence of the disability movement in the UK met with a critical response from disabled feminists who pointed out how disability had been defined according to the prioritising of issues concerning the workplace and public spaces over and above issues of reproduction and the politics of the domestic sphere (e.g. Morris, 1996). In a similar vein, second wave feminism met with a critique by black feminists who were able to demonstrate how an apparently universal category of 'woman' reflected distinctly white middle-class interests over those of women belonging to black, minority ethnic and working-class communities (e.g. hooks, 1981; Lorde, 2007). And, in a more fundamental critique of gay rights campaigning, queer theory has sought to emphasise the fluid, contingent and ultimately exclusionary nature of identity categories which have a disciplinary effect as well as a celebratory quality (e.g. Seidman, 1993). These differing critical responses to a discourse of rights and recognition have all questioned the need for a fixed and stable category upon which it is premised, even as they have acknowledged its power both to mobilise and unite. The question they raise in the context of an emerging rights-based agenda for dementia is just how universal a category can dementia be? The continued invisibility of LGBT* perspectives in policy and practice in Scotland and elsewhere perhaps highlights the limitations of a category-oriented rights-based approach.

At the level of practice, a category-based approach to difference has already been widely critiqued in other areas of health and social care and not least in relation to how 'gay', 'lesbian', 'bisexual' or 'transgender' have in the past led to well-meaning checklist-style responses to working with service users (Ward and Jones, 2010). The inherent problems associated with such an approach underline the difficulties of seeking to engage with questions of difference through emphasis upon a single category of identity in isolation from any others (see Hulko, Chapter 3 in this book for in-depth discussion of this problem). Associated with this approach is an equally over-simplified understanding of questions of inequality and disadvantage in health and social care. Category-based approaches have supported an additive way of thinking about issues such as discrimination, marked by the language of 'double-jeopardy' or 'triple whammies', where the dynamic interplay and interlocking nature of different forms of oppression is overlooked (Ward and Bytheway, 2008).

From equal rights to the queering of dementia

A core feature of queer theory has been the shift in focus away from homosexuality as a unified identity and toward the unmarked nature of heterosexuality as a socio-political organising principle:

> Queer theorists argue that identities are always multiple or at best composites with literally an infinite number of ways in which identity-components (e.g. sexual orientation, race class, nationality, gender, age, able-ness) can intersect and combine. Any specific identity construction, moreover, is arbitrary, unstable and exclusionary.
>
> (Seidman, 1996: 11)

Hence, queer theory extends beyond a focus upon sexual and gender identities to consider more widely the workings of power and knowledge in a social context (see King, Chapter 4 in this book for a more detailed discussion of its development, impact and implications). In the latter section of this chapter we go on to consider the lessons from a queer critique of a rights-based approach and, in particular, three key messages from queer thinking regarding an approach to tackling inequalities:

1   First, according to more recent perspectives on power as diffuse and circulating, there is a need to consider the interplay of advantage and disadvantage in the situation of any group or individual;
2   Also, that a narrow focus on a single category of identity means that dominant interests are often left unmarked and hence under-analysed;
3   And, consequently, there is a need to broaden the lens from a focus upon categories of identity in order to problematise normativity at a wider level.

These messages from queer theory point to a more radical agenda for dementia policy, practice and activism and a consequent need to re-examine what dementia means and signifies.

'Disoriented in time and place'

This section focuses upon the politics of time and place in order to argue that such a line of thinking offers a useful alternative to a rights-led approach to dementia. In particular, a queer perspective invites a broadening of the lens from a focus upon 'dementia' to a consideration of the dominant interests embedded within our social and physical environments that affect all of us and highlights the importance of analysing how these are upheld.

The recent shift in dementia policy to a focus on the community as a resource and place of care marks what Power (2014) describes as a 'new geography of care and support'. It has spurred interest in dementia-friendly communities and the promotion of other forms of affiliation through projects such as Dementia Friends where efforts are currently being made to increase the visibility of dementia within communities based upon an appeal to and assumption of good-will and munificence. By contrast, a queer approach heralds a more fundamental problematising of the dominant interests that currently shape the material and social properties of local communities, one that acknowledges conflict and imbalances of power.

For instance, in beginning to think about the relationship between dementia, place and space much can be learned from ideas of 'queer space'. In early work on the queering of space, Bell and Valentine (1995) argue that 'the presence of queer bodies in particular locations forces people to realise that the space around them, the city streets, the malls, and the motels have been produced as (ambiently) heterosexual, heterosexist and heteronormative' (p. 18). In other words, day-to-day queer experience leads to an awareness of the dominant interests embedded within, and reproduced by, public spaces but also serves to de-naturalise what is seen as natural. The authors underline that identities are inter-twined with the social and material environment (see also Valentine, 2007). Such an approach points to a very different way of thinking about the emplaced experience of dementia.

Ahmed (2006) has similarly sought to explore the intertwined nature of identity, place and space by rethinking notions of orientation and comfort. Focusing on the relationship between whiteness and space, she argues that spaces allow certain bodies to extend into them more easily than others – 'those spaces are lived as comfortable as they allow bodies to fit in' (p. 135). Ahmed uses the analogy of a comfortable armchair that moulds itself to the contours of a particular body shape to argue that social spaces also carry the impression of certain bodies. Hence, non-white bodies experience a lack of fit and discomfort in some types of place, something that Ahmed describes as disorientation:

> Disorientation can be a bodily feeling of losing one's place and the effect of a loss of a place.... Disorientation involves failed orientations: bodies inhabit spaces that do not extend their shape, or use objects that do not extend their reach. At this moment of failure, such objects 'point' somewhere else or they make what is 'here' become strange.
>
> (Ahmed, 2006: 160)

For Ahmed, notions of comfort and orientation provide a way of interrogating the link between social and physical spaces and the identities of those who inhabit them. Discomfort constitutes what she describes as a 'queer effect' – one that arises from the juxtaposition of queer bodies with normative spaces. Such thinking suggests compelling parallels with an experience of social and physical spaces by people with dementia. The design and use of the built environment rarely considers the perspectives of the person with dementia and, as a result, creates a sense of discomfort and disorientation. To understand this discomfort as a 'queer effect' is to mark an environment as exclusionary and hostile to difference, a process that is educative because it renders visible the 'unseen' and unmarked ways in which spaces favour some bodies over others.

Alongside queer perspectives on space and place are ideas about queer time, for example, as explored in the work of Halberstam (2005) (see also Edelman, 2004 and Kafer, 2013) who draws attention to normative understandings of time and timescales. Halberstam argues for the need to deconstruct 'the naturalization of modes of temporality' and draws attention to those who live outside of heteronormative constructions of time and space such as 'reproductive and family time'. Halberstam takes as an example the lived experience of time for gay men with HIV and AIDS before the advent of drug therapies where a constantly diminishing future created a new emphasis on the here and now:

> And yet queer time, even as it emerges from the AIDS crisis is not only about compression and annihilation; it is also about the potentiality of a life unscripted by the conventions of family, inheritance and child-rearing.... Queer subcultures produce alternative temporalities by allowing their participants to believe that their futures can be imagined according to logics that lie outside of those paradigmatic markers of life experience – namely, birth, marriage, reproduction, and death.
>
> (p. 2)

Halberstam's notion of queer time draws attention to how certain ways of living 'in time' have been naturalised around what has traditionally been the heterosexual lifecourse, but also how notions of time and timescales can work in a disciplining and regulatory way upon people's lives. As such, Halberstam is keen to underline the potential rewards and learning to be derived from living outside of these 'modes of temporality'.

Some useful parallels exist here with recent efforts to understand the temporal experience of people with dementia and an emerging interest in 'dementia time'. For instance, Bartlett (2014a) draws particular attention to the temporal dimension of life with dementia that includes the progressive nature of the condition and hence the implications of a much shortened life expectancy for how time is experienced and what it means. She points out that dementia can also affect a person's perception of time and in this way 'unsettles basic sociological assumptions about people's relationship to clock-time' (p. 3). The Scottish Dementia Working Group Research Sub-Group has also addressed issues of dementia time in the context of advising principles for research involving people with dementia:

- Researchers need to consider 'dementia time' in their expectations of research, including finding out the best time and how each individual keeps track of time.
- Researchers should always re-cap on previous conversations or interviews each time they meet with people with dementia.
- It is important that researchers find out from us and from people who we trust, what is going on in our lives, especially if they are getting in touch after a gap in contact.
- It is important that researchers remind us the day before that they will be meeting with us, using the communication that we indicate is best and arrive at the time they said they would.
- Researchers should not stay for longer than agreed, unless the person with dementia invites them to.

(SDWG, 2014: 684)

This practical advice underlines the importance of attending to the lived experience of time for a person with dementia, but also highlights the way that certain approaches to time are naturalised in day-to-day interactions and social relations.

Queer theory thereby offers some useful and alternative ways of thinking through issues of difference and inequality in the context of living with dementia. It highlights the potential for people with dementia to draw attention to normativity in many different aspects of everyday living and to make apparent the naturalised and hence unmarked and often hidden operations of power. Like queer bodies, the bodies of people with dementia provide a standpoint for a critique of the unequal and unthinking ways in which the social and material environments we all inhabit are skewed toward the interests of some over others. Their day-to-day experience and habitation of these places and spaces is educative and revealing but is also a basis to problematise and challenge normative assumptions embedded in areas such as design, architecture and urban planning (see also Heylighen *et al.*'s (2013) exploration of how disabled people can offer a distinctive expertise of the designed environment).

Implications for policy and practice

So what are the implications of queer thinking for ongoing developments to dementia policy and practice?

In terms of recent efforts to reconceptualise dementia this chapter has highlighted the way in which it is evolving into a fixed and stable category of identity in a debate on the rights of people with dementia. Such a perspective seems at odds with a condition that is marked by such diversity and experienced in a fluid and changing fashion over time. The critical response to the journey of other rights-based campaigns suggests that a category-oriented approach to dementia may also be unhelpful for practice. Instead, there is a need to disaggregate 'people with dementia' by paying closer attention to 'social location', and through this 'to move beyond observation of difference to specify relations of inequality between [different] groups' (Calasanti and King, 2015: 193).

Linked to this is the need to question an overwhelming emphasis upon consensus in mainstream research and policy. An approach that foregrounds commonality of experience over difference and potentially conflicting interests has proven unhelpful in spotlighting the particular experiences and perspectives of individuals from minority groups and communities affected by dementia. Indeed, such an emphasis is a key element in a process of minoritisation. This implies the need to ensure inclusivity in areas such as user involvement, and co-productive working as well as in recruitment strategies and the design of research but also to acknowledge and learn from conflict and points of departure within these initiatives.

Current policy that rests upon these assumptions of consensus and the presumed willingness to help and support people with dementia is also at odds with the lived experience of many LGBT* individuals and lacks supporting evidence. In this respect, the collective experiences of LGBT* individuals affected by dementia may offer a counter-narrative from which to critique many of the ideas that drive policy and commissioning in the field of dementia care but can also serve as a litmus test for inclusive practice.

Finally, the experiences of people with dementia of what Ahmed (2006) calls a 'queer effect' could and should provide a basis on which to rethink our view of place and space, to understand the norms that shape the built environment and uncover those dominant interests that are currently taken as natural and which remain unquestioned. This would represent a radical departure from current thinking on dementia, design and the environment. Their experience could also help us to look beyond normative constructions of time and the unquestioned temporalities that shape our everyday lives and to understand how life can be approached differently when a greater emphasis is placed upon the here and now and closer attention is paid to the pace and tempo within day-to-day social encounters.

Looking ahead: towards a more radical critique

In drawing these arguments to a close and looking ahead to what might lie 'beyond' discourses of citizenship and equal rights, an alternative roadmap exists in building connections between dementia studies and the more radical approaches outlined not only within queer but also feminist, post-colonial, and crip/critical disability studies.

As I have sought to demonstrate in this chapter, creating these connections can shed light on those areas within dementia studies that remain under-analysed and indeed can help to steer the debate on dementia into alternative and uncharted territory. This applies not least to broader questions of normativity. There is currently no term or language to describe an equivalent within dementia studies to what 'heteronormativity' means to the analysis of sexuality, or what 'ethnocentricity' means to the debate on race, or 'phallocentricity' to gender.

Indeed, an entire layer of analysis (and associated lexicon) is largely missing from dementia studies, the absence of which is thrown into relief when we begin to draw connections to these other fields of social critique.

By way of a conclusion, I would argue then for the potential benefits of developing this more critical dimension to the debate on dementia. In this context, the diverse experiences of people living with dementia could provide the basis for a much broader (and deeper) analysis of current social conditions and of the inequalities, forms of disadvantage and sources of privilege that currently shape all our lives. Crucially, such a development could mark the opening of a radical critique of 'able-mindedness' as an organising principle and normative influence upon the social, political and material environments inhabited by us all.

Notes

1 The SDWG is a network comprising and led by people with dementia: www.sdwg. org.uk/.
2 The Care about Rights programme includes training resources for practitioners: www. scottishhumanrights.com/careaboutrights.
3 The Dementia Friends Scotland initiative is aimed at promoting awareness and support for people with dementia by building a network of trained 'friends': www. dementiafriendsscotland.org/.

References

Ahmed, S. (2006) *Queer phenomenology: orientations, objects, others*, Durham NC: Duke University Press.

Alzheimer Scotland (2009) *Charter of rights for people with dementia and their carers in Scotland*, accessed online 1 May 2015: www.scottishhumanrights.com/application/ resources/documents/FINALCharterofRights.pdf.

Alzheimer Scotland (2011) *Promoting excellence: a framework for all health and social services staff working people with dementia, their families, and carers*, accessed online 1 May 2015: www.gov.scot/resource/doc/350174/0117211.pdf.

Alzheimer Scotland (2012) *Delivering integrated dementia care: the 8 pillars model of community care*, accessed online 1 May 2015: www.alzscot.org/assets/0000/4613/ FULL_REPORT_8_Pillars_Model_of_Community_Support.pdf.

Alzheimer Scotland (2015) *Rights-based approach to dementia*, accessed online 1 May 2015: www.alzscot.org/campaigning/rights_based_approach.

Bartlett, R. (2012) Modifying the diary interview method to research the lives of people with dementia. *Qualitative Health Research*, **22**, 12, 1717–1726.

Bartlett, R. (2014a) The emergent modes of dementia activism. *Ageing and Society*, **34**, 4, 623–644.

Bartlett, R (2014b) Citizenship in action: the lived experiences of citizens with dementia who campaign for social change. *Disability & Society*, **29**(8), 1291–1304.

Bell, D. and Valentine, G. (1995) *Mapping desire*, London: Routledge.

Calasanti, T. and King, N. (2015) 'Intersectionality and age' in J. Twigg and W. Martin (eds) *Routledge handbook of cultural gerontology*, London: Routledge, pp. 193–200.

Council of Europe (2011) *Discrimination on grounds of sexual orientation and gender identity in Europe* [2nd edition], accessed online 1 May 2015: www.coe.int/t/Commissioner/ Source/LGBT/LGBTStudy2011_en.pdf.

East Dunbartonshire Council (2014) *Present in East Dunbartonshire: co-production with people living with dementia*, accessed online 1 May 2015: www.jitscotland.org.uk/wp-content/uploads/2015/04/Present_Project_Report_2014.pdf.

Edelman, L. (2004) *No future: queer theory and the death drive*, Durham NC: Duke University Press.

Halberstam, J. (2005) *In a queer time and place: transgender bodies, subcultural lives*, New York: New York University Press.

Heylighen, A., Van Doren, C. and Vermeersch, P. (2013) Enriching our understanding of architecture through disability experience. *Open House International*, **38**(1), 7–19.

hooks, b. (1981) *Ain't I a woman: Black women and feminism*, Boston: South End Press.

Joint Improvement Team (2012) *Talking points: personal outcomes approach*, accessed online 1 May 2015: www.jitscotland.org.uk/wp-content/uploads/2014/01/Talking-Points-Practical-Guide-21-June-2012.pdf.

Kafer, A. (2013) *Feminist, queer, crip*, Bloomington: Indiana University Press.

Kelly, F. and Innes, A. (2013) Human rights and citizenship in dementia care nursing. *International Journal of Older People Nursing*, **8**(1), 61–70.

Keyes, S. E., Clarke, C. L., Wilkinson, H., Alexjuk, J., Wilcockson, J., Robinson, L., Reynolds, J., McClelland, S., Corner, L. and Cattan, M. (2014) 'We're all thrown in the same boat...': A qualitative analysis of peer support in dementia care. *Dementia*, accessed online 28 October 2015: http://dem.sagepub.com/content/early/2014/04/04/1471301214529575.abstract.

Lorde, A. (2007) *Sister outsider: essays and speeches*, New York: Crossing Press.

Morris, J (ed.) (1996). *Encounters with strangers: feminism and disability*, London: Women's Press.

Nolan, M., Hanson, E., Grant, G., Keady, J. and Lennart, M. (2007) 'Conclusions: realising authentic participatory enquiry' in M. Nolan, E. Hanson, G. Grant and J. Keady (eds) *User participation in health and social care research: voices, values and evaluation*, Maidenhead: Open University Press, pp. 183–202.

Power, A. (2014) 'Eroding the collective "places" of support: emerging geographies of personalisation for people with intellectual disabilities' in K. Soldatic, H. Morgan, H. and A. Roulstone (eds) *Disability, spaces and places of policy exclusion*, Abingdon: Routledge, pp. 163–177.

Scottish Dementia Working Group Research Sub-Group (SDWG) (2014) Core principles for involving people with dementia in research. *Dementia*, **13**(5), 680–685.

Scottish Government (2010) *Scotland's National Dementia Strategy*, accessed online 1 May 2015: www.gov.scot/Publications/2010/09/10151751/0.

Scottish Government (2013) *Scotland's National Dementia Strategy 2013–2016*, accessed online 1 May 2015: www.gov.scot/Topics/Health/Services/Mental-Health/Dementia/DementiaStrategy1316.

Seidman, S. (1993) 'Identity and politics in a postmodern gay culture: some conceptual and historical notes' in M. Warner (ed.) *Fear of a queer planet*, Minneapolis: University of Minnesota Press, pp. 105–142.

Seidman, S. (1996) 'Introduction' in S. Seidman (ed.) *Queer theory/sociology*, Oxford: Blackwell, pp. 1–30.

Tait, L. and Lester, H. (2005) Encouraging user involvement in mental health services. *Advances in Psychiatric Treatment*, **11**, 168–175.

Valentine, G. (2007) Theorizing and researching intersectionality: a challenge for feminist geography. *The Professional Geographer*, **59**(1), 10–21.

Ward, R. (2000) Waiting to be heard: Dementia and the gay community. *Journal of Dementia Care*, **8**(3), 24–25.

Ward, R. (2012) 'Conclusion: making space for LGBT lives in health and social care' in R. Ward, I. Rivers and M. Sutherland (eds) *Lesbian, gay, bisexual and transgender ageing: biographical approaches for inclusive care and support*, London: Jessica Kingsley Publishers, pp. 196–209.

Ward, R. and Bytheway, B. (eds) (2008) *Researching age and multiple discrimination*, London: Centre for Policy on Ageing.

Ward, R. and Jones, R. L. (2010) 'Introduction' and 'Conclusion' in R. L. Jones and R. Ward, (eds) *LGBT issues: looking beyond categories*, Edinburgh: Dunedin, pp. xi–xvi; 82–88.

Ward, R., Pugh, S. and Price, E. (2010) *Don't look back? Improving health and social care service delivery for older LGB users*, London: Equality and Human Rights Commission.

Ward, R., Scottish Dementia Working Group and River, L. (2011) 'Between participation and practice: inclusive user involvement and the role of practitioners' in J. Keady and S. Watts (eds) *Mental health and later life: delivering an holistic model for practice*, London: Routledge, pp. 9–21.

Webb, S. A. (2008) Modelling service user participation in social care. *Journal of Social Work*, **8**(3), 269–290.

Wintrip, S. (2009) *Not safe for us yet: the experiences and views of older lesbian, gay men and bisexuals using mental health services in London*, City Bridge Trust, accessed online 1 May 2015: www.ageofdiversity.org.uk/NotSafeForUsYet.

Glossary

Biphobia   Prejudice and discrimination towards bisexual people.

Cis   An abbreviation for cisgender (e.g. cis-man, cis-woman).

Cisgender   Women and men who identify with the sex/gender assigned to them at birth.

Gender   A social and cultural construction of normative behaviour based on notions of femininity and masculinity.

Gender identity   The gender(s) with which one identifies.

Heteronormative   The assumption that heterosexuality is the normal way of being.

Heterosexism   The privileging of heterosexuality.

Homophobia   Prejudice and discrimination towards lesbian, gay and bisexual people.

LGB   Lesbian, gay and bisexual.

LGBT*   Lesbian, gay, bisexual and trans*.

Sex   Biological sex assigned at birth.

Sexual identity   The sexual identity with which one identifies, among those who understand sexuality in terms of identity, e.g. lesbian, gay, bisexual, heterosexual.

Sexual orientation   The gendering of sexual desire, based on which gender(s) one finds sexually attractive/desirable, among those who understand sexuality in terms of orientation i.e. orientated to 'same', 'different', 'both' or multiple gender/sexes.

Sexuality   A term which encompasses sexual identity, sexual orientation, sexual performance and sexual desires.

Trans*   An umbrella term which covers the gender identity spectrum: including (but not limited to) transgender, transsexual, transvestite, genderqueer, genderfluid, non-binary, genderless, agender, non-gendered, third gender, two-spirit and bigender (Tompkins, 2014).

Transition   To undergo a process (or part of a process) by which a person changes their physical sex characteristics and/or gender expression to match their inner sense of being male or female (or other). This process may include a name change, a change in preferred pronouns, and a change in social gender expression through things such as hair, clothing and mannerisms.

It may or may not include hormones and surgery (adapted from Lambda Legal, 2013: 1).

Transphobia Prejudice and discrimination towards trans* people.

Transsexual A medical term describing people whose gender and biological sex do not line up, and who often seek medical treatment to bring their body and gender identity into alignment. There are several terms used to commonly describe transsexual people, including MTF (abbreviated term for male-to-female transsexual people), FTM (abbreviated term for female-to-male transsexual people) and trans man and trans woman (common language terms used to describe FTM and MTF transsexual people) (Stonewall, 2015).

Transvestite A term used to describe people who dress in clothes associated with their opposite sex, as defined by socially accepted norms, but still identify with their biological sex. An erotic transvestite is a person who gets sexually excited by the dressing. A social transvestite, however, simply feels more comfortable in such clothes (Stonewall, 2015).

References

Lambda Legal (2013) *Creating Equal Access to Quality Health Care for Transgender Patients: Transgender-Affirming Hospital Policies.* New York: Lambda Legal. Available at www.lgbtagingcenter.org/resources/resource.cfm?r=625#sthash.I8VkGiwq.dpuf [downloaded 16 June 2015].

Stonewall (2015) *Transgender*. Available at: www.stonewall.org.uk/sites/default/files/transgender_booklet_2004.pdf [downloaded 13 October 2015].

Tompkins, A. (2014) Asterisk. *TSQ: Transgender Studies Quarterly*, **1**(1–2), 26–27.

Index

Page numbers in **bold** denote figures.

 Taylor & Francis eBooks

Helping you to choose the right eBooks for your Library

Add Routledge titles to your library's digital collection today. Taylor and Francis ebooks contains over 50,000 titles in the Humanities, Social Sciences, Behavioural Sciences, Built Environment and Law.

Choose from a range of subject packages or create your own!

Benefits for you

» Free MARC records
» COUNTER-compliant usage statistics
» Flexible purchase and pricing options
» All titles DRM-free.

 REQUEST YOUR FREE INSTITUTIONAL TRIAL TODAY

Free Trials Available
We offer free trials to qualifying academic, corporate and government customers.

Benefits for your user

» Off-site, anytime access via Athens or referring URL
» Print or copy pages or chapters
» Full content search
» Bookmark, highlight and annotate text
» Access to thousands of pages of quality research at the click of a button.

eCollections – Choose from over 30 subject eCollections, including:

Archaeology	Language Learning
Architecture	Law
Asian Studies	Literature
Business & Management	Media & Communication
Classical Studies	Middle East Studies
Construction	Music
Creative & Media Arts	Philosophy
Criminology & Criminal Justice	Planning
Economics	Politics
Education	Psychology & Mental Health
Energy	Religion
Engineering	Security
English Language & Linguistics	Social Work
Environment & Sustainability	Sociology
Geography	Sport
Health Studies	Theatre & Performance
History	Tourism, Hospitality & Events

For more information, pricing enquiries or to order a free trial, please contact your local sales team:
www.tandfebooks.com/page/sales